# FROM BOSSUET TO NEWMAN

BY

OWEN CHADWICK

SECOND EDITION

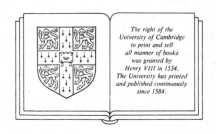

The right of the
University of Cambridge
to print and sell
all manner of books
was granted by
Henry VIII in 1534.
The University has printed
and published continuously
since 1584.

## CAMBRIDGE UNIVERSITY PRESS

CAMBRIDGE
LONDON   NEW YORK   NEW ROCHELLE
MELBOURNE   SYDNEY

Published by the Press Syndicate of the University of Cambridge
The Pitt Building, Trumpington Street, Cambridge CB2 1RP
32 East 57th Street, New York, NY 10022, USA
10 Stamford Road, Oakleigh, Melbourne 3166, Australia

First published 1957
Second edition 1987

Printed in Great Britain at the
University Press, Cambridge

*British Library cataloguing in publication data*

Chadwick, Owen
From Bossuet to Newman. – 2nd ed.
1. Theology, Catholic – History
I. Title
230′.2′0903    BX1747

*Library of Congress cataloguing in publication data*

Chadwick, Owen.
From Bossuet to Newman.
Includes index.
1. Dogma, Development of – History. 2. Newman, John
Henry, 1801–1890. Essay on the development of Christian
doctrine. 3. Catholic Church – Doctrines – History.
I. Title.
BT22.C43 1987    230′.2′09    86–28389

ISBN 0 521 33462 4 hard covers 2nd edition
ISBN 0 521 33676 7 paperback

# CONTENTS

# ABBREVIATIONS

BL    Bodleian Library

BM    British Museum

BP    Brownson Papers, University of Notre Dame

CUL    Cambridge University Library

DHGE    *Dictionnaire d'Histoire et de Géographie Ecclésiastiques*

DTC    *Dictionnaire de Théologie Catholique*

ET    English Translation

OM    MSS. of the Oratory, Birmingham

OML    MSS. of the Oratory, Brompton

PG    Migne, *Patrologia Graeca*

RHE    *Revue d'histoire ecclésiastique*

ST    *Summa Theologia*

TQ    *Theologische Quartalschrift* (Tübingen)

VA    Vatican Archives

VL    Vatican Library

# PREFACE TO THE FIRST EDITION

On 9 October 1845 John Henry Newman, one-time leader of the Oxford movement in the Church of England, was received into the Roman Catholic Church by Father Dominic the Passionist in the little private oratory at Littlemore. Less than two months later he published as the reason or account or vindication of this step a justly celebrated book—the *Essay on the Development of Christian Doctrine*, which hereafter I shall describe with brevity as the *Essay on Development* or even as the *Essay*. My purpose has not been to reassess the dogmatic validity or otherwise of that book, since such reassessments have been common enough. As is appropriate in lectures upon the Birkbeck foundation, my purpose has been primarily historical, to set that book in the context of intellectual history.

I have confined my attention to the comparatively narrow field of the idea of doctrinal development. The wider question I have not sought to tackle, the idea of philosophical development as it was maturing from Leibniz through Lessing to Herder and Hegel and then to Darwin: the destruction or transformation of older cosmologies like 'the Great Chain of Being', the rise of the idea of progress, the change from the partially unhistorical theories of the Enlightenment to the more deeply historical consciousness of the nineteenth century (now believed to be less of a radical change than was at one time thought)—these are subjects which impinge upon my own but which have been discussed by many in recent times, not least by members of our own Faculty of History. I shall need to ask how far this wider swing in European thought conditioned the narrower swing in doctrinal thought. But I hope that by confining my attention to the narrower, I may be able to shed a little, little ray of light upon one side of the wider. And if further justification is needed, perhaps I may take two texts. Lord Acton once wrote that

Newman's *Essay on the Development of Christian Doctrine* did more than any other book of the time to make the English 'think historically, to watch the process as well as the result'. And Mark Pattison, a devout disciple of Newman in the years from 1842 to 1846, a man who almost followed him into the Roman Catholic Church but who slowly reacted against him little by little until he turned first into an ardent liberal and then into a cynical liberal—Mark Pattison, in his old age Rector of Lincoln College Oxford, wrote to thank Newman for a present, a copy of the third edition of the *Essay*. 'Is it not a remarkable thing' wrote Pattison to Newman, 'that you should have first started the idea—and the word—Development, as the key to the history of church doctrine, and since then it has gradually become the dominant idea of all history, biology, physics, and in short has metamorphosed our view of every science, and of all knowledge?'[1]

Though I am dealing with the problem of 'doctrinal mutability' within the thought of a particular Church, the same problem faced all the Christian churches, with the partial exception (as yet) of the Eastern Orthodox Church. The idea of development is a peculiarly interesting illustration of a move from static towards dynamic throughout Christendom. It is peculiarly interesting partly because it is far easier to isolate it from external influences like Hegelianism; and partly because the characteristic notions of infallibility and definition rendered the problem unique. The new historical studies, the new criticism, might have turned a conservative society towards absolute obscurantism, towards a total rejection of the validity of historical evidence, towards a destruction of the critical doubt by refusing to allow historical inquiry to be relevant to religious faith. Plenty of evidence from the Ultramontanism of the middle nineteenth century and after shows that this peril was not imaginary. Greatly

[1] Acton in CUL Add. MSS. 4987, 60; Pattison to Newman, 5 April 1878 (OM).

to its credit, the conservative community refused to follow several seductive proposals of this kind. To this refusal Newman contributed more than any other Catholic.

The style appropriate for lectures differs perceptibly from the style appropriate for a book. But I have preserved the lecture-form in which they were designed, and the chief difference here is that the exigencies of time compelled me to compress chs. IV and VI into a few paragraphs.

I owe thanks to the Master and Council of Trinity College for giving me this opportunity, and to a number of most courteous librarians and archivists who have given me their time, friendly assistance, advice, critical disagreement, and even, at times, generous hospitality.

CAMBRIDGE                                                  O.C.

1957

*Figures in the text refer to the notes
beginning on page 196*

# INTRODUCTION

To be asked to write an introduction to one's own book, which was written thirty years ago, is to be set no easy task. An author is aware how much has been written on the same theme since he published his book. He knows of those who agree with him and why they agree, and of those who doubt, and why they doubt. But the book is still cited in the many debates on the theme; the bibliography of the subject lengthens all the time[1]; and people still ask for copies of the book. For the subject of Christian thought, changing in its expression through the movement of history and society, has become far more central to the debate even than it was in 1956–7. The relation of Christianity to history is seen to be entangled with questions about the truth of Christianity, and the various ways in which its faith is formed and formulated.

Catholicism had a special interest in the question; for it was, and is, particularly conscious of Christian continuity through the centuries since the New Testament. Protestants too, are conscious of that continuity. But since the Reformation, they have placed less emphasis upon it, and in very recent times it became a problem also to Protestants. Because Catholicism had a special interest, the figure of John Henry Newman grew in importance. He is more important to Christianity as a whole, now, than he was when this book was written in 1956; precisely because of the question which this book sought to analyse. He was among

[1] The reader will gain especial help from the following:
H. Hammans *Die neueren katholischen Erklärungen der Dogmenentwicklung* Essen 1965,
N. Lash *Newman on Development* London 1975.
J. Stern *Bible et tradition chez Newman* Paris 1967.
J. H. Walgrave *Unfolding Revelation* Eng. trans. London 1972.
M. F. Wiles *The Making of Christian Doctrine* Cambridge 1967.

the first small handful of Catholics to face the new questions for Christianity raised by the advance of historical research; and as time passed his thought on the subject became much the most influential, and his person much the most famous, among that small handful of Catholic thinkers early in the nineteenth century who first faced those questions.

*   *   *

Jesus was born and lived. He said various things about God and man. He founded sacraments. He died and the disciples perceived that he rose again. They started to frame their understanding in words; Son of God, Lamb of God, who died for us and opened the gate of the kingdom of heaven.

The message or gospel which the disciples took into the world had power. It converted others, then many. They ordered the community which grew. They gave it ministry. They gave it words and ritual for the sacraments. Various ways of Christian life were found acceptable, others were found unacceptable. 'The Catholic Church' discovered its inheritance: a Bible; a memory of Christ with a sense of his continued presence; the sacraments which were founded; a ministry passed down from the apostles; various customs with varying degrees of importance; from the keeping of Sunday as a holy day, to the clothes which the porter of the church was expected to wear.

They knew that they had a message for the world. A message which carried with it the saving from sin, and the way to a holy life. Some people expressed the truth in one way and some in another. What was true was felt to be bigger than the words which expressed what was true.

But some words or phrases were found by Christian feeling to be unworthy of the truth which they knew. If someone said in a sermon 'Christ the Son was like God His Father', it was true.

It could not be denied that it was true. And yet it felt inadequate. Before long they felt it to be corrupt. Christ was one with his Father, that they knew from St John's Gospel. To say that he was *like* was to deny that he was one. They framed doctrine; not only to say what they believed to be true, but also to deny what they believed to be untrue.

Therefore Christian doctrine 'developed'. By the end of the fourth century the Catholic Church had a creed far more defined than at the end of the second century. The process did not stop in the fifth century. It went on in every century; influenced by popular ways of prayer, and the attempts to control superstition, and phrases afterwards branded as 'heretical', and argument by schoolmen, and insights of new philosophers. A Church in history, with a message partly about a piece of history, must explain itself to new generations, in a world of new knowledge, and new phrases, and new ways of enquiry. To be a Church in history was to develop. Not only in less weighty things, like the clothes worn by clergymen, or the number of saints' days, but in the doctrines of the faith.

Until the beginning of the nineteenth century no Catholic fully saw or admitted this fact. That was the time when the European intelligence at last acquired a sense of the continuous change in human affairs. Among Catholics the first to see it were a group of South German Catholics and, quite independently, John Henry Newman at Littlemore outside Oxford.

In retrospect it is extraordinary that it took so long to see. But that is the same as to say how extraordinary that it took humanity so long to acquire a historical sense.

Christianity had a special consciousness which made historical change harder to discern. From the first the message or gospel was handed down, father and mother to children, congregation to congregation. Stand in the old ways. Be faithful to the past. The apostles walked and talked with the Lord. They alone understood how to interpret his mind. They passed their understanding to us, his Church. Follow no novelties. Accept what is handed down. The Latin word for the act of handing down is *traditio*, tradition. We keep Sunday as our holy day instead of Saturday; if anyone says that it should be Saturday, he does not understand the mind of the Lord. We baptize infants; if anyone says that no baby should be baptized because faith must always be conscious, he is not loyal to what we have received from those who understood the mind of the Lord.

The earlier Christians, and the Catholics of the Middle Ages, whether in Eastern Europe or Western, felt no discrepancy between Scripture and tradition. The idea of *orthodoxy* was very quick to arise. A local church faced with an innovation could consult the surrounding churches. It particularly wished to consult churches known to be founded by apostles. So they discovered whether the novelty was faithful to the general mind of the Church. By the middle of the third century they had forged an instrument for declaring the mind of the Church on disputed questions—the Councils of Bishops, whose consensus guarded and represented the consensus of the whole Church.

Councils could say what was the custom of the Church, and what its consensus. Their judgment was not thought to add anything to the deposit of faith. They stated the Church's mind. But the Church knew its mind. It did not need to discover what it thought.

Therefore this sense of tradition—a deposit—a rule of faith—a gospel unchanging through the centuries—became part of faith. It was the clearest way in which the uneducated layman or laywoman could understand what was authority in the Church. Being deep within the idea of authority, it was deep inside faith. It was part of Christian devotion.

During the fourteenth and fifteenth centuries many studies realized the discrepancy between Scripture and tradition. When they studied the documents, some of them found that the Pope's authority was not so marked in the early centuries of the Church. Some of them discovered that the word transubstantiation, which sought to describe what happened to the bread and wine in the mass, was not accepted by all Christians in early times, not even by a Pope. Some of them discovered that common practices, like the sale of indulgences, could find no justification in earlier centuries.

This argument was not settled. Or at least it was settled by two sides differing but not agreeing to differ. Protestants said that the only guide to the doctrines of the Church must be the authority of the Bible. Catholics of the Counter-Reformation said that the only safe guide is what the Church does now, for the Church is guided by the Holy Spirit to keep the faith. Their strongest argument against Protestants was to point out that Protestants changed not only what had been done for three or four hundred years, but even what had been done for more than a thousand years.

Therefore, to the Counter-Reformation of the sixteenth century, the notion of tradition, as a kind of authority supplementary to Scripture, was even more important than to their predecessors. It was an embattled idea of tradition. Stick to what is. Stand firm in the accepted ways. They have always been the ways, must always have been the ways, for the Church does not err.

When they came to consider the evidence of earlier centuries, they found it more helpful than some of them perhaps feared. If we were to take the fully developed Catholicism of the end of the fourth century, there might be argument about some Catholic practices. But there must be even more argument over some Protestant convictions, like (for example) the belief that monks are wrong and should be forbidden; for in 400 A.D. the Roman Empire was populous with monks.

This then, was the background to our problem. Tradition was embattled. We never change. We never have changed. And then, two centuries and more afterwards, we discover that everyone thinks how everything changes, and all the time. Slowly, cautiously, and painfully, we must adapt; restate; open the eyes to what is proven; recognize the truth now established; until 1973, *Mysterium Ecclesiae*, the Congregation of the Doctrine of the Faith distinguished the meaning of a doctrine—which is always true—from the words in which the Church expresses that doctrine; words which are true for those able to understand them, but words which are not indispensable to the meaning which they seek to express; and which may be changed in the light of new usages of words, or new historical ideas.

In this study, Bossuet stands foursquare, and untroubled, at the end of the seventeenth century, confident or over-confident that we never change. Newman stands hesitant and troubled, in the fourth decade of the nineteenth century, putting forward an idea of change which was the first Catholic idea of change to come anywhere near the heart of this difficult problem: to see, and preserve, and keep, the essence of the faith and simultaneously to see how the language changed and with the language some of the ideas. The question of this book is how, during the 150 years that lay between Bossuet's book and Newman's book, the ground for the possibility of Newman's theory was prepared. In the context of that age it was a revolutionary theory. No one can be surprised that it took a century or more before it was widely accepted. But it was of the first importance to the future of Catholicism, and ultimately to its intellectual integrity.

It is an axiom shared by everyone treated in this book that words can express truths about God and the soul. Those words will always express the truths badly, in the sense of incompletely, inadequately. The truth about God is bigger than words could ever encompass. But the shared axiom is that words, so far as they go, are capable of expressing truth. People who think that the truth about God can only be known by confronting Him wordlessly (whatever that means) need not attempt this book.

For in that case the problem of change does not exist; since words have become only helps to prayer, and a stimulus towards the wordless confrontation, and need correspond to nothing in reality. Then you may change the words as often as you like, so long as they help you to sense the numinous.

It is also an axiom, not of all the people mentioned in this book, but of all the Catholics mentioned in this book, that God gave his revelation once for all; during a definite and limited period of years; which ended with the death of the one of the twelve apostles who was the last to die. When the last apostle died we do not know; perhaps as late as 100 A.D. The ground for this is the uniqueness of revelation, which is the uniqueness of Christ. The apostles alone knew his mind. They alone knew his teaching, and how he wanted to perpetuate his message. What came after the death of the last apostle was only explanation; not an amplifying. God did not reveal his truth in this way to St Augustine, or St Bernard, or Martin Luther, or Bossuet, or Newman. The time of revelation ended; and we must live by what we were then given, until another world come upon us.

Divided by 150 years, Bossuet and Newman shared an important quality for the purpose of tackling the problem of revelation and change, which is the problem of history and the gospel. Both were theologians, but both were also historians. Both specialized in the history of the Church during its early centuries. Therefore the difference between them is less a difference between two persons (very different though they were in personality) than between two ages of historical enquiry. What we have to chart is in one respect the development of the historical profession, of its range and its effectiveness.

Newman perceived, much more clearly than Bossuet, the assimilative power of Christianity. It enters the world with Jewish axioms. It moves out into the Jewish dispersion among the Greeks, then among the Latins. It has to commend its gospel in a society where intelligent men use the language of Greek philosophy, Platonic or Stoic. Its missionaries start to talk that language, then to think in that language. This is a very sure way of throwing up what, very early, the Church called 'heresy', that is, ways of expressing the gospel which were felt to be unfaithful to the authentic gospel; an attempt which tried and failed to express the truth. But it also gave the Christians a lot of new insights and modes of expression which were felt to be authentic; and in this way some aspects of Greek thought could be assimilated by the Church, so that St Augustine, eminent Christian father and teacher, could be and feel himself to be a Platonist. And so also when it came to the revival of Aristotle, or the renaissance of Greek learning, or the coming of the new historical studies. Newman had a conviction about this strength in Christian thought to assimilate all that was right and good in the thought of the non-Christian world. His mind had the faculty of reaching outward continually. He bubbled with vitality of mind. It was a property which he shared with Bossuet. But Bossuet's mind was more solid, perhaps more rounded; Newman's the more sensitive, and much more probing. They were both great preachers in their different ages. You could not have preached Bossuet's sermons in Newman's pulpit; and the reason was not only French taste versus English taste, not only classical versus romantic. The reason was a sign of that development of society, and of faith within the society, which Newman freely recognized and Bossuet was hardly willing to recognize.

The problem was not only a Catholic problem. It touched Catholics more directly, and Eastern Orthodox still more directly; because the Catholic West and the Greek or Russian East had so deep-felt a conviction of an unchanging heritage of truth. But Protestants had the same problem; the impact of historical change on truth and the presentation of truth.

Protestants were inclined, perhaps, to think that Newman and his arguments were unimportant. They had little sense of an unchanging tradition, or fancied that they had none. They believed that they could appeal to the Bible, and the Bible only, as the source of the religion of Protestants. Maurice Wiles in a brilliant though difficult book, *The Making of Christian Doctrine*, Cambridge 1967, took up the problem from the Protestant point of view. It started by declaring his fascination with the story of the Catholic development between Bossuet and Newman as described in the first edition of this book; but said that 'it is like reading a debate about the movements of the planets before the intervention of the telescope'. 'The general problems with which they were concerned are real problems; but the particular problems to which they addressed themselves so vigorously are not ours; and, more emphatically still, the way in which they approached them is not and cannot be ours' (pp. 1–2).

And yet the Catholic is not so remote from the Protestant, nor the Christian of the later twentieth century so remote from the Christian of the earlier nineteenth century, as that verdict might suggest.

Professor Wiles asked in what ways Christian doctrine was made during the first five centuries after the New Testament. He asked himself, in fact, the question which the Jesuit Denis Petau (see below, p. 58, etc.) asked himself during the earlier seventeenth century, and which still later Newman asked himself in the most important part of his essay. His presuppositions were not at all the same. He had not the feeling of Petau that Plato was an enemy. He had not the feeling of Newman that he needed to show the modern Roman Catholic Church to be the natural outcome in history of the age of the Fathers. He was more free in his enquiry. Petau and Newman were sure that the development of doctrine which happened was right. They were sure, for example, that the creed made by the Council of Nicaea in 325, and framed in the Nicene Creed, is 'true'; a true expression (so far as it goes) of the Christian faith. Maurice Wiles is not sure that the development is right. At least he feels we may ask ourselves whether it is wrong.

Of course there is bound to be a difference between a Roman Catholic and a Protestant on this matter. It is essential for a Protestant to show that developments in a Church ruled by Popes may be wrong. The original protest, of Martin Luther, rested upon a conviction that a single development—the creation and sale of indulgences—could be shown to be wrong. Some developments of doctrine are corruptions. That is the belief of the Reformation, and is hardly to be denied, now, by anyone, whether Catholic or Protestant. Certainly it cannot be denied by the Eastern Orthodox, who for centuries complained, and still complain, of the Western addition of the phrase *And the Son* to the Nicene Creed.

When the Reformation happened, the Protestants were attacked by conservatives for making schism in the Church, and for departing from the historic faith of Christianity. They did not reply, Yes, certainly that is what we are doing; we are starting afresh, and making a new Church, with insights into the Scripture better than those which you possess. On the contrary. They replied that they were the historic Christian community, professing the historic faith. Dr Cave, for example, vindicated the Church of England from the charge of schism. It retained the ancient creed (including the Nicene and Athanasian creeds), as the confession of faith. It specially reverenced the first four General Councils, and taught no doctrines which could not be proved by the word of God and 'the general consent of the Fathers'. Next to the word of God, the Church of England reverenced antiquity. It appealed to both, and 'decrees by both to be ruled'.

Such a statement might feel to our critic to lack the plain insight that the Churches have already altered their teaching more drastically than by redrafting one phrase of the creed. By the middle twentieth century the church of Dr Cave, and of Professor Wiles, not only made the Athanasian Creed voluntary. It accepted that the Bible is not historically true in all its parts.

During the last hundred years it allowed developments in doctrine which are not just additions to an old creed, but contradict some bits of what all Christians used to accept as part of their faith. These developments are not like indulgences, or like the doctrines about the Blessed Virgin made of obligation by Pope Pius IX and Pius XII. That is, they are not innovations growing out of medieval devotion. Nor are they like the word transubstantiation, an innovation growing out of the devotions of the age of the Fathers. Nor are they like the phrase *of one substance*, an innovation growing out of the devotions of many in the primitive Church.

In each of those cases these doctrines arose out of a people's devotion. But in these modern developments the doctrine has not arisen out of prayer. It has come from the necessity for integrity of mind. No one who studies the Bible, with the equipment which we now possess, can believe all of it to be historically true. That makes a difference to prayer and devotion; a very big difference, certainly a much bigger difference than was made to prayer by the use or non-use of the phrase *of one substance*. But the change was not due to devotion. In earlier centuries the way of prayer was normally the law which governed doctrine. In these modern developments the law which governed doctrine decisively affected the ways of worship.

Professor Wiles makes the weighty point that a doctrine which develops or is developed is more likely to be *legitimate* and *valuable* rather than necessary. This must be right, at least often. Take for example the addition to the Nicene Creed—so much attacked by the Eastern Orthodox Churches—of the words *And the Son*—the Holy Spirit proceeds not only from the Father but from the Son. The circumstances of Spanish heresy in the eighth century made it necessary to add the word *Filioque* to the creed, in order to protect the revelation of God through a Son and Saviour. Those who made this addition could find ample ground for it among the theologians, and believed that they had sufficient ground for it in Scripture. From Spain it was accepted as right by Rome and then by all the Western Church.

This addition precisely met the test of a development that was *legitimate* and *valuable* in the circumstances in which it was made; no less than the addition of the phrase *of one substance* four hundred years before. But though *legitimate* and *valuable*, was it also necessary in the sense of *necessary for all time*, or *necessary to the true faith of a true Church*? Evidently not; for no one in the West, since earlier and more ignorant days, blamed the Eastern Orthodox Church for keeping to the words of Nicaea and not adding the thought *And the Son* to the Nicene Creed. Modern divines of both East and West have recognized that no difference is made to the doctrine of God, whichever formula is used. The addition was valuable, in the society in which it arose. That could not (in theory) stop the Western Church removing the clause for the sake of a Christian peace and communion with its Eastern families of Christians. Naturally the West would be very reluctant to make such a change (1) because if circumstances arose in which it is valuable, who knows whether such circumstances might arise again? (2) because if no difference is made to truth by the addition, why bother to change?—never change anything for the sake of *diplomacy*, only for the sake of truth (3) because the words of the Nicene Creed in their Western form are hallowed in the usage of more than a thousand years. The development was *legitimate*, and *valuable*. Surely it was not 'necessary' to the Church. But since it happened as a development, and was accepted, and grew sacred by time, it is an 'unnecessary' thing which could not be changed without 'necessity'.

Professor Wiles (p. 7) raised the possibility that *bishops* were such a development. The Church started life with the apostles and a jumble of order and disorder; apostolic leaders or committees of responsible men, single heads of congregations, or strong chairmen of committees, or weak chairmen of committees.

The force of apostolic authority, as it was inherited, steadily made the apostolic leaders the norm, and before long the form of ministry *necessary* to the being of a Christian congregation. Here was a development. Since the Reformation some Christians held the development to be a corruption, and believed that the polity intended by Scripture rested upon committees of responsible men (in modern times, men and women). Other Christians accepted the doctrine which primitive Christians reached—*no bishop no church*. Wiles asks whether this is just such a development; legitimate and valuable in its time; bringing order into Catholicism and preserving its faith; but not *necessary* for all time, in different generations and different circumstances. That is, circumstances alter cases. The Church 'developed' the authority of bishops for a particular and necessary purpose. It is not bishops which are necessary, but the purpose which is necessary. He asks whether there may come circumstances (some areas of the Reformation were such a set of circumstances) where the purpose of the early bishops is better fulfilled without bishops than with bishops; and then no one can say any longer, *no bishops, no church*.

On this view a statement of doctrine needs to be understood in its context; the state of society, the world-view of the age, even the philosophies of the time, through which the Church lived. Newman was among the first of the Catholics to recognize that society changes all the time; that the world-view of an age is constantly adapted to new knowledge or new habits of thought; that there is a fashion even in philosophy. He was also the first to recognize the inherent problem for Christianity: if Churches, whose purpose is the saving of humanity, need to adapt their words or practice to a changing society and changing morals or philosophy, they need to be sure that they 'develop' their teaching and practice by their own inward laws of development, and not be blown about, hither and thither, by the intellectual fashions of an age.

Wiles raised another weighty question. A doctrine may be

'true'—postulate the phrase *And the Son*. It is 'true' in its time—it serves a purpose in correcting a Spanish error. It becomes 'necessary'. But when in the course of centuries the controversy out of which it arose is dead, it becomes irrelevant—true but of no importance to Christian faith or life? On this view a 'true' statement of Christian doctrine can never lose its 'truth' but can lose its 'relevance'. Can a doctrine be simultaneously *necessary* and *irrelevant*?

The question touches people who need to think about relations between the different Churches. It is hard to say where *relevance* ends or begins. *Of one substance* was a phrase arising out of a controversy which some think, though only some, to be as dead as possible. Does that mean it is now irrelevant as a phrase? Not necessarily. The controversy out of which it arose contended about something which was cast by both sides into words of that time, and the forms in which both sides put the argument grew arid as time passed. But the ultimate about which they contended was deeper than the language in which they contended. A phrase like *of one substance* could continue to be relevant even though it was drafted to meet an argument no longer relevant.

The modern student of the early Church sees five different ways in which doctrine developed during the first centuries; (1) the presentation of the Christian message to a non-Christian world with its own non-Christian axioms and philosophers; (2) statements by some Christians held by other Christians to be misleading or false—that is, 'heresies'—and therefore to be repudiated by definition; (3) a desire of the Christian intellectual to think through more deeply the intellectual and spiritual implications of the faith; sometimes, as with Origen of Alexandria, the more daring results of intellectual speculation carried development not by positive statement but by repudiation, as under (2) above; (4) the influence of the Bible, Old Testament as well as New; for example, expressions of the ideas of priesthood; (5) popular piety; this was particularly true of the development of the cult, and therefore, the doctrines, of the Blessed Virgin Mary and of the Saints, but could affect expressions of language about the sacraments or even the doctrine about the Christ. In his own way, and his own language, Newman recognized all these ways of development which the modern historian of ideas finds.

Like Newman, Professor Wiles lays down as 'test of a true development' (p. 177): 'not whether it preserves all the distinctions of the old in their old form', but whether it continues the objectives of the Church in 'her earlier doctrinal work in a way which is effective and creative in the contemporary world'.

Or again (p. 181), 'We are more likely to prove loyal to the past in the important sense of the word loyal', if we think not so much in terms of the translation of old formulas into new sets of words as in terms of the continuation of the same task of interpreting the Church and Scriptures, her worship and her experience of salvation. In out attempts to pursue that task we may still go badly astray. But it is only as the Church as a whole gives herself with full seriousness to the task that true development becomes a genuine possibility. And the only test of whether the development in question is a true one is for the Church to ask herself repeatedly whether she is expressing as fully as she is able the things to which her Scriptures, her worship and her experience of salvation bear witness.

Professor Wiles seems to dismiss Newman as irrelevant. But Newman accepted—he was the first to accept—all this statement of what true development of doctrine should be; and he would scruple only at two things in it. First, he would not have allowed the adjective *only* in 'the only test of a true development'. He would say that the tests of true development were more complex and more varied than is here supposed. Secondly, he might not have liked the proposition that the Church should repeatedly ask herself whether she expresses her truths as fully as she is able. He might have wondered whether, once Christians gained some truths for themselves, they need to go on and on asking themselves whether they are sure that they are true; whether their conscience, as well as their minds, would not do better to get on with the job of trying to live Christian lives without undue fuss, as least until they are brought up sharp by some event which forces them to ask whether they are being faithful to the mind of Christ. He did not think that the best mind of an individual moves best by a constant examination of its own logic. The mind moves in harmony with the conscience, and in response to experience, which is partly more knowledge, but which is above all the experience of God and his ways. As he thought this way to be the way a single mind moved, so he thought that this was how the mind of the Church moved. Not by constant re-examination of the logic of what it was saying, but slowly and gently; with the corporate mind moving in harmony with a moral and intellectual response to the experience of the day, which was partly more knowledge but even more, the experience of God and his ways.

Among the Christian Churches of the later twentieth century, the issue here discussed is at the base of questions which are weighty; and in various ways.

First, and most obvious: the ecumenical harmony between Churches. A word like *transubstantiation* is seen to be a technical definition trying to explain a conviction of a people's devotion arising out of a particular philosophy of a particular epoch. The devotion matters more than the technical term. Protestants repudiated it because they thought the development to encourage superstition, or magical ideas, or even idolatry, among the common people. At least they found such superstition to exist, and suspected a theory like transubstantiation of being its cause. If the devotion matters more than the technical term, it is easier—not much easier but rather easier—for those who value the term to respect those who have scruples against it, either because of its past history, or because they think that the philosophy which created the technical term is not now credible. And it is easier—not much easier but a bit easier—for Protestants who see that it no longer encourages superstition (if it ever did) to respect those who value its use. That could be important in the harmony of Christendom.

If a Church can develop an expression of truth, it can develop it further. The most awkward of all doctrines, in the harmony between the Churches, is the doctrine that the Pope is infallible— when speaking officially, and on matters of faith and morals. This was defined in 1870, as an attempt to give the Catholic Church a forcible speaking authority amid the intellectual confusions and moral anarchies of the modern world. Of course it was believed, by that majority of bishops which defined it, to be no innovation in Christian doctrine but an expression of what true Catholics believed since the days of St Peter.

The definition had not the desired effect. It made the Pope's voice no more authoritative amid the intellectual and moral confusions. Certainly the authority of the Pope within the Catholic Church developed further after 1870. But that was because there were now newspapers, and then radio, and then television, and faster communications across the world. His increase of authority did not depend on what the bishops of 1870 defined about him, as a development of doctrine.

Newman, by then a Roman Catholic of twenty-five years standing, had no difficulty in accepting the truth of the bishops' definition about the Pope. He had not wanted it to happen, lest Protestants be put off from the Catholic Church. But he believed the Pope to be infallible and instantly accepted what the bishops declared. Only, he still did not know quite what was meant. He saw at once that the authorities of his Church had developed a statement which was in his eyes true so far as it went, but was partial; and sooner or later must be explained ('developed') further if it was to be fully intelligible in Christian terms.

A Church with a more Protestant tradition needs the same

kind of adaptation or development. It finds the process a little easier, but still not easy. Its doctrines are, so to speak, its trust deeds. If you alter them, you raise the question of identity and legitimacy. In 1571, the Church of England declared it necessary to the Church that we believe that Athanasius's Creed can be proved by most certain warrant of holy Scripture and must thoroughly be received and believed. Four hundred years later hardly any members of the Church believed any such thing. But the statement could not be retracted. Its sting had to be drawn; first by a declaration that ministers of the Church were not committed to any particular assent but a general assent to the 39 Articles in which this is contained; and secondly, by changes in liturgy (1974 onwards) which freed everyone from any necessity, or even direction, to use the creed as though they thought that it should be thoroughly received and believed.

In this way, the idea of development could become a liberating force among static formulas now obsolete or partial. As one of the best modern Catholic minds on this theme has written, 'The irrevocability of dogma does not entail the immutability of dogmatic formulas. All dogmatic statements are open to correction and adjustment so that they may express more adequately what they mean'. (J. H. Walgrave, *Unfolding Revelation* (1972), 38.)

In 1688 Bossuet would have rejected those sentences. Doctrine was static, and nothing but static except in minor explanation. In 1845 Newman could have accepted them, though he would not have expressed these sentences in that form. That is, Newman helped to bring more understanding; more integrity; a more realistic sense of history; a freer outlook to the Catholic mind, and through it to the mind of Christendom.

A book is a statement of someone's opinion at the time when he wrote. If he is invited to re-issue it nearly thirty years later, he will do well not to ask himself whether now he would write

xxx

as then he wrote. But what others have written since that time cannot but affect his mind. The second Vatican Council happened after the book was published, and gave an impetus to thinking on these theme.

Probably I would wish to show more anticipation of the schoolmen among the earliest Christians. The doctrine of Tertullian in the early third century, about the way in which the Spirit of God leads the Church into all truth, is remarkable, and a sign how deeply, and how early, the problem took hold of Christendom; in Tertullian's case, by meditation on the texts of the gospel of St John. The successors of Origen in the East had something of the same ideas, though in the manner of Greeks they cast it into a more intellectual form. Augustine (*de baptismo* 2, 3) recognized that the decisions of earlier 'plenary' councils of bishops were corrected by later councils, in the light of experience. St Vincent of Lérins was a conservative like Bossuet; yet the formulation of his conservatism was made in such a way as to recognize development in thought and understanding. His successors saw the conservatism far more clearly than they saw the idea of 'progress' with which Vincent surrounded it.

There is one point about Newman which others have made since and which I should wish to have made more clearly. In the earlier less formed centuries of Christian thinking, ideas of progress and development in religion were not purely intellectual. The soul reaches out to God in faith, and little by little finds the intellectual consequences of what is felt; and so with the Church. The process by which this happened is not purely intellectual, but also religious. The later medieval schoolmen, and still more the Spaniards of the Counter-Reformation, wanted to bring clarity into so loose a definition. The only way to make it clearer was to make it a process of the intellect, and not a reaching out in feeling, or in a sort of 'wordless' cognition. Therefore in defining the idea of development, they made it arid. Newman's contribution was not only to develop the idea of development in such a way that history could speak. He brought back feeling, conscience, religious experience, into the process of development. The word *development* was one of the least exciting of all words. The word *evolution* was one of the least exciting of all words. Darwin took the word *evolution* and made it speak to the human race. Newman took the word *development* and made it speak to Christendom.

Since Newman's day Christendom, Catholic or Protestant, has agreed on one thing. The experience of God in humanity is not only an experience of a gift given in a series of words; whether those words are the words of the Bible, or the words of preaching in a Church. This was always accepted as true about the individual. Always the Christian was believed to possess an immediacy in meeting God, as well as a guide, in his Bible, to the nature of that meeting. Protestants and Catholics came to find that the same is true, not only of the individual, but of the Church. The sense of possession of God is guided by the texts but not confined to the texts. Almost all are now agreed that the object of faith is not a series of sentences made up of words, whether the words are found in the text of the Bible or in the determinations by Churches. The object of faith is God alone. The knowledge of him is presented in a series of sentences; but the sentences point to the reality, they do not encompass the reality. The apprehension of a devout soul reaches out beyond the sentences to find that which is.

Therefore everyone, or nearly everyone, is now agreed on the possibility of better expressions of truth, in new circumstances or with new insights; not to reject the old but to explain the old; to make it no longer arid or irrelevant in a new age. A doctrine of development became necessary to Christendom. And in Catholicism, thanks to Newman, and to the meditations of others after him, the doctrine of development became associated with matters of the highest importance—devotion, and teaching, and above all the possibility of adapting both devotion and teaching to new times and new needs.

# CHAPTER I

## SEMPER EADEM

'The Catholic faith'—what is it? An unchanging gospel, handed down by pen and mouth from age to age, generation to generation, mother to child, teacher to taught, pulpit to pew. An inexhaustible treasure deposited in a bank, so that all may draw from it. That which has been believed in every place, in every century, by all Christian men and women. *Semper Eadem.*

So Christians affirmed in 1700, whether they were Catholics or Protestants. And so, 200 years later, Christians affirmed, whether they were Catholics or Protestants. But the affirmation did not, and could not, mean precisely the same in 1900 as it meant in 1700. In 1688 the mighty Bossuet, publishing his mightiest onslaught upon the Protestants, declared his axiom that *variation* in the teaching of the faith must be a sign of error, and was robustly confident, even to his own discomfiture, that no Christian could disagree with him and remain a Christian. Two centuries later, no Christian who seriously meditated upon the problem, could assent to the axiom with quite the assurance of Bossuet: and some Christians might have refrained from assenting until they had explained more precisely what they meant. The circumstance that during the last 200 years thinkers have varied in declaring what is meant by an unvarying truth and an unvarying doctrine, proves that the axiom is to us less axiomatic than it was to Bossuet. It would be paradoxical to assert 'I believe that Christian doctrine never changes but by that proposition I do not mean what my ancestors meant.'

Sir Henry Wotton (we are told by Izaak Walton) visited the church of a friendly priest in Rome to hear the vesper music. And the priest, 'seeing Sir Henry stand obscurely in a corner', sent to him a choirboy with a small piece of paper on which he had written 'Where was your religion to be found before Luther?' And presently Sir Henry wrote underneath 'My religion was to be found then, where yours is not to be found now, in the written Word of God.'

It was the most troublesome question of the early seventeenth century, the question which stretched the controversial muscles of the Society of Jesus or of King James' college of theological warriors at Chelsea. It was troublesome because both sides accepted a strictly immutable axiom. The apostles have given to their successors, and through their successors to us, a corpus of teaching which the Church must preserve if she is to remain the Church. Thereafter we should be able to discern this corpus being taught in all the centuries between the apostles and the year 1600; *quod ubique, quod semper, quod ab omnibus.* Where do you find in the tenth century or the thirteenth century, cried the Counter-Reformation, your teaching about the Eucharist or about justification by faith alone? The extant documents are rare and infrequent, answered the reforming defence, because the others were suppressed and destroyed by persecuting and un-Christian inquisitors. Where do you find in the second or third century, cried the Protestants in riposte, your teaching about transubstantiation or papal authority? The extant documents are rare and infrequent, replied the conservative defence, because the others were suppressed and destroyed by persecuting and un-Christian emperors. Can you find your faith in the Bible or the Fathers? asked the Protestants. Was there a thousand years at which God winked? retorted the Counter-Reformation. 'Though we, or an angel from heaven, preach any other gospel unto you than that you have received, let him be accursed'—how can the Council of Trent justify itself before the Pauline text? 'Upon this rock I will build my Church and the gates of hell shall not prevail against it'—how can the Lutherans and the Reformed justify themselves before this text when *ex hypothesi* their doctrine vanished out of historical record for centuries? So the argument swung, text and counter-text, historical example versus historical example, syllogism and counter-syllogism, jingle-jangle, the ingredients of an irresolvable deadlock.

On 27 June 1623, the Anglican Dr Featley fought a battle with the Jesuits Sweet and Fisher in a London dining-room, the prize being the allegiance of Edward Bugges Esquire. Fisher urged Featley to show ('from good authors') persons through the centuries who believed as Featley did: and he refused to be content with generalized assertions of continuity but pressed for names. Featley, who was no historian, desired at all costs to refrain from producing a list of names, and replied by asking for a list of persons ('from good authors') who in all ages had believed the doctrines of the Council of Trent. Fisher refused to be drawn. He would produce his list *after* Dr Featley had produced the Protestant list. Featley attempted to shift the discussion from the uncertain ground of historical inquiry to the more solid ground of theological syllogism. The manœuvre failed. 'Names, Names, Names' chanted a chorus of Fisher's sympathizers. 'Name visible Protestants in all ages.' 'What!' said Dr Featley, 'will nothing content you but a Buttery-book? You shall have a Buttery-book of names if you will stay awhile.' He began confidently at the first century and proceeded cautiously into the second century: and then refused to go further until Fisher had mentioned some Tridentines of the same centuries. Fisher declined: and the meeting ended, like most such meetings, in stalemate.[1]

The debate is characteristic of a particular epoch in the history of controversy. Both sides tried to avoid the awkward, ugly, irreducible snag. The Jesuit at first sought to hold the debate on the question 'Where was your church a century ago?' and to avoid the evidence of antiquity. The Protestant at first sought to hold the debate on the question, 'Where was your church in the time of the gospels?' and to avoid discussing the perpetuity of the faith. But arguments of this kind could not be contained within the decorous channel of a syllogistic debate. Each side was forced, sooner or later, to accept the historical challenge of the other. The Protestants must seek to prove historical continuity through the ages or they must alter their notion of continuity. The Roman Catholics must seek to prove the faithfulness of the Tridentine Church to antiquity or they must alter their notion of continuity. On the one side the massive tomes of Flacius and the Magdeburg Centuriators, tracing with scrupulous care the steady 'corruption' of the Roman Church, contained every single thinker of the medieval centuries who might in any sense be regarded as anti-Roman: Flacius inserted St Thomas Aquinas, Duns Scotus, and William of Occam into his catalogue of witnesses—one wonders what the zealous Oxonians, who tore folios of Scotus and sent wisps of paper fluttering round the quadrangles, would have said if they had known that a left-wing Lutheran could include even Scotus among the witnesses to the truth. On the other side the equally massive tomes of Cardinal Baronius, showing with scrupulous care the unchanging nature of tradition, contained every scrap and hint from antiquity which might be an early anticipation or example of a later doctrine or practice. From these scraps and hints Baronius attributed to apostolic times the celibacy of the priesthood, the institution of the feasts of Christmas and Epiphany, saints' days, the use of holy water, the cult of images which derived from the miracles wrought by the passing of St Peter's shadow.

The centre of theological gravity was shifting from the Bible into the field of ecclesiastical history. The Reformers, in appealing from the contemporary ecclesiastical authorities to the Bible and the Church of the first three, or the first six, centuries, had implicitly appealed to fair historical investigation. The defenders of the Counter-Reformation, on their side, needed history not only as a weapon and a shield, needed *Annals* to set against *Centuries*: they needed common ground with the Protestants if they were to argue with them. They could find a bridge for communication and debate neither in the Bible, since for one side

4

its data must be supplemented, and for the other side must not be supplemented, by tradition, nor in the decisions of ecclesiastical authority, since Protestants appealed from them to the Bible. But the bridge, the common ground, they could find in the scholarly study of antiquity. The Reformers, to prove that the Bible meant what they said it meant, should show that it had been so received in antiquity. The Counter-Reformers could sustain their argument from tradition only if sufficient evidence from antiquity could be discerned to favour it. Upon the evidence of antiquity, therefore, both sides were prepared to reason and to listen. It was not surprising that eminent Catholic scholars from Melchior Cano to Mabillon put ecclesiastical history in the van of theological study. Melchior Cano had written that theologians not expert in church history do not deserve the name of theologians. A theologian who knows not history, said Alexander, 'is scarcely as much as half a theologian'.[1]

Of this controversial appeal to historical inquiry as the evidence for an unchanging tradition of doctrine, Bossuet was the most celebrated representative.

When Edward Gibbon went up to Magdalen College, Oxford, to spend fourteen months, 'the most idle and unprofitable' of his whole life, he borrowed from another undergraduate Bossuet's two works, the *Exposition of the Catholic Doctrine* and the *History of the Variations of the Protestant Churches*. 'I read, I applauded, I believed....I surely fell by a noble hand....My conqueror oppressed me with the sacramental words *Hoc est corpus meum*, and dashed against each other the figurative half-meanings of the protestant sects.' For a century or more the *History of the Variations* was one of the sharpest weapons in the armoury of Catholic apologetic.

Bossuet had declared the axiom that variation in religion is always a sign of error; that the Christian religion came from its Lord complete and perfect; that the true Church had maintained immutably, *must* have maintained immutably, the deposit of truth which had been given to it. He stated this axiom in its most absolute and provocative form: not because he intended to provoke, but because he believed that no one who contradicted the axiom could remain a Christian. He did not suppose that the Protestants would accept his interpretation of the axiom. He was not so naïve as to expect Protestants to admit that their religion had varied in substance, nor so sanguine as to imagine that everyone would allow the unqualified claim of the church of Rome to immutability. But the axiom itself he proclaimed with an absolute confidence as common to all parties. He used the phrase 'without fear of contradiction'.

Why was Bossuet so confident?

He was confident, first, for certain reasons peculiar to himself, certain idiosyncrasies of his mind and training, certain special features of his situation. To notice these idiosyncrasies is important inasmuch as they detract from his representative character as the protagonist of a controversial school.

Of all those who have written upon Bossuet, Henri Bremond enjoys the widest reputation in England. Bremond was possessed of gifts which enabled him to understand the religious mind of the French seventeenth century as few others have understood it. A delicacy of mind, an enthusiasm for the development of spirituality, a critical and questioning approach, a sensitive style, a wide sympathy and comprehension of men and the world—all these were gifts which enabled him to set forth pre-eminently the religious lights and shadows of that age. Yet, where Bossuet was concerned, Bremond suffered from certain prejudices, or at least disadvantages. He was witty, sometimes too witty. There is just enough of the appearance of a balloon about Bossuet to make any humorist wish to prick him: and Bremond was naturally equipped with a satirical pin. Bremond was born with a rebellious imp, Bossuet was the dignified voice of authority. Bremond wielded a rapier, Bossuet a bludgeon. Bremond admired and pursued scholarly investigation, Bossuet feared and resisted innovation. Bremond passionately studied the life of prayer and mystical theology, Bossuet had triumphantly assaulted Fénelon. Bremond disliked Bossuet more than any other figure in the long span of Christian centuries except perhaps Rancé. His portrait therefore is not far short of a caricature. He seized upon undoubted facets of Bossuet's mind and, like a clever cartoonist, drew them in high relief.

Consider this judgment. 'We cannot regard Bossuet as an authoritative theologian, unless we regard as authoritative the chemist who repeats line by line all the opinions of Lavoisier.'[1] The judgment is blinkered and anachronistic. It is blinkered because it demands that the thinker of a deductive epoch should treat theology as an inductive science. It is anachronistic because it expects originality from a theologian. In the seventeenth century the last quality desired by a Gallican theologian was originality. Jansen once expressed the Gallican theory epigrammatically by asserting that theology was an affair of the memory, not of the reasoning faculty, and the contents of his famous book upon St Augustine proved that his practice was consonant with his theory. A man who believes in rational inquiry may disagree with a man who thinks he can repose upon deductions from texts accepted as final authorities. But to turn disagreement into contempt is to close the eyes to the intellectual revolution of two hundred years.

Bossuet's mind, it is true, was static. If you rummage assiduously among the forty-three volumes of his works, you can without difficulty discover him to contradict himself and if you failed to do so you would regard it as miraculous. But the outlook, the principles, the method, spring to birth, like Gibbon's style, full-grown. From his work as a young priest at Metz and his controversy with Ferry to the correspondence with Leibniz in his old age, he adopted the same general ground, measured everything with the same yardstick. Touch the bell anywhere and it sends forth the same note, deep and serene, across the fields.

7

Through the thorniest years of the Gallican controversy and the defence of the four articles, a time of stress and argument when, if ever, a thinker's mind might be expected to move, Bossuet did not budge.[1] A static mind is sometimes static because its owner is stupid, or complacent, or arrogant. Bossuet was not stupid, nor complacent, nor arrogant. Hallam, it is true, thought that Bossuet was arrogant. But Hallam had read little more than superficially into Bossuet and as a good Whig was sometimes tempted to equate with arrogance a Tory's confidence that he knows the right answer. Certainly Bossuet was inclined to admire his own arguments when he later re-read them. But this was not the strident conviction of a Tertullian. It was the quiet unstrained confidence of an integrated and rounded personality who is assured that he has built his faith upon a rock. He was, I think, a 'naturally' religious person: and the doubt which a Pascal conceived to be inseparable from faith did not enter his make-up. If you were to take Bossuet as the alpha and Newman as the omega, Bossuet's certitude was a rounded union of intellectual and moral certainties, an integrated philosophy of life: Newman's certitude was moral, a certitude of the conscience—at the bare intellectual level he spent part of his life stretched on the rack of doubt.

The national circumstances of Bossuet's lifetime reinforced his assurance. Louis XIV revoked the Edict of Nantes in 1685. Throughout Bossuet's life the Huguenots were on the run. He became the religious mouthpiece of a conquering political party. When John Jewel preached his famous sermon at St Paul's Cross on 26 November 1559, he challenged the conservatives to produce any evidence from the first 600 years of Christian history to support their case. The moderate excess was natural to the mouthpiece of a triumphant group of returning exiles. *Mutatis mutandis* Bossuet fell into similar exaggerations. He habitually occupied a pulpit and habitually introduced into his writing an element of the preacher's dogmatic force: *nous pouvons dire, sans craindre d'être repris.....* His genius was didactic, magisterial, endowed with the ability to convince and carry by a rich combination of authority and persuasiveness; a genius dependent on what has been called his 'immobilité impérieuse'. It has been said, and by no enemy, that Bossuet was 'l'homme de toutes les autorités et de toutes les stabilités'. He had never been in opposition: he had never pleaded his case among a crowd of hostile spectators: he had seen eminent Protestants, from Marshal Turenne downwards, respond to the religious arguments and the social pressure of the age of Louis XIV. But we must not attribute the assurance to a respectable and intellectual version of the dragonnades.

Bossuet was a theologian, not a historian. Yet, as a historical investigator, he was not contemptible. Rébelliau, in the book of 1891 which is even now the most instructive guide to Bossuet's relations with the Protestants (*Bossuet, historien du Protestantisme*), proved, astonishingly, that for their epoch the inquiries used in the *History of the Variations* were advanced and critical. Living in the century of scholars like Petau, Mabillon, Morin, Tillemont, Basnage, Leclerc, Daillé, Ruinart, Montfaucon, he could not remain untouched by the critical spirit. But Rébelliau also showed, incidentally, that he was a critical historian only in his history of the Protestants. The reason is interesting. He was looking for variations and trying to display them: and he was therefore fully conscious, all too conscious, of the changing conditions of 'heretical' thought. But when he came to write universal history, or the history of the Catholic Church, he was so much on the watch for unvariations that history was lost in dogmatic interpretation and a pattern was imposed. The *Discourse on Universal History* is stamped with an ecclesiastical pattern, a smooth ebb and flow, a structure of interpretation. As a true Augustinian Bossuet saw Providence, in supreme dominion and transcendent wisdom, guiding and controlling the historical series, hurling down empires and raising them up, delivering to the sword a Rome obdurate in her heathenism and intoxicated with the blood of the martyrs, creating a new and Christian Rome like a phoenix from the ashes. 'Let us talk no more of chance, or of fortune, or talk of them only as of a name with which we cover our ignorance.'[1] The world and its history is a marvellous concatenation, a fascinating and complex design, like the stupendous edifice of Solomon's Temple. Bossuet's history has little room for the rugged, the unexpected, the anfractuous. If we do not see this plan stamped upon the face of history, we deserve to see nothing, but to be delivered up to our hardness of heart. Behold in this providential history the progress of the Church, ever assailed and ever triumphant, ever the same from the beginning of the world. If again you take Bossuet as the alpha and Newman as the omega, Bossuet was an incurable historical optimist, Newman an incurable historical pessimist. Newman saw little in history but disaster, destruction and despair, the crimes and follies of mankind. Bossuet saw little in history but St John getting safe from the boiling oil.

So much for idiosyncrasies. It is important to put these on one side, or at least to be aware of them, in order to distinguish more accurately the representative character of this apologetic. For the *History of the Variations* was the classic representative of the historical school of Gallican apologetic.

This Gallican apologetic was un-scholastic: it was made possible by the needs of Counter-Reformation controversy: and it was fostered by a partial illusion of historical inquiry.

Bremond thought that if Bossuet had dared to speak his mind he would have accused St Thomas Aquinas of asking too many questions. But Bremond supposed that Bossuet was eminent among those who write more sumptuously than they think, that he was damming the river of living theology, that his prose might suitably be compared to a dazzling fog. These hyperbolical condemnations rest upon two truths about Bossuet which a less antipathetic critic might eye more benevolently. Bossuet's mind was pastoral. As he worked away in his study, surrounded by folio volumes and turning with affection the pages of the Benedictine edition of St Augustine or gazing at the Augustinian texts inscribed on his table, he could never quite forget the souls of his diocese and the souls of France. He did not believe that academic research was necessary to salvation. When he observed the results of the Biblical critic and ex-Oratorian Richard Simon, he was inclined to believe that research hampered salvation. But, still more, Bossuet's mind was un-scholastic. (Un-scholastic, rather than anti-scholastic, is the right word: for Bossuet respected the schoolmen, at least until they became nominalistic logicians, because he thought them so splendidly patristic.) This neglect of the schoolmen he shared with many of the Gallican apologists of the seventeenth century. Perhaps it would hardly have been possible to hold this particular form of the doctrine of immutability without neglecting the schoolmen.

The conservatives had shared in the general reaction of the sixteenth century against the schoolmen. The Protestants were not alone in accepting the nominalistic assumptions, in distrusting the forms which rational inquiry had taken, in questioning the superstructure which reason had built upon patristic thought. Many conservatives of the new school of apologetic, rising from 1530 onwards, found that against the scriptural arguments of the Protestants the time-honoured distinctions of the schools blundered and misfired, and they therefore looked for common ground in Biblical exegesis and in patristic theology. This neglect of the schoolmen was not to be found in the more traditional religious disciplines. In course of time we can see a cleavage appearing between those who believed that the Fathers were the criterion of all controversy, and those (like many of the Dominican and Jesuit theologians) who believed that the Catholic tradition could not be sustained without the help of the scholastic theologians. It is possible to trace at a conservative university like Louvain the growing discrepancy between the two approaches.[1] The patristic school was in part encouraged by the needs of controversy. To refute the Protestants one could not merely reassert old dogmas.

To convince the Protestants there must be common ground in the argument. And while the Protestants always asserted that the evidence of the early Church must be controlled by that of the Bible, they were often ready to argue upon the correct interpretation of patristic evidence, since they were confident that the patristic evidence favoured them. The conservative scholars engaged on the publication of the primitive and patristic sources, a work culminating in the eight folio volumes of the *Bibliotheca Patrum* published at Paris in 1575 by Marguérin de la Bigne, canon of Bayeux. De la Bigne intended to provide a store-house of ammunition to prove against the Protestants the continuity of patristic and Counter-Reformation theology: and its utility is shown by its frequent and enriched editions during the next century.

Part of the strength of the movement away from the scholastics towards the Fathers thus rested upon the needs of controversy. But it also derived something of its power because so many conservatives had implicitly accepted some of the assumptions of the opposition. Often trained in nominalist ways of thought, they suspected the scholastic opinions almost as deeply as the Protestants. When the Protestants utilized scholastic theology to prove the incompatibility of modern dogma with ancient dogma, there were Catholics who readily defended themselves by throwing scholastic theology overboard. 'As for the gew-gaws of schoolmen...,' wrote Thomas Harding to John Jewel, 'I utterly despise them.' A theologian and bishop like Jansen believed as firmly as any Protestant that the scholastics had corrupted the primitive doctrines of the Church.[1] There was never a sharp division between those who continued the scholastic tradition and those who were going behind the scholastics to the Fathers. But a Suarez or a Melchior Cano on the one side, a Castro or a Catharinus on the other side, represent different attitudes: these different attitudes derived, not from discrepant doctrines of tradition, but from the diversity of approach between any systematic theologian and any apologist. There was no hard and fast

line. Bellarmine and du Perron had been subject to both influences: and many other theologians, who for the Protestants'
sake appealed to the Fathers, approached antiquity after a scholastic
training and found scholastic points of view. It is fair to say,
however, that nearly all the Gallican apologists surrounded themselves with a vaguely un-scholastic atmosphere. Even Mabillon,
not (perhaps) in the constitutional sense a Gallican, and a scholar
who honoured the schoolmen more highly than many of his
contemporaries, yet considered the *Summa* too long and too time-
absorbing, and believed that in spite of its excellence the student
could probably use his time more profitably in reading the
scriptures, the Fathers and the Councils.[1] In the classical *apologies*
of the seventeenth century, scholastic thought played almost no
part. The Jansenists Nicole and Arnauld were both eminent
patristic scholars who appealed to the perpetuity and stability of
the Catholic tradition: and Bossuet approved their plan and its
execution.[2]

Anyone who reads in the little handbooks of controversy,
lively little handbooks published by the troopers of the Counter-
Reformation, will see that, howsoever the argument may be
adorned and illustrated, the key apologetic weapon is the appeal
to an unchanging tradition. Protestants have varied in the faith:
you have changed the doctrine and practice of a thousand years.
You are a new religion. Where was your church before Luther?
This tactic of attack or defence had been countenanced, though
not canonized, by the decree of the Council of Trent upon scripture and traditions. It was widely believed, as Bossuet believed,
that if you admitted change you had admitted what the Protestants
called *corruption* of primitive Christianity. More than that: if you
admitted change, you appeared to be undermining your own
bastion against the onslaughts of the Protestant controversialists.
Among those who were accusing the Reformers of altering everything, it was a natural and an insidious temptation to exaggerate

13

the static and immutable quality of their own thought and practice. The critical acumen of the *History of the Variations* brings into higher relief the dogmatizing qualities of the *Discourse on Universal History*.

The argument, the appeal, was useless unless the documents supported it. To many conservatives the documents of antiquity appeared sufficiently to support them.

It may be that the documents appeared to support them a little more vigorously than later they proved to do. For the primitive documents still included some forged documents, the spurious nature of which had not yet been proved, though in most cases it had been suggested. The works of Dionysius the Areopagite, the Isidorian decretals, the Clementine Recognitions, the Apostolic Constitutions, part of the Athanasian Corpus—these and others had been challenged by humanist or reformer, but were still thought by many to be genuine. Only during the second half of the seventeenth century, only during Bossuet's lifetime, did medieval scholarship become competent enough to reach assured or almost assured conclusions about authenticity. The general picture of the primitive Church was still confused by the existence of documents which did not date from the century which they claimed to represent. This is not to say that Protestant scholarship was better equipped because it challenged the authenticity of these documents. Throughout the sixteenth century and into the seventeenth century many reputable Protestants, and indeed some reputable Roman Catholics, accepted as authentic the scandalous legend of Pope Joan, despite the weighty arguments to the contrary. John Jewel and other learned Protestants looked favourably upon legends that Joseph of Arimathaea came to Glastonbury, or that St Paul visited England on his circuitous route to Spain. Neither side possessed equipment or experience to sort these problems definitively until the years after 1650, even more after 1680. Gallican apologetic still partly rested on conditions of historical inquiry which were beginning to change momentously even while Bossuet was writing.

14

The argument from an unchanging tradition therefore looked more defensible than it was to prove to be. But strong it certainly was. It was strong, in part, because it was Gallican. They were pushing the schoolmen quietly and politely aside: they were not defending the papal supremacy as a primitive doctrine: they were not seeking to maintain theories of indulgences and the like which had appeared late in Christian history. Provided that they remained sturdily patristic in their scholarship, they were admirably entrenched. Throughout the seventeenth century, the Gallican use of history went far to counter the proverb that no man was ever converted by an argument. How formidable was the fortress may be judged, among other signs, by the Protestant Daillé's work *De usu patrum*, published in 1631. Daillé was among the most eminent patristic scholars of the century. So far from wishing to throw overboard the Fathers, he devoted his life to the attempt to prove that substantially they were on the side of the Protestants. Nevertheless he was driven, by the arguments of du Perron and others, to write the *De usu patrum* which in undermining the Roman Catholic appeal to patristic authority equally undermined his own appeal to patristic authority, and more than any other single book would be utilized by the Latitudinarians to show the weakness of any appeal to the Fathers. The purely historical argument brought in converts as did no other arguments of the century. Even Isaac Casaubon admitted in a letter to Uytenbogaert that the Calvinists' departures from the faith of the Fathers were a grave source of perturbation to his own faith. Chillingworth became a Roman Catholic for a time because he found an opposition between the doctrine of the Fathers and the doctrines of the Protestants— he went over, he said 'because the doctrine of the Church of Rome is conformable, and the doctrine of Protestants contrary to the doctrine of the Fathers, by the confession of Protestants themselves'. François Pithou told Father Sirmond that he had been converted through reading the Fathers of the Church, especially the *Commonitory* of St Vincent of Lérins. (During the seventeenth century the *Commonitory*, with its celebrated canon *quod ubique quod semper quod ab omnibus*, ran through twenty-three editions and twelve translations in France alone.) Another convert told Mabillon that 'nothing had contributed more to disabusing him of his error than the study of ecclesiastical history'.[1]

The fortress was not unlike the Tractarian fortress of 1830 to 1850. Bossuet would have understood Pusey or Liddon better than he would have understood Newman or Ward, better than he would have understood Duns Scotus or Gabriel Biel or Suarez. Indeed the fortress was not unlike the doctrine of tradition in the contemporary English school of Caroline divines. Bossuet and his friends acclaimed George Bull's works in defence of the Nicene faith: Mabillon, among his list of books suitable for monastic libraries, recommended Anglicans like Bull, Pearson, Ussher, Henry Hammond. For the defence of the Fathers against Daillé's onslaught, more than one continental theologian sent his readers to the apology for the Fathers by the high Anglican Matthew Scrivener.

No man can be unaffected by the assurance of his age. The glory of Catholic France: the revocation of the Edict of Nantes: the power of Gallican apologetic: the sufficient success of the efforts to convert Protestants and to controvert their pastors: the Augustinian doctrine of Providence: the preacher's authoritative tone: the quiet stability of his character—all these contributed to the static quality of Bossuet's mind. Other writers had pleaded before him the argument of variations. But only a writer with this background and this outlook could have written so persuasively and so trenchantly the *History of the Variations of the Protestant Churches*. As philosophers seek to prove the ego by declaring that change is only intelligible to a something which is itself unchanging, the book—even the title of the book—was possible only to a man who knew that he stood in the immobile, unvarying tradition of a continuous system of doctrines.

The Church's doctrine [he wrote] is always the same.... The Gospel is never different from what it was before. Hence, if at any time someone says that the faith includes something which yesterday was not said to be of the faith, it is always *heterodoxy*, which is any doctrine different from *orthodoxy*. There is no difficulty about recognizing false doctrine: there is no argument about it: it is recognized at once, whenever it appears, merely because it is new....[1]

Heresy merely because it is new? Surely, someone will say, Bossuet must have allowed some progress in doctrine, he must have allowed that the Church has defined some doctrines more clearly than they were at first defined? Was he not familiar with every line of the *Commonitory* of St Vincent which contains such an idea? How else can one account for the decrees of the Council of Trent, or even the canons of the Council of Nicaea?

A learned scholar (M. Struman)[2] has examined this question and answered it, almost without qualification, in the negative.

If you had told Bossuet that doctrine had 'progressed', he would have agreed. But he would normally have understood the word to mean that it had spread like a mustard-seed, that the word once taught in Palestine and delivered to the saints now resounded through the earth as the waters cover the sea. By the progress of doctrine he normally meant that the faith had crept or flown from city to town and town to village and village to hamlet, from father to son and schoolmaster to pupil, from one generation to another. By the progress of doctrine he meant, not a deeper *understanding* of the word once delivered, but evangelistic success and missionary heroism. Doctrine progresses not by Christians perceiving that it contains implications not hitherto known, but when more Christians receive it accurately.

Then what happens when the Church defines doctrine? What happens when the authorities of the Church insert the words 'of one substance' into the 'Nicene' Creed and declare that Arianism is a heresy?

Put the question another way. Was Arianism a heresy before the Church officially and authoritatively said it was a heresy? Or did it only become a heresy in consequence of the definition? Was Arius 'guilty' of anything until after the Council of Nicaea?

Put the question another way. The bishops who troubled the finances of the imperial postal service by travelling from far and wide to an ecumenical council, were they attending the council simply to declare what their Church believed already, or were they attending the council in order to form a corporate mind upon a matter where uncertainty, indecision and variety of opinion were reigning? If a thinker, a spirited or pertinacious or daring or unbalanced thinker propounds a new theory or speculation startling to his fellow-Christians—let us say, that the Book of Genesis is not in all points to be understood as an accurate description of historical events—is this new speculation known to be heresy by the fact that it is new, or does the Church need to meet, to discuss, to meditate, in order to find a corporate mind upon a theory which has seldom been propounded before? (In the case of Genesis, in the *Essays and Reviews* case of 1860–4, some members of Convocation, like Archdeacon Denison, urged that the speculation was heretical simply because it was new: other members of Convocation urged that it was heretical, not because it was new, but because its consequences could be regarded as destroying the traditional idea of revelation.)

It might be argued that the answer to this question depends entirely upon the speculation put forward. Some new speculations can be seen immediately, by any instructed person, to be incompatible with Christian faith and therefore do not need defining as right or wrong. Other speculations appear immediately to be legitimate points of debate and difference among Christians, and therefore unsuitable for definition as right and wrong. The pinpoint of the difficulty is only those speculations which are not obviously incompatible with Christian faith, but the consequences and ramifications of which prove subsequently to be so incompatible. Then there needs to be meditation, discussion, inquiry, by the representatives of the Church.

Bossuet would, I think, have recognized these distinctions; though, like St Bernard of Clairvaux, he would have shrunk from admitting that doctrinal speculation could in many circumstances be wholesome or profitable. But in the difficult case he would have insisted that the Church was perfectly conscious of her mind upon the general question in debate, and that all she was doing in a discussion before defining was *applying* her mind to the particular question. In no sense would Bossuet have said that the Church needed to 'make up her mind'. She never makes 'new' articles of faith. She only declares what she has always believed— explicitly, consciously, and continuously believed.

Put the question still another way. In several celebrated texts St Augustine asserted that heresies are 'good' for the Church, useful to the Church. Heresies are useful to the Church because they help her to explain herself more fully. If heretics are useful to the Church, may it be said that heretics are helping her to 'make up her mind'? Bossuet, the Augustinian, rejoiced in these texts of the master. Heresies have helped the Church to explain herself. But it is to *explain* herself. She knew the truth all the time, but she had not always found the most appropriate words to communicate and expound that knowledge.[1]

To describe this good by-product of heresy, Bossuet used two words—clarification and explication. The phrase 'explication of doctrine' (we shall find) was used by others to mean a notion quite different, is used by others to signify an idea akin to the idea of development. Bossuet did not mean that. What he mainly meant was *translation into clear language*. The Church knows what she believes. The heretics help her to find new language to express that belief. It is as though an American visitor were to enter a shop in England and ask for a pair of 'suspenders'. He knows precisely what he wants: to himself he can express his want perfectly. But the behaviour of the shop-assistant shows him that in England the sentence is liable to ludicrous misunderstanding, that he is not offered what he wants. He therefore engages in a short discussion or inquiry, after which he can express himself in more accurate English and get what he wants. He was always clear what he wished to buy. He did not enter the shop undecided, not knowing whether he might not buy an elastic belt or a piece of string, only to be convinced by argument that he wanted 'suspenders'. But he needed a little inquiry before he could make his desire as clear to the shop-assistant as it was to himself. This is a symbol of the process which Bossuet thinks to happen when the Church defines a doctrine. The view that heretics help the Church to 'make up her mind' he once called a 'crude illusion'. The view that heretics help the Church to communicate her mind he warmly and vigorously embraced. He was far too instructed a historian to suppose that the word *consubstantial* was apostolic or that the word *transubstantiation* was primitive. But it was the words, not the ideas, which had changed. These new words, admittedly new words, were the clearest means of communicating truths which the Church believed before ever the words were invented.

And so Bossuet was able to give to the *History of the Variations* its trenchant, provocative, unconditional, infuriating, asking-to-be-refuted preface—

If by such proofs they show us the least unconstancy, or the least variation in the dogmata of the Catholic Church from her first origin down to us, that is from Christianity's first foundation; readily will I own to them that they are in the right, and I myself will suppress this my whole history.

He would have been surprised and shocked if he had learnt that, only a few years before, a theologian in Prague had been teaching one of the most extreme theories of development ever put forward by a reputable Catholic thinker.

# CHAPTER II

# LOGICAL EXPLANATION

From the vigorous, warm, gusty oratory of the Gallican apologists, we pass into a thinner and cooler and quieter atmosphere, that of the Spanish lecture-room. In the universities and religious houses of Valladolid, Salamanca, Alcalá, Coimbra, Saragossa, the problem could be debated on its merits as a theological problem, unhampered by the needs of Protestant controversy. Representatives of a tradition of inquiry, of teaching, of exposition reaching steadily back for full 500 years, the heirs of the schoolmen were continuing their rigorous and unimpassioned investigations.

The American wealth of Spain had enabled adequate professorial endowments and new collegiate foundations like Alcalá to stimulate theological inquiry. Through the sixteenth century, in dogmatics, exegetics, mystical and ascetical thought, casuistry, canon law, Spanish theologians were steadily extending their analytical range, their patristic and philosophical equipment, their speculative power. The political influence of Spain carried the prestige of their thought to Rome, north Italy, the Netherlands, to Ingolstadt and southern Germany. Though the Nominalist and Scotist traditions continued in particular chairs (it was said that 'Spain gave sanctuary to the theology of Paris') the University of Salamanca had initiated a renaissance of Thomism, a philosophy which was canonized and disseminated when the Dominican Pope Pius V elevated St Thomas Aquinas among the doctors of the Church. The *Summa* was being substituted for the *Sentences* of Peter Lombard as the matter for academic comment. The new Jesuit order had adopted Aquinas as its theological patron: and by the end of the sixteenth century the promise shown by men like Lainez and Salmeron had been fulfilled in the most learned, acute, analytical and original theologians of the Jesuit order, Molina, Suarez, and Gabriel Vasquez, to be followed shortly by John de Lugo. The originality included, it must be allowed, a readiness to treat St Thomas more freely than was customary among the Dominican commentators. A Suarez or a Lugo felt at liberty to admit contradictions or obscurities in the master, to examine, criticize and depart from his judgments where they did not understand them or believed that later information or later controversy had rendered something in the *Summa* obsolete or unintelligible. The Dominicans suspected this freedom, sought to counter it, persuaded the authorities of Salamanca in 1627 to forbid teaching which was not the authentic teaching of St Augustine and Aquinas. The rivalry between the two schools—the faithful Thomists and the Thomists like Suarez who felt free to modify, was not without its graver consequences. The Jesuits, perhaps, were more conscious than the Dominicans of the problems raised by the Protestants, more conscious that new arguments had been thrown into the debate which could not leave the old answers unexamined. And in the argument over grace and justification this consciousness of the Protestant claim could change cool discussion into heated controversy. But the Jesuits were not framing their theology in order to controvert the Protestants. They were working in the true and authentic tradition of scholastic thought. It was the latest flowering of medieval divinity.

In the long list of questions which they had asked themselves was our question, the question how an immutable revelation is compatible with the historical definitions of the Church. If, as all Christians are agreed, the revelation given to men is absolute and final and cannot be supplemented, how is it that the Church has defined doctrines, that is 'made new articles of faith'?

The masters of their tradition—thinkers like Duns Scotus or Bonaventure or Aquinas—had suggested a possible answer. They had used logical words. In defining a doctrine, the Church was not putting into the revelation a truth which was not there before the definition. It was displaying more clearly the inner content of the revelation, explicating what was implicit.

The schoolmen had introduced these notions, first in considering the status of the heroes of the Old Testament. According to the *Epistle to the Hebrews*, it was *by faith* that Abel offered to God a more excellent sacrifice than Cain; by faith Enoch was translated, by faith Noah prepared an ark, by faith Moses kept the passover and the sprinkling of blood. What faith was this?

It was certain that without faith none could be saved. Everyone believed that the patriarchs and prophets, the fathers and ancients of Israel, had been saved or were being saved or would be saved in the Judgment. By common consent these fathers were members of the true Church, by common consent they might legitimately receive the name of Christians. *Una est fides novi et veteris Testamenti.* They must therefore (in some measure) have believed and assented to the doctrines of the Christian Church, at least to the 'substance' of those doctrines. It was obvious that they had not consciously assented to truths which the Church had only learnt to teach after hearing them from the lips of the apostles. That they were saved by faith in Christ seemed evident from the language of St Paul: yet their faith in Christ could not have been openly formulated, could not have included conscious acceptance of the articles of faith which the Christian Church taught as necessary to salvation.

Medieval theologians met the difficulty by an analogy between the unformed faith of uneducated Christians and the unformed faith of the patriarchs. The peasant child on the manor, the woman with the issue of blood in the gospel, the rough warrior in a crusading army, believed the gospel—in general terms. They could not read the Bible, they could not describe the detailed articles of their faith, still less comprehend the relations of those articles. They gave a vague, general, diffused assent to God and 'what the Church teaches'. They possessed faith sufficient for

salvation. But this faith was not open faith, articulated faith—
it was *fides velata* rather than *fides distincta*, as Peter Lombard had
described it in the *Sentences*;[1] *implicit faith* rather than *explicit faith*
as a row of commentators developed and analysed the idea.

The schoolmen did not frame the distinction with one eye
upon the doctrine of tradition. It arose ultimately from meditation upon the plight of the Old Testament patriarchs, and was
more precisely formulated after meditation upon the nature of an
uninstructed faith. But, once framed, it was eminently adaptable
to explain the increase of doctrinal precision in the Christian
Church. The *homoousios*, it was now argued, was but 'explicating'
what the ante-Nicene Christians, or some ante-Nicene Christians,
had believed less explicitly. A modern theologian might hesitate
before applying to the corporate faith of the Church a distinction
so useful in defining the faith of an individual. The medieval
theologian felt no such difficulty. He did not even raise the
question whether the analogy was legitimate. For among his
doctrinal assumptions was the idea of continuity between the new
Israel and the old. Indeed he did not distinguish the new Israel
from the old. For him the Church was born, not at Pentecost,
but in Abraham or in Adam. He was rarely aware that change and
explication appeared in the history of the Church since the
apostles. But he was frequently aware that the Church of the Old
Testament had grown in the knowledge of Christ. Because the
Church of the Old Testament was continuous with the Church
of the New Testament, the analogy of implicit faith was easily,
inevitably transferable from the one to the other. To 'transfer'
something one needs to be conscious of *A* versus *B*: and they were
only aware of the continuous existence of *A*, under two different
dispensations.

Words like *explicit* and *implicit* have a history in traditional
logic. Their logical status was not the reason why they had been
brought in to serve this particular purpose of explaining how and
why doctrine changes. But as soon as the analysts sought to

expand or illustrate the analogy, they turned naturally to logic, to the syllogism. The deduction from two premises is *implicated* in those premises. The conclusion of the syllogism is an *explication* of a truth which before was implied by, but perhaps concealed in, the premises. Already Aquinas and Scotus had pointed to the logical element in the explication which was the Church's unfolding of its doctrine. For logic afforded the precise analogy which was needed—to explain how there could be *addition without change*. If it is revealed that $2 + 2 = 4$, then it may in a sense be said to be an addition if the Church suddenly tells us that $4 + 4 = 8$. Yet nothing has been added to the original revelation. The Church, being inerrant, could pronounce definitions of disputed articles. The Church believed doctrines before it formally defined them: but that the definition is in some sense an 'addition' is proved by the vagueness of patristic language upon some dogmatic points, and the inability of ancient language to defeat modern heresies. Therefore the definition, if it is not a mere declaration of what is manifestly the faith, is a declaration of its implications—those inferences which must follow by necessary conclusion from the revealed data of the faith. If definitions were necessary inferences, they were perhaps adding a 'something', a clarification to Christians of the faith: yet no one could assert that they were additions to the meaning of the revelation—from eternity they followed necessarily from the revealed data. It was like (this is not a medieval comparison) the slow opening of the petals of a rose-bud.

The medieval schoolmen, to whom the issue was speculative, rarely did more than point to the logical analogy and offer occasional illustrations of it. Their successors of the Counter-Reformation proceeded to investigate more analytically the properties of 'logical explication' when it was applied to the doctrines of the Christian Church.

Was the idea of logical deduction a parable, an analogy, or did the Church actually infer something from the premises revealed to it? Were they saying, when the Church defines a doctrine, it is not adding *ab extra* to the revelation, *in the same way as* the conclusion of a syllogism is not adding *ab extra* to the premises? Or were they saying, when the Church defines a doctrine, it is not adding *ab extra* to the revelation *because* its definition is a conclusion contained in the revealed premises? The divines of the late Middle Ages plunged into the second of these intellectual pools. For to say that the definition *was like* a logical deduction explained nothing: it was a simple tautology, a different way of saying precisely what you were trying to show. To say that it *was* a logical deduction solved the chief paradox of dogmatic history, the paradox that an unchanging revelation had been changed.

This proposition, once asserted, was like the peak in Darien which stout Cortes climbed. It opened a sudden view into an ocean of new possibilities.

If you were to go, in imagination and in sympathy, to a Spanish lecture-room of the middle or early seventeenth century, say to the University of Salamanca, perhaps the most eminent of the Spanish universities of that age, and had listened to a discussion of the article *de fide*, you would have heard an analysis of the varieties of syllogism available to the theologian. Though the atmosphere of the lecture-room would have been lively and enthusiastic, with students ready to applaud or to stamp their feet, the reasoning of the lecturer would have been cool and exact in its learned analysis.

A necessary deduction from two premises is as certain as the premises. A revealed premise is certain, absolutely certain, certain with the certainty of revelation, certain *fide divina* as the theologians expressed it. If therefore two revealed premises may be put together to produce a consequence, the consequence must be as certain as the premises, and it can only be as certain as the premises if it has itself the certainty of revelation...

It is revealed that God was in Christ.

It is revealed that Christ was very man.

It is therefore a necessary inference that in Christ were two natures. The conclusion is as certain as the premises, certain with the certainty of revelation. It was held, therefore, that the council at Chalcedon of 451, in determining its Christological formula about the two natures of Christ, had not innovated upon the data revealed by scripture: it had declared the inner content, or the necessary consequence, of scripture. It was held to be impossible to deny the two natures without denying at the same time the revelation in scripture.

But suppose that one of the premises is not revealed, is not certain with the certainty of revelation.

For example: there might be a revealed major premise and an unrevealed minor premise, thus:

All infants validly baptized are regenerate.

I am morally certain, I have immediate knowledge, that I fulfilled the requisite conditions today in baptizing this baby.

Is it therefore revealed to me, *de fide* to me, that this baby is regenerate? Is it revealed, not only that all babies validly baptized are regenerate, but that this particular and individual baby is regenerate?

Spanish theology (for the most part) replied that it was so revealed. If the universal is revealed, all the particular instances contained in the universal must be revealed. And there is in this instance immediate and indubitable knowledge that the particular is a true instance of the universal proposition.

But there are other unrevealed propositions which as minor premises contain a greater element of doubt, and are no longer resting upon an immediate apprehension or experience:

In every Mass validly celebrated the Host is truly consecrated (revealed major).

This Mass which I am attending is being validly celebrated (unrevealed minor).

Therefore—is it *revealed* to me that in this Mass the Host is truly consecrated?

Not so certainly. For this is not only dependent upon immediate experience. The conditions laid down for valid celebration include certain conditions about the status of the priest, conditions like whether he has been truly baptized or truly ordained, conditions about which the communicant cannot satisfy himself with an immediate certainty. Most Spanish thought therefore held it probable that individual consecration in an individual Mass could only be known by moral certainty (or very high probability, like the moral certainty with which a man knows that the city of Constantinople exists though he has never visited it), not by *de fide* certainty so as to become part of that which was revealed to the individual.

The Spanish lecture-rooms illustrated the similar doubt about the unrevealed minor by an historical illustration:

All men are born in original sin (revealed major).

Historical investigation proves that Cicero was a man (unrevealed minor).

Therefore—is it revealed that Cicero was born in original sin, and not only that Cicero (if he was a man) was born in original sin?

For some Spanish thinkers the moral certainty, or (philosophically speaking) very high probability, established by the historical inquiry was enough. Others could not see how the conclusion of a syllogism could be more certain than one of its premises. Arriaga, the Spanish Jesuit who was teaching at Prague in the middle of the seventeenth century and who distrusted the reliance upon logic in accounting for the development of doctrine, illustrated the weakness of the syllogism by saying that since the conclusion of the syllogism was believed to be *de fide* and therefore possessed the certainty of revelation, and since the existence of Cicero was unrevealed and therefore highly probable, it is more certain that Cicero was born in original sin than it is that he existed.[1]

A third type of syllogism consists of a major premise which is unrevealed and a minor premise which is revealed: and the classical instance had been inherited from the medieval lecture-rooms—

All men smile (unrevealed major).

Our Lord was very man (revealed minor).

Therefore—is it revealed, though the New Testament does not tell us so, that He smiled?

How do we know that all men smile? Is it a proposition collected by induction—we have observed men and women smiling, and so we elevate this inductive observation into a universal? If it is an induction, then the logical inference is not certain, and the proposition that He smiled *cannot* be *de fide*. But it might be argued that this is not precisely an induction. When it is revealed to us that He was very man, it must also be revealed to us that He possessed those qualities and capacities which (also by induction) we know manhood to possess, like hungering and thirsting and weeping and smiling. And if we are thus to be subtle in distinguishing what can be revealed and what cannot, we might assert (with more than one Spaniard) that while the capacity to smile is revealed to us because it is contained within the totality which is manhood, the historical circumstance that He did in fact smile is not revealed to us because the universal on which it depends is an induction.

These three types of syllogism were affirmed to be the logical means by which the Church has developed her doctrine. Development is a drawing out of the logical and necessary consequences of the scripture—or of the consequences of the consequences of scripture. This logical theory allows more room for genuine explication than the Gallican theories of authors like Bossuet. The Church, you may say, is truly having to 'make up her mind'; her leaders need to meet, to discuss, to thrash out the dialectical question—what is the precise expression of the truly logical inference? The theory can find room for the theologian and his work. In Bossuet's system, the theologian is more a historian than a theologian. For he is a registrar of what has always been

believed and what has not, and is therefore a theologian in so far as
he is an ecclesiastical historian. The only 'advances' possible in
divinity are advances in historical research. Since 'progress' in
theology suggests the introduction of new ideas, and since new
ideas are heretical because they are new, it is hardly possible for a
Bossuet to find room for such 'progress'. In this logical system,
by contrast, the theologian has his traditional place. To draw the
consequences of the revelation is his true work, and his high
vocation.

But here another question enters to complicate and trouble our
thought. Is the logical inference revealed to an individual, or only
to the Church? Suppose that long before 451, when the Council
of Chalcedon defined that our Lord was one person in two natures,
an intelligent theologian, a Theodoret or a Leo the Great, had
perceived that this definition was a logical and necessary inference
from scripture—can it be said to be *revealed* to him, can it be said
to be revealed to Theodoret or to Leo the Great before the teaching authority in the Church declares it to be revealed, determines
that this is the true interpretation of what scripture contains?
This is recognizably a question raised in the first chapter but
thrown into another context. Then we had the question, can
heresy be heresy before the Church has declared it to be heresy?
Here we have the question, can orthodoxy be orthodoxy before
the Church has formally and officially declared that it is orthodoxy?

This question is a crux. If a theologian is to maintain a traditional theory of tradition, if he is to maintain that the revelation
was given once and for all, then he must answer this question with
at least a 'substantial' yes. He must assert that to an individual
thinker who infers correctly, the inference is revealed before any
definition by the authorities of the Church.

For how do logical inferences occur? If the Church is making
inferences which are true inferences, then she is bound by the laws
of thought like any individual thinker, and with her corporate

mind she is only doing what any instructed Christian is potentially capable of doing. Many minds, truly, are better than one mind. The harmony and structure of the whole body of doctrine is often too majestic and too comprehensive for the single mind to grasp. The most instructed and perceptive mind may be deceived about the force of its own reasoning. But that the single mind can sometimes grasp the truth even before the corporate mind is proved, not only by historical examples, but by the nature of the case. A corporate mind is not an entity in the air: it is influenced by the decisions and the judgments of many individuals. Theodoret and Pope Leo and others needed to judge truthfully before the Council of Chalcedon could pronounce the definition. Further, the heretic would not otherwise be condemnable or blamable: and the ancient Church certainly blamed Arius and Eutyches before the Councils of Nicaea or Chalcedon had determined the doctrines which those robust ecclesiastics had impugned.

All the Spanish, of whatever school, were therefore agreed that explicit revelation was known to be revealed to the individual whether the Church had formally declared it to be so or not. And many thinkers agreed that together with explicit revelation, some 'confusedly' explicit revelation (as Suarez put it) might be allowed to be known by the individual before any official judgment by the Church. A priest has immediate knowledge that the child he has validly baptized is regenerate. He does not need to wait, absurdly, for an official declaration. The particular instance is contained, directly known to be contained, in the revelation of the general proposition that all infants validly baptized are regenerate. An individual theologian believes *de fide* that our Lord was capable of smiling. For since it is revealed to him that our Lord was very man, the properties which compose manhood are revealed to him though the Church has neither defined nor considered the question whether He could smile.

So far there was fairly general agreement. But what of the explication of the implicit where one of the premises is unrevealed, is a premise established by natural reason and yet not immediately apprehended? Here appeared a rift in academic opinion.

For example, in the Monothelite controversy of the early seventh century, the Church declared it heretical to assert 'one will' in Christ and orthodox to assert two wills, divine and human. If this definition be a logical inference, it is not an inference from two revealed premises. Unless it is argued that the idea of a will is as obviously contained within the idea of a nature as the capacity to smile is included among the properties of manhood, one of the premises may be held to be unrevealed—namely, the proposition, 'a nature, to be a nature, must include a will' (or words to that effect).

One school argued that the Church, in thus defining, was only doing what the individual theologian could have done, in short that there was no difference in logical principle between the condemnation of the single nature at the Council of Chalcedon and the condemnation of the single will two centuries later. This school, headed by the Jesuit Gabriel Vasquez, contended that the inference made from one revealed premise and one premise which was morally certain was also *de fide*, and *de fide* to the theologian who inferred it even before the Church had declared that it was *de fide*. A man might have been orthodox about the two wills before the condemnation of Monothelitism, and if he was so orthodox then the doctrine was revealed to him before the Church asserted that this doctrine was contained in the revelation.[1]

This view maintained the traditional theory of tradition, and the uniqueness of the revelation. Its weakness consisted in the contention (too sweepingly maintained) that an inference from one revealed premise and one unrevealed but morally certain premise was itself revealed. And during the twenty years before and after 1600 a battery of critics was subjecting this sweeping contention to shrewd examination.

A second school, headed by the Jesuit Molina (celebrated for his systematic attempt to prove the error of the Augustinian doctrines of grace) contended that definition by the Church like that which condemned the Monothelites could not in any sense be said to be revealed. The Holy Spirit was not given to the Church so that she might make additions to revealed doctrine. The definition, though known to be true because the Church had declared it, was not a declaration of what is revealed: it is known with moral certainty, as a theologian knows something certainly though that something is not revealed.

How we are able to distinguish that which is 'theologically certain' (because the Church has defined it) from that which is revealed, Molina and his successors did not discuss. But at least his theory possessed the merit of clinging, like the theory of Vasquez, to the traditional theory of an immutable tradition. To many thinkers, however, this statement of the case appeared to question the infallible authority of the Church in defining doctrine, though this was far from Molina's intention.[1]

The third school, in criticizing both Vasquez on the one side and Molina on the other, came nearest to expressing, in logical terminology, what would later be called a theory of development.

Against Vasquez, it was clear to Suarez and his disciples that in many syllogisms where one premise was unrevealed, the conclusion could humanly speaking be no more certain than the less certain of the two premises. If this was true of any doctrine which the Church had historically defined, then the definition had provided a new certainty, a revealed certainty, which was not available to the individual theologian before the definition. The definition of the Church has compensated for the weakness of the unrevealed premise.

How does a man discover that certain propositions are revealed? He needs to make inquiries, he needs to examine whether an alleged revelation may be received as a true revelation, he must have evidence that the authority which he is trusting is a trustworthy authority and neither mistaken nor lying. And when he has decided that the authority is trustworthy, he makes an assent of the will, or an assent of the 'practical judgment', the assent or faith.

It was evident to all theologians of that age that the decision 'this authority is trustworthy' and the act of faith were in some way disparate, acts (one might say) on different planes. Faith, the thinkers of the Counter-Reformation believed, is an absolute God-given certainty, an assent of such a nature that there can be no room for high probabilities, still less for doubt. By a bouleversement of language they held that 'faith' was more certain than unrevealed 'knowledge'. The Church tells me that valid baptisms regenerate. I know that I did fulfil the conditions laid down for validity when I baptized that baby. One might have supposed that my immediate knowledge of what I did was certainty— while the general proposition that valid baptisms regenerate, being dependent on an act of faith, was not without the touch of probability attaching to any act of human faith. For all these Spanish thinkers that is a precise reversal of what is true. The revealed proposition is certain absolutely: the human immediate knowledge is certain ('merely' certain) morally. Faith is a higher certainty than knowledge.[1] For faith is an assent to God revealing, an assent which, because it is made to God revealing, knows in the act itself that it cannot be deceived, for God is true. This is *fides divina*, *fides infusa*.

Still, you need to inquire before you assent. Though the act of faith is an act assisted or created by God's grace, if the act of faith is isolated from all intellectual preparation, from all argument or discussion, you will have nothing which you can say to lead a man towards conversion, you will find it difficult to give a reason for the hope which is in you, and you will probably be unable to blame a man for rejecting the gospel when it is put before him. Though faith is an act of assent to a divine authority which transcends reason, you still need to inquire.

But this inquiry, this 'speculative' preparation for faith, does not produce the certainty of faith. Of course there are certainties and certainties, and most theologians held that the natural reason could 'demonstrate' the existence of God. But even if some theologians find themselves able to 'demonstrate' the existence of God, in most people the assent is a 'moral certainty' at its highest, an acting upon probability at its lowest. Even in the demonstration, there is a difference between the kind of certainty produced by an argument which is asserted to lead by logical stages to God's existence, and the certainty believed to be produced by an assent to God's truth and God's authority. The contribution of the human mind to faith arrives at results no more certain, in the absolute sense, than the more 'certain' results achieved by natural science.

True faith, God-given faith, cannot therefore be the same as human faith: *fides divina* is not *fides acquisita*. A theologian examines the argument from design or from miracles, investigates the 'proofs' for the existence of God, and concludes that God is. This conclusion is based upon human evidence, and has no more certainty than the evidence upon which it rests. But divine faith is certain infallibly (so they argued), because it rests upon the infallible promise of God. Suarez is responsible for extending an old question in the scholastic series. How can an assent be infallible when it is based upon evidences which are probable? It is the question with which Newman was to wrestle all his life, chasing that elusive answer which, just as he was about to catch it, 'plunged into a thicket, curled itself up like a hedgehog, or changed colours like a chameleon'; the chase which ended in walks with Ambrose St John on the hills above the Lake of Geneva and a return to the hotel to begin writing the *Grammar of Assent*. Suarez tried to solve the problem with a theory which comes perilously near to fideism. The only absolute certainty is the certainty of faith. We cannot therefore discover any sure grounds for the assent of divine faith except faith itself. God reveals: in the act of revealing, he displays his own existence and truthfulness. We should and must investigate the arguments from miracles or from prophecy or from causation, arguments which lead us towards faith. But in the act of divine faith these probable arguments are put aside: we make a simple assent to the revelation because it is the revelation. Suarez was prepared to use strong language to assert that the probabilities produced by human reason are high probabilities, 'morally certain' probabilities, far more probable than any propositions to the contrary. But, because he was convinced that the certainty of faith, to be certain infallibly, must rest upon the divine revelation and upon that alone, he was more ready than his predecessors to allow the weakness of the 'human certainty' produced by rational argument.

Throughout the work of Suarez appears the hunt for certainty: the consciousness of the faint doubts attaching to premises of natural reason: the sense of the chasm between logical assent and supernatural assent. Vasquez and others had likewise allowed that the assent of the reason and the assent of faith were distinguishable: but for Vasquez they were invariably associated, they were two facets of a single act of faith, the one a requisite for the other. Suarez admitted that 'normally', 'commonly', 'ordinarily', inquiries were a necessary preliminary to faith, but with the admission he sought always to insist that they could not be the cause of true and infallible faith, perhaps not even the condition.

Here is another example of the same quest for certainty. Can an ignorant believer make an act of *fides infusa* in an article which is in truth not an article of the Catholic faith but is heretical or erroneous, though the believer knows it not? For a man to make an act of true faith, the revelation has to be sufficiently proposed to him by human authority, by the ministers of the Church, for 'how shall they believe without a preacher?' A simple layman receives the faith from the priest in his parish, from the pulpit or in the school. This is the way in which the revelation is sufficiently proposed to the great majority of Christians, and in no other way.

Must not the act of faith be of the same quality and nature to whatever articles the layman assents? The layman, if he is incapable of testing the statements preached to him in church, is morally bound to be obedient to them, just as the conscience is bound to perform a wrong action if the conscience, being misinformed, is convinced that the action is right, or just as the individual worshipper has a moral duty of worshipping at the Eucharist without being able to discern whether this Eucharist is in fact a valid Eucharist. And suppose that a priest, himself uninstructed or consciously heretical, preaches untruths to the congregation, the ignorant among the congregation are bound to believe those untruths—do they then believe them with *fides infusa*, with a faith of infallible certainty?

To imagine so is nonsensical. If the assent of divine faith could be based upon an untrue 'revelation', all the assurance of faith would collapse. Anyone could doubt whether the revelation in which he believed was genuine. Therefore there is legitimate reason, according to Suarez, for supposing that the layman may doubt whether a particular proposition is in accordance with the inerrant doctrine of the Church, and that only those particular propositions which can be shown with certainty to be in accordance with the inerrant doctrine of the Church can be matter for *fides infusa*, since these are the only propositions which can be said to be 'sufficiently proposed'.[1] The solution is unsatisfying (and it was clearly half-unsatisfying to Suarez) because if the layman can as easily doubt about the precise teaching of the Church as he can about alleged revelations (perhaps more easily) the assurance of certain faith is still failing. Suarez had to assume that on particular points of faith the inerrant teaching of the Church is always and easily discoverable. But, again, the solution shows the trend of his mind. The authority of the Church is needed to compensate for the lurking doubts of *fides acquisita*.

Can you ever be 'infallibly certain' of a premise of natural reason? Suarez is convinced that you cannot. Infallible certainty is something confined to supernatural assistance and grace. If you took all the theologians, even all the saintly theologians, and could establish a common mind, a consensus of opinion upon some theological point dependent upon natural reason, this would not (according to Suarez) suffice to establish and confirm a doctrine infallibly:[1] these are but men, they are frequently deceived, they are working with the discursive human reason, the results which they achieve are in the last resort upon a different plane from the supernatural certainty which he believed to be necessary to the doctrinal teaching of the Church.

Can a heretic make an act of divine faith, of *fides infusa*? Can a heretic be infallibly certain of those doctrines which he believes correctly, however many other doctrines he may disbelieve, or believe incorrectly? According to Vasquez and his tradition of thought, the heretic must be able, from the revelation, to draw the revealed inference, to accept as of divine faith those articles of faith which he perceives truly. His partial orthodoxy is, so far as it goes, orthodoxy before the Church has declared that it is orthodoxy. It is an argument in support of this view that one of the doctrines of orthodoxy is the proposition that what the Church teaches is true: and evidently a man need not believe that what the Church teaches is true before he arrives at the belief that what the Church teaches is true. But for Suarez (following here some hints of St Thomas Aquinas) the habit of divine faith is upon a different plane from any such partial acts of faith. According to his view, the heretic can believe only by *fides acquisita*, by the arguments of discursive reason and human probability, because his only means of transcending these probabilities is the infallible authority of the Church. To deny one article of faith therefore denies all 'implicitly', just as 'a man who for God's sake detests one sin detests all implicitly'.[2]

In 1601–2 Spain beheld a more concrete illustration of the same trend of thought which sought to allow the definition by the

Church to compensate for the weakness of the premise of natural reason—a little storm in the academic teacup of Spain.

The Spanish court and people, in this century, were treating theological controversy with the same popular interest which the Arian controversy had received in the fourth century. Conquest in theological debate was celebrated by the towns with junketings and fireworks and bullfights. When the news of a papal decision came through in 1607, the walls of Salamanca were placarded with posters in honour of Molina's victory. The argument focused upon the doctrine of grace, that fundamental problem which the Protestants had posed to the Counter-Reformation. On the one side were the strict Thomists, Augustinians to a man, led by the Dominican Order and its chief theologian Domingo Bañez, the favoured director of St Teresa of Avila and, until his retirement in 1601, the leading professor at Salamanca. On the other side were the Jesuits, led at first by Molina from his chair at Coimbra, conscious that the Augustinian theology of grace might be thought to favour the Protestants, anxious to re-state the theology of St Thomas Aquinas in such a way that its Augustinian elements might be modified or transformed. Around this main theme floated a host of lesser controversies—attacks upon the Jesuit constitution and institutes, questions over theories put forward by the theologians of either side. Anyone who has read in the history of a university like Salamanca, where both sides were strongly entrenched, will recognize that around the year 1600 controversialists in either party were beginning to acquire the mentality of heresy-hunters.

In July 1601 Father Gaspar Hurtado, of the University of Alcalá, defended as thesis for his doctorate a number of propositions: among them, that 'It is not *de fide* that a particular person, e.g. Clement VIII, is the successor of St Peter'. The troubles did not ensue until spring 1602, when an informer complained in a series of letters to the Papal Secretary of State, and still more, after 7 March 1602 when a theologian of the Jesuit College at Alcalá,

Oñate, maintained the same thesis in a public act under the presidency of another Jesuit, Luis de Torres. The Jesuits, in a spirit of reverence, carefully refrained from inserting the name of the reigning Pope.

The thesis bears directly upon our problem, the problem of immutability. For it offers a peculiarly interesting question about the nature of the logically implicit and its relation to moral certainty. Is the belief that this man is the Pope simply a particular contained in a universal, as you deduce that this baptism regenerates from the proposition that all baptisms regenerate? If so, you may argue that it is implicitly revealed and therefore *de fide*. But this is difficult to maintain. For you are not asserting that you believe this Pope to be the successor of St Peter because all popes are the successors of St Peter: that would be a true particular contained in a universal. You are asserting that this individual man is the Pope: and it appears that you cannot secure the proposition without the inquiries of natural reason comparable to those inquiries which are not immediate but inform us after investigation that Cicero was a man. This premise, whatever 'moral certainty' might be attached to it, could not claim the immediate certainty which might alone be held to justify the 'revealed' inference. The premise depended on the probable, highly probable, fulfilment of a complex series of practical and mental conditions. It was not easy to demonstrate that he who was accepted as Pope had been validly baptized, validly ordained, and canonically elected without simony.[1]

Consequently the Jesuit Fathers did not suppose that they were saying anything startling or original when they presented their public thesis. They did not allow for the atmosphere of theological suspicion and distrust which was then hanging like a mist over Spain. A number of their antagonists accused the Jesuits of doubting whether Clement VIII was Pope. They even supplied a motive for the thesis—the Jesuits believed that the Pope would decide against them upon the doctrine of grace, and were already preparing their future line of retreat. The Jesuits replied, with a becoming firmness, that they had no idea in the world of questioning whether Clement VIII was the Pope. The question was not at all whether this statement was true. The question was whether it was revealed to be true in the original deposit of faith.

The matter was complicated by the opinions of Pope Clement VIII himself. His Papal Secretary of State was that coughing, asthmatic, pock-marked Pietro Aldobrandini of whom Ranke drew so lively a picture. Aldobrandini, a born and effective administrator, appears at first to have been incapable of understanding the theological point, incapable of distinguishing between 'true' and 'revealed to be true'. He was not the only administrator to feel muddled. It is odd, said the Papal Nuncio satirically to the Grand Inquisitor, that after eleven years of pontificate, when even the Turks and the heretics believe Clement VIII to be Pope, there should be doubt only in Spain. Under Aldobrandini's terrible indictment of the Jesuits, the Spanish Inquisition, obediently but reluctantly, moved into half-hearted action. They imprisoned Oñate, de Torres and two other Fathers from the College at Alcalá, the Rector of the College and the gentle Vasquez himself, one of the most eminent theologians in Spain.

The investigations of the Inquisitors did not run smoothly. None of the theologians whom they consulted would classify the opinion as heretical, even if it were admitted to be scandalous. The Jesuits produced many approved authors who had maintained the doctrine. Better still, they proffered to the papal nuncio the commentary upon St Thomas Aquinas by the Dominican leader Bañez, open at the page where Bañez had maintained something like the same doctrine. After only a month and a half, on 17 June 1602 the rector of the College and Vasquez were released, and the two others were allowed to return home to a temporary house-arrest.[1]

A little controversy of this sort probably convinces no one. Eminent theologians like Vasquez on the one side or Suarez on the other were unmoved by popular and diplomatic clamour about scandal, they were concerned only with what they conceived to be the nature of revelation. While it is possible that the side of the Alcalá theses may not have received as stout a defence as it may have deserved out of a desire to avoid popular misunderstanding, it is certain that both opinions continued to be held.[1] Yet, apart from the incidental excitements, to which all theologians are sometimes liable when misunderstood by their episcopal superiors, there was a real argument about the nature of theological inferences. The papers of the Roman censors show that several theologians thought they perceived an overriding necessity, in a matter so momentous, for an unfailing and absolute certainty. And if this certainty could not (as was at first asserted) be secured by the plea that an inference from one revealed premise and one premise of natural reason was itself revealed, then it must be secured through the infallible authority of the Church which has received this Pope as the Pope.[2]

It may be objected, then, that the Church's definition is a new piece of revelation. If the Church can make an inference 'supernaturally certain' when by natural reason it is not more than 'morally certain', then the Church is no longer unfolding the inner content of the revelation, is no longer declaring what is (in the strictest logical sense) implicit. She is bringing into the revelation a statement from outside it. She must be adding to, supplementing, the revelation once given by God.

Suarez did not shrink from the necessary consequence. He admitted it boldly. A definition by the Church is 'equivalent' to the revelation, is a completion or 'consummation' of the revelation. It had the same authority and was to be accepted by the assent of *fides divina* in the same way. And he admitted, even (contrary to the dominant tradition of thought) that an alleged 'private revelation' to a Christian individual could become binding upon all the faithful provided that the Church accepted and approved the private revelation.[1]

The thought of Suarez's successor and critic, Cardinal John de Lugo, showed still more clearly what was happening. In Suarez the belief that the definition of the Church was compensating for the weakness of an unrevealed premise is necessary to his argument, but it is partially concealed. Lugo displayed the consequence, as the only apparent means of avoiding Suarez's language about 'equivalence' to revelation, new revelation. He knew that all Christian tradition denied the possibility of new revelation to the Church. He held that Suarez was therefore wrong in effectively allowing the possibility of new revelation. God reveals nothing which he has not revealed at least 'in confuso'. Yet Lugo stated the same doctrine as Suarez in other, and tautological, words. God does not reveal new truth: but He does reveal that the Holy Spirit guides the Church to correct definitions. There is therefore new truth: and we know it to be true, not because God reveals it immediately, but because He reveals the instrument of defining it to be inerrant. Instead of one revealed premise and one unrevealed premise, there are now two revealed premises, one of which is the proposition 'that which the Church defines with the assistance of the Spirit cannot be untrue'. The theory of Lugo is like a courteous bow, a raising of the hat in token of respect to the fair lady Immutability whom he was about to abandon to her fate. He need not have been so reluctant to admit Suarez's wording.[2]

Both Suarez and Lugo tried to safeguard their opinion from the charge that it was against any sound Vincentian theory of an unchanging tradition. They both continued to assert that the apostles knew *explicitly* all the doctrines which the Church would later draw from the teaching passed from the apostles to the Church implicitly, that the apostles were *explicitly* aware of such doctrines as the two wills or transubstantiation. They believed that to no Christian was it possible to assert that the Church now knew more of truth than the apostles had received from their Lord. They both contended that definitions were always concerned with defining the true sense of scripture or drawing out its implications or applying the once-given revelation to particular and new contingencies. But, as a fact, they knew enough history to admit that the Church had sometimes defined, though one premise was of natural reason: and if the definition was to be a proclamation that a doctrine was revealed, this could only be secured if the definition in some way overcame the lurking weakness of the natural premise, and therefore it was necessary to postulate that the definition was 'equivalent' to the revelation.

The theory lay open to a grave objection from the point of view of the traditionalists, an objection which Lugo himself raised and faced but did not answer. If this particular theory of definitions is true, historical inquiries are superfluous. It is no longer necessary for the ecclesiastical authorities to inquire into what the scripture says explicitly, or what the ancient Church taught and did. There is no longer need to inquire what is tradition. For any rational theory of tradition, some safeguard must be found to show that scripture and tradition do in due measure control or limit what definitions are possible to the Church. The language of Suarez and Lugo provided no such safeguard. Some of their more conservative contemporaries, facing the same difficulty, argued that the Pope was only infallible in definition when he had made due and diligent inquiry into scripture and tradition.[1] Such a restriction was impossible for Suarez and Lugo upon the principles which they had adopted, and their language, however they might assert the unchanging nature of Christian tradition, could offer no safeguard that the tradition was truly unchanging.

In Suarez, and in Lugo, it is clear that the attempt to explain the development of doctrine by a logical explanation was breaking down. They both continued to maintain the logical language.

They both continued to assert that the Church was defining what was 'virtually' revealed, what was implicit in the gospel given by the apostles to the Church. But these words and notions, 'virtual' and 'logically implicit' had ceased to be so significant because theological inference was becoming less important than ecclesiastical definition: divinely assisted definition could dispense with logically certain inferences. The attempt at a logical explanation was breaking down because with their notions of the certitude of faith, and with Suarez's widening of the gap between reasoning and *fides infusa*, the explanation had ceased to cover what it was intended to explain. Another Spanish Jesuit, Arriaga, who taught at the University of Prague (he died in 1667 when Bossuet had already won his reputation in the Paris pulpit) avowed it wholeheartedly.

Arriaga distrusted the natural premise even more than Suarez. Deductions which Suarez had freely allowed to be revealed *in confuso*, Arriaga rejected. It may be true that I am certain that I validly baptized this infant—but I manifestly suffer from an invincible capacity for self-deception. What is revealed never transcends the conditional—*if* this infant was validly baptized, he is regenerate. In order that a deduction from the revelation may be *de fide*, it must be identical with the revelation. If *Christus est homo* is revealed, then *Christo es hombre* is revealed: if 5 is revealed, then 2 plus 3 is revealed. But unless the identity cannot be contradicted without nonsense, that identity must itself be revealed if the deduction is to be believed to be revealed. It is revealed to us that Christ had a soul and a body. But this is not revealed to us as an inference—

> Christ was very man.
> All men have souls and bodies
> *Ergo*...

It is revealed because it is contained in scripture, and no natural premise is needed. There are many propositions which can reasonably be deduced with moral certainty from revealed premises. But not all things are *de fide* which are true. It is *de fide* that a dove flew out of the ark: the precise zoological description of this dove is not *de fide*. This potential weakness, this potential self-deception of the reasoning faculty, is illustrated by the incoherent behaviour of the theologians. Theologians frequently work with syllogisms founded on one revealed and one unrevealed premise. But experience shows that theologians frequently disagree: and therefore either the natural premise was less well-founded than they believed, or they have been deceived about the validity of the inference.

Then we must allow that in the definition of the Church and the Pope, there is revelation. Arriaga admits that this is not (according to the linguistic uses of theology) 'properly speaking' revelation. But his argument is designed to equate the two kinds of revelation, and he several times used the word 'revelation' of that which is contributed by the authorities of the Church. For the only alternative is to suppose that definitions subsequent to the apostles are implicit in the apostolic message. But in fact these doctrines, or facts, which are now revealed to us are *not* implicit in the scripture, and it is a misuse of language to say that they are. It is necessary that it is *de fide* that the Council of Trent was legitimately assembled, that Innocent X is now the Pope, that St Luke is in heaven. Scripture does not tell us that St Luke died in a state of grace. And if it be argued that the function of definition is to declare the true sense of scripture or to apply it to contingent circumstances, Arriaga replied that you cannot even determine the true sense of scripture without additional 'revelation' of some kind. 'The scripture itself does not say, I have this sense and not another.' And though theological usage distinguishes the 'revealing' action of the Holy Spirit from the 'assisting' action of the Holy Spirit upon the mind of Pope and Council in defining, this distinction is more verbal than real, since the logical explanation has been rejected. According to Arriaga, all revelation is explicit: no revelation is implicit or virtual: and so

46

the proclamation of doctrine, or sufficient proposition by the Church, is the making explicit what was not explicit, and need not have been implicit, earlier.[1]

In Spain the main scholastic tradition, headed by the Carmelites of Salamanca, repudiated these innovations of Suarez. Arriaga's contentions had almost no influence upon the course of the argument. In Italy a strongly reviving school of commentators upon Duns Scotus represented the older, more static outlook.[2] The majority of thinkers in the seventeenth and eighteenth centuries were disciples either of Vasquez, who believed that inferences from one natural premise could be *de fide* before the Church defined them, or of Molina, who believed that these inferences could never be *de fide* because the Church was not given the assistance of the Holy Spirit in order to increase the body of revealed truth. But Suarez, Lugo and Arriaga are portents that the medieval notion of logic was creaking under the strain which was being placed upon it. Once you have allowed a definition to be 'equivalent' to a new revelation: once you have denied that some doctrines of the Church are 'implicit' in scripture —then the idea of logical explication has ceased to account for all doctrinal development. It might reasonably account for *some* development: but unless it has accounted for all it is no full and sufficient explanation. It has become an analogy, a metaphor, a poetic parallel.

Suppose that it were argued, as Suarez would have allowed, like this: before you make a definition, you need theologians to make inferences. And suppose that after the definition is declared, the grounds for the inferences of the theologians are found to have been weaker than was thought, perhaps even nugatory— then this does not affect the truth of the definition. They may prepare, perhaps must prepare, for the definition: but the definition is not dependent upon them. If this view is taken, the inference has lost its old place in doctrinal development: and if anyone continues to assert that all doctrinal development is a form of 'logical explication', we should do well to inquire critically into the logical status of that word 'logical'.[1]

The Gallicans knew nothing, or almost nothing, of this tradition of thought. Bossuet possessed the volumes of Vasquez and Suarez on the shelves of his library, and sometimes he read extracts from them. But Gallican scholarship was historical. Historians, concerned as they are with what is rugged and unique and unrepeatable, investigating a theme where generally valid laws are impossible, often dislike logic with its dependence upon universals. Nor did Newman know anything of this tradition until he had finished and published his *Essay on Development*. And here is a portent. For centuries Catholic theologians had explained doctrinal development by the use of logical inference. Yet the Christian public now associates the idea of development with a thinker whose suspicion of Dr Hampden or the Reverend Charles Kingsley was as nothing compared with his distrust of the syllogism.

# CHAPTER III

# THE CATHOLIC CRITICS

Father Hardouin travailed with unrelenting and passionate endeavour over the sources for the history and antiquities of the Church. He published a text of the councils which for long remained the definitive text, an edition which marked an epoch in the study of the canons. He examined the ancient coins and was among the first to apply numismatic evidence systematically to the writing of ancient history. And his eccentricities are one of the rare tragedies in the history of modern scholarship.

In a work of 1693 he hinted; in a work of 1709 he affirmed; in posthumous works of 1729 and 1733 he shouted—a bewildering but simple thesis. Apart from the scriptures—that is the Latin scriptures—and six classical authors, all the writers of antiquity, profane or ecclesiastical, were forged by a group of writers in the thirteenth or fourteenth centuries. This group of forgers he never defined or discussed, but always referred to them generically as 'the impious crew', 'maudite cabale'. Of the Latins only Plautus, Pliny, the *Eclogues* and *Georgics*, Horace's *Satires* and *Epistles* were authentic; of the Greeks only Homer and Herodotus.[1] It was patent to the eye that the *Aeneid* had been written by a Christian pseudo-Virgilius as an allegory of the coming of Christianity to Rome after the burning of Jerusalem. The killing of Turnus and the suicide of Amata were allegories upon the destruction of Judaism and the abolition of the synagogue. Any instructed reader of the *Aeneid* will see at once the poor grammar, the Gallicisms and the thirteenth-century solecisms. The prophecy about the Carthaginians in Book IV, so far from being a reference to the Punic wars, signified the hatred which the Mohammedans of the North African coast would bear to the Christians. The prophecy of a conquered Greece in Book I is not a reference to Mummius' destruction of Corinth, as the commentators have supposed, but to the sack of Constantinople by the crusaders in 1204. The reader of Horace's *Odes* will see that Lalage represents Christianity with the gentle joy which it brings. These fabricators needed unsparing effort to create almost all the documents of an alleged antiquity. They possessed indefatigable, adamantine, brazen-bowelled scribblers. They manufactured a multitude and variety of books and documents because they knew that, the more there were, the more difficult the conspiracy would be to detect. They forged the Fathers, both Greek and Latin; they then had to forge a background of antiquity in which the Fathers could be supposed to exist; they had to provide imaginary adversaries like Arius or Pelagius, they had to create decretals, diplomas, charters, monastic annals; they had to invent variant readings, inscriptions like the canon of Hippolytus, and liturgies under the names of SS. Basil and Chrysostom to prove that the Greek liturgies were older than the Latin. To opponents who argued that it was absurd to suppose that so vast a number of ancient documents could have been fabricated by a single group, Hardouin replied that the total size and weight of all antiquity was less than the total weight which the Reformers of the sixteenth century published, and even than the aggregate from Vasquez, Suarez and five other writers from the Society of Jesus.[1] To opponents who urged their surprise that this lamentable fraud had been allowed to remain undiscovered so long, Hardouin replied that it was not at all surprising. Only during the seventeenth century had the manuscripts from the libraries been edited properly, and so for the first time we were seeing an authentic picture of antiquity. Scholars had indeed proved, to the satisfaction of nearly everyone, that numbers of documents supposed to be ancient were in fact forgeries—the pseudo-Isidorian decretals, the Clementine Recognitions, the Apostolic Constitutions, the Canons of the Apostles, the Protevangelium of St James, nearly half the supposed works of Athanasius, all the supposed works of Dionysius the Areopagite—

one could continue a long catalogue of the works which eminent scholars had now abandoned. Hardouin claimed that he was only carrying to its rightful conclusion this process of sifting which modern printing and modern scholarship allowed. Asked by the Oratorian Father Le Brun why he was publishing such extravagant theories, he is said to have replied 'Do you think I get up at four o'clock every morning in order to say the same as everyone else has said before me?'

Hardouin is typical of no one, illustrates nothing. But madness is sometimes an obsession with a genuine and sane preoccupation. To investigate conservative apologetic among Hardouin's contemporaries is to see at once that he is a fanatical and grotesque representative of one trend of thought in the apologetic of that age.

Hardouin converted to his views disciples, a few from among the younger members of the Society of Jesus. Nor did he lack distinguished and eminent support. A member of the French Academy and its historian, the ex-Jesuit Abbé d'Olivet, Voltaire's tutor, was responsible for the posthumous publication of several of Hardouin's manuscripts and himself accepted part of Hardouin's theory.[1] This was the kind of madness which suited a few thinkers who were not mad. Classical scholarship, pure and unaided, had not led Hardouin to his conclusions. It is therefore worth asking the question, what were the intellectual pre-suppositions? Hardouin himself needs no theoretical justification—you cannot put an oddity into a category. But why were his rare disciples prepared, if not to suppose the theory to be true, at least to eye it with the faint and wistful hope that it might be true? Gallican apologetic was dominantly patristic: in its confident and scholarly appeal to the Fathers lay its power. Yet here was a minority of French thinkers and savants markedly losing their confidence in the appeal to the Fathers.

Amid the complex and untidy pattern of academic thought in that age, three strands can be discerned which contributed to this decline in the reputation of the Fathers—the fight against Jansenism: the fear of philosophy: and the new power of the historical critics.

Though it might be denied that St Augustine had been a Jansenist, it could hardly be denied that some of his language proffered too ample an umbrella for the Jansenist theses. The prolonged, see-saw fight through the second half of the seventeenth century between the defenders and the assailants of the Augustinian Jansen did not concern only the theology of Augustine. Informed distrust of Jesuit moral theology, uninformed distrust of Jesuit papalism or theories of tyrannicide, fear of puritanism and devotional or moral rigorism, suspicion or defence of Gallican constitutionalism, the Church as the elect and holy congregation versus the Church as the gentle mother who embraces sinners—the so-called Jansenist controversy contained far more than an assault upon St Augustine. The opponents of the Jansenists denied that they intended to assail St Augustine. Most of them had begun by trying to distinguish between the disciple and the master, by trying to proscribe the one and acquit the other: and the confident attempt to refute this distinction, to prove that he who condemned Jansen condemned in the same breath St Augustine (if not St Paul) was the keep of the Jansenist castle. The Archbishop of Rouen, though militant against the Jansenists, declared with pompous hyperbole in 1661 that he was ready to sign with his blood everything contained in all ten volumes of St Augustine; and the fatal oath, designed to catch Jansenists in 1655, contained a solemn avowal that the doctrine of Jansen 'is not that of St Augustine, whom Jansen has wrongly expounded'.

But whatever was claimed or intended, howsoever they might seek to dislodge the heresiarch from the doctor of the Church upon whose capacious shoulders he claimed to be sitting, the strife relentlessly but inevitably weakened (with one party) the authority of St Augustine. Other motives—moral, ascetic, devotional— were entering in. Just as Anglicans like Jeremy Taylor and Henry

Hammond and George Bull were seeking from 1650 to refute the Augustinian theory of justification which their Protestant forebears of the sixteenth century had canonized, so some French theologians, from Molina and St Francis de Sales onwards, were beginning to nibble away at the Augustinian doctrine of grace. And since in western thought Augustine bestrode the Fathers like a Colossus, to weaken the authority of Augustine was to weaken the force of any appeal to the Fathers whatsoever.

The attack upon Jansenism therefore helped, in part, to undermine the Gallican theory of tradition; contributed to the sense of scepticism about historical appeals to traditional authority; contributed to the awareness that the Fathers were not wholly reliable guides unless there was a living and authoritative voice to interpret them. In those Jansenist days, Madame de Sévigné was not the only person to be puzzled by the reading of St Augustine. A young Jesuit student used Augustine as an entertaining experiment to test his superiors. He copied out a large extract from Augustine's work on free will, but he placed no title at the top. He then carried it round to his teachers, and asked them to give their opinions of its theology. One allowed that its tendency was to Platonism: one of them, walking in the gardens of the Luxembourg, hazarded the guess that the book was written by some Dutch Protestant preacher: a third said that Father Hardouin ought to leave the Fathers alone and attack this sort of book instead. The student obtained his most piquant pleasure by observing the variety of different routes along which his superiors sought to extricate themselves when he revealed the true author of the book.[1] It cannot be doubted that the quarrel over the Jansenist propositions was indeed affecting the attitude of some to St Augustine. To weaken the authority of the Fathers, as a decisive court of dogmatic authority, is to weaken Bossuet's notions of immutability. The Gallican idea of unchanging tradition depended as much as the early Tractarian theory upon maintaining confidence in the dogmatic authority of the Fathers.

In the last twenty years of the seventeenth century, some theologians were beginning to sense that the Age of Reason was advancing upon them, and they did not like what they expected. Pascal, who had deserted 'the God of the learned and the God of the philosophers' in the awful night of 23 November 1654, had uttered some of the most anti-intellectual cries ever uttered by a great intellectual—*se moquer de la philosophie, c'est vraiment philosopher*....But Pascal's scepticism was more passionate than rational, more personal than detached. By 1690 the desire to show the uselessness of the intellect had become intellectual, cool, systematic. In all ages when metaphysics are in the melting-pot, devout spirits shrink from the tumult of theological and philosophical argument and find their rest in 'simple faith'. In the religious world of the late seventeenth century Rancé founded the Trappists with something of this spirit in mind. The Benedictines were pursuing scholarship: they had created the finest monastic school of scholarship that the west has ever seen, the congregation of St Maur. From 1683 Rancé was vehemently attacking the Benedictines of St Maur—attacking them not only because they were unfaithful to the Rule of St Benedict but because scholarship hampered devotion and often harmed the Church: Rancé compiled a quaintly solemn catalogue of the eminent heresiarchs, from Nestorius to Luther, who had begun their career as monkish scholars.[1] Knowledge breeds heretics. Rancé ransacked the centuries for quotations from the irrationalists, paraded all the old proof texts of Tertullian—*Quod simile Philosophus et Christianus...Platonem omnium haereticorum condimentarium.*

From Rancé in his cell to Huet and d'Olivet among the scholars, among a whole group of religious thinkers, the reaction was appearing. It is as intelligible as the rise of the Evangelical Movement in an England ruled by Hoadly and the memory of Archbishop Tillotson. The Lord did not choose twelve philosophers to be his apostles: he chose fishermen. Lean upon faith. Lean upon the revelation. Distrust metaphysics.

In Catholic and unscholastic France, the metaphysicians in possession (so far as any could be said to be in possession), were the disciples of Descartes. From Descartes had descended a progeny assured of the power of human reason to justify the ways of God to man, a progeny ecstatic with mathematics, with clear ideas, with certain inferences. It is easy perhaps to exaggerate the Cartesian influence upon the Jansenists and Gallicans. One eminent critic even contended that the Cartesian influence upon the Gallican divines is a legend based upon a misunderstanding by the nineteenth century. You can find ardent Cartesians among the Benedictines of St Maur. You can find ardent Cartesians in the ranks of the Jansenists. If you therefore inferred (as was once inferred) that the metaphysic of Malebranche was in any sense a kind of official metaphysic to the divines of Bossuet's age, you would be sadly mistaken. In the same ranks you could find stout assailants of Cartesian theory.

With the philosophical reasons for rejecting Cartesian doctrine —the nature of perception, the ontological assumptions—I am not concerned. But the theological consequences of the attack upon the Cartesians are relevant. The Cartesians seemed to be leading theology towards an immanentism which minimized the uniqueness of Christianity. They seemed to suppose that when by ontology and the examination of the human reason they had inferred the necessary existence of Perfect and Infinite Being, they had taken a long stride to proving by reason the existence of the God of the Christians. Malebranche, without being pantheistic, pushed Cartesian theory relentlessly towards the pantheism of Spinoza: for an approach to the doctrine of God from the doctrine of Infinite Being ran immediately into the problem of the nature of transcendence.

In the years round 1700 conservative thinkers were peculiarly sensitive to any doctrine which appeared to minimize the uniqueness of the Christian revelation. For this was the time when other races and other religions had invaded Christian theology and invaded it successfully. Until 1680 Christian thinkers had never needed to take non-Christian religions seriously. Closer acquaintance with other religions led to a more charitable attitude towards them. Men were now studying what Mahomet or Confucius said, and not what the Christians said they said. In China the Jesuits, criticized for the alleged laxity of their missionary policy, were setting before the western public the merits of Chinese civilization, Chinese morality, Chinese religion. Twenty years after it was published, Bossuet's *Universal History* was beginning to seem narrowly European. From 1700 the Persians and Zoroaster, from 1703 the 'noble savagery' of the American Indians, from 1705 Mahomet—in an age when the moral aspect of Christian life was rising in the scale in comparison with the dogmatic aspect, the high morality found in other religions might be used by the attacking deists and rationalists. It might also be used by the Christian apologists to defend the argument from universal consensus.

God, contended Christian apologists (who had sometimes, but not always, received Cartesian influence), bestowed the foundations of his revelation upon all mankind. Comparative inquiry discerned traces, now clear, now faint and partial, in the religions of China and of Greece and of America: vestiges of the primitive revelation to Adam or Noah or Moses. The rising tide of classical scholarship could not fail to disclose the loftiest moral teaching in the ancient philosophers. What Aristotle was to the Thomists, Plato was to Malebranche and the Cartesians. When they found Platonism in St Augustine and the Fathers they were not dismayed. They seized upon the fact and displayed it as a sign of the harmony between the Christian revelation and natural revelation. Thomassin *par excellence*, Huet of Avranches at one stage of his thought, and a crowd of lesser apologists, threw a girdle round the earth in the hunt for natural parallels to Christianity. Thomassin displayed the parallels with pagan antiquity as signs that the revelation had been universal; signs that the revelation entrusted to Moses or

Noah had indeed been passed in fragmentary form to other peoples.[1]

To the Kierkegaards of that age, to the thinkers determined at all costs to preserve the uniqueness and absoluteness of Christianity even at the expense of its rationality, the faith was being undermined. They were beginning to suspect metaphysics wherever they found them: they disliked Thomassin and the argument from universal consensus. The most trenchant of all Hardouin's posthumous works—and that is saying a good deal—is a work entitled *The Atheists Unmasked.* Who are these 'atheists'? Descartes, Malebranche, Thomassin, Nicole, and the other Jansenists: there are even three tendentious pages denouncing Pascal. They are 'atheists' because they have introduced impersonal, philosophical, immanentist concepts into their account of God our Father: and if they are able to quote from St Augustine and others to support their use of Plato and the pagan philosophers, that is for Hardouin a piece of evidence supporting his thesis that the works attributed to St Augustine are spurious.

The Fathers—there's the rub. St Augustine, if not a Christian Neo-Platonist, used the philosophy of Plato. Worse, the second-century apologists lay bleeding in the same trap into which Thomassin was about to decoy Catholic apologetic. They had used the Logos-language, not in its restrained post-Nicene application, but in a quasi-Platonic or mediatorial application to argue that all truth is of God. A correspondent of Huet, Father Martin, was gravely distressed at the argument from a universal consensus. Huet wrote him a consoling letter: 'You are not the first to be shocked by this argument....But St Justin Martyr used the same argument in two places, and this kind of reasoning is normal among the ancient Fathers when they are combating paganism.'[2] If the Fathers utilized and approved the philosophy of Plato, so much the worse for the Fathers. By the early years of the eighteenth century both Protestants and Catholics were hotly debating the relationship between the Fathers and pagan philosophy.

We find a curious contrast between the Protestants of England and the Roman Catholics of France. In both churches, among a section of thinkers, the reputation of the Fathers was sliding down-hill between 1680 and 1730. In England that section was the left wing, the Latitudinarians; in France it was the right wing, the anti-Gallicans. For some of the English the Fathers were too dogmatic and not philosophical enough. For some of the French the Fathers were too philosophical and not dogmatic enough.

Denis Petau was a French Jesuit of learning and diligence who had died in 1652. He had written more than one book of refer-ence which Bossuet, in common with every other educated clergyman, could not avoid using. He represented harmoniously in his own mind both the streams of Counter-Reformation thought—the appeal to historical inquiry on the one side, the scholastic discipline upon the other: yet in the French way he was oddly unscholastic, almost humanist: at bottom a patristic theo-logian and not a schoolman. In spite of his classical and patristic learning, he was no historian, in the sense in which the coming centuries were to understand the word 'historian'. He had none of the quest for 'scientific history', or 'impartial history', no sense of continuity or of change.

But in reading the ancient Fathers, Petau had formed in his mind a particular historical theory. He believed that Platonism was the bane of the Christian religion. He supposed that every ancient heresy, culminating in Arianism, derived from the Platonic infection. He began his treatise *De Trinitate* with a survey of the quasi-Trinitarian doctrines found among the Platonists.

A man who believes Platonism to be the source of all error will not read the early Christian Fathers with a wholly uncritical approval. In five successive chapters Petau surveyed ante-Nicene Christianity, showed how heresiarchs like Marcion and Tatian depended upon Platonic presuppositions, displayed the cloven hoof peeping out beneath the togas of Justin Martyr and Clement of Alexandria and Origen. Though learned, the thesis was perhaps a little crude, unsubtle, oversimplified.

A divine of the fifth century like Augustine or Jerome; a school-man of the thirteenth century like Aquinas; a Spanish theologian of the Counter-Reformation—none of these would have been seriously perturbed by these admissions, even if they had rejected the theory of a Platonizing corruption of doctrine. The Gallicans of France were dismayed. They had sought their common ground with the Protestants in an appeal to the immutable tradition derived from the Fathers, and the immutability of the Fathers' doctrine was being weakened. Petau (possibly, though not certainly, at the request of his superiors) added a preface to explain himself. The preface appeared to contradict the text. It asserted that some of the holiest Fathers had used unsuitable language because its perils were not yet observed, but that they had all maintained unchangeably the 'substance' of the faith. It is in fact an error to set Petau's theory of explication in opposition to that of Bossuet, as though Petau's theory contained some kind of anticipation of a later idea of development. Petau was to play an insignificant part in the movement of Newman's mind 200 years later. But it is a mistake to suppose that Petau possessed either a sense of historical change or any idea of development. He possessed neither of these assumptions. What he did possess was so fixed a belief in the poisonous influence of Platonism that he was ready to admit error among the ante-Nicene Fathers—an admission not so easily assimilable by the Gallican theory of tradition. And he believed that Platonism was poison long before Malebranche had become famous or Thomassin had proclaimed the argument from universal consensus.

The consequences are celebrated—how Unitarians in England and France appealed to Petau: how the Protestant Jurieu hurled Petau's name at Bossuet to counter the theory of Catholic immutability on which Bossuet based his *History of the Variations*: how the second edition of Petau's *Dogmatic Theology* was issued by another Protestant, Jean Leclerc: how the Anglican George Bull undertook the *Defence of the Nicene Faith* against Petau and later received the honour, unusual for an Anglican divine, of applause from the French clergy.[1]

In France there was another reason for the decline of the Gallican theory of an unchanging tradition. If Petau was not a historian, the first persons to whom the modern age has agreed to accord the name 'historians' are Frenchmen of the late seventeenth century—the Benedictines of St Maur and the great school of scholarship which surrounded them.

It was the age when first appears that well-known character of the academic world, the scholar whose spider-ridden house is so piled with books that he cannot go to bed and has to sleep in an arm-chair: the little, personal, disorganized sign of the disinterested passion for truth about the past. It was the age when first appears, as a type, the 'pedant', and when appear also the first delicate satires upon pedantry. It was the age when the social status of the pure scholar had risen to heights hardly known since the days of Erasmus—when the Duke of here and the Marquis of there courted the Benedictines of St Maur, when the Guide-Book to Paris mentions a number of savants among the important and interesting sights of that city. It was the age when for the first time since the Reformation we can discern an international amity of scholarship which leaps over the walls of religious prejudices as well as the barriers of national antipathy. Mabillon, in drafting a list of books recommended for monastic libraries, inserted a number of works by eminent Protestant divines. A benighted historian of the nineteenth century needed to defend Mabillon by arguing that you must study the enemy in order to defeat him. The defence was folly. Mabillon inserted Protestant scholars, not because he wished to controvert them, but because he found them useful in research. It is an epoch.

The modern study of ecclesiastical history had sprung out of the needs of controversy. History was being used to a particular dogmatic end. And although in the face of criticism and counter-criticism the writing of history had been improved, developed, deepened, it was still being used by the theologians. In England Bull and Pearson were using their patristic researches to defend the Anglican Church: in France Nicole and Arnauld were using their patristic researches to defend the Roman Catholic Church. They were surer, less propagandist, less inaccurate, in handling their material than Flacius Illyricus or Cardinal Baronius in the previous century, but essentially they were still standing in the same tradition of historical scholarship, the tradition that Newman's *History of the Arians* and many another work was yet to illustrate. But with Mabillon, Montfaucon, Ruinart, Tillemont, we seem to have passed beyond all consciousness, even remote consciousness of the possible theological or controversial effects of their researches. They are confident that truth will prevail: that truth cannot be incompatible with truth: that the problems are to be solved 'for their own sake': that the argument must be followed where it leads. And so they were laying the foundations of modern history.

Let us pause for a moment on Mabillon, the gentlest and humblest scholar of them all. For him study was as far as possible from the manufacture of powder and shot. It was the old manual labour of the Rule of St Benedict—a fruitful way of keeping the mind occupied; a useful employment of one's time: a method of performing that general penitence to which monks are called.

If you look a little at the trouble involved in copying, composing, revising, comparing the works of the Fathers and other ecclesiastical authors, correcting proofs, etc., you will readily agree that this can take the place of manual labour, provided it is done in the spirit of religion, of humility, and of penitence, seeking only the glory of God and the profit of the Church and of our neighbour. These occupations are penitential.

His opponents argued that reading was only useful for sanctity if it was pious reading; Mabillon replied that 'All truth is of God, and by consequence one must love it. All truth can carry us to God...', even if it is truth acquired through the disciplines of philosophy, history and mathematics. In short, historical research was being put forward by Mabillon and St Maur not as a useful agent of theology, but as a study for the glory of God—which in later and less Christian terminology is to say, a study as an end in itself.

Historical scholarship undertaken as an end in itself does not always reach conclusions which the researchers originally expect. Morin had shown that the commonly accepted theories both of ordination and confirmation were not the theories of antiquity. There was argument whether the present theory of the relation of the viaticum to extreme unction was faithful to antiquity. Documents hallowed by tradition—the works of Dionysius the Areopagite above all—had followed the pseudo-Isidorian decretals and so many other medieval documents into the limbo of fabrications. The only serious conflict which Mabillon incurred with authority arose from his criticism of the credulity about relics to be found in the city of Rome. The Carmelites, convinced that the distant origins of the order dated from Elijah and the Old Testament, had declared war upon the *Acta Sanctorum* of the youthful school of Bollandists and secured the condemnation (happily a temporary condemnation) by the Spanish Inquisition of the March, April and May volumes. Richard Simon was startling the Biblical scholars by his resolute and critical theories about the text-history of the scriptures. Every Catholic was convinced that an ox and an ass were present in the stable at Bethlehem: that Jesus was conceived on 25 March and born on 25 December: that the Wise Men were three in number, and that they were kings. Sober, pious, Catholic historians like Tillemont and Baillet were relegating these stories and many like them to the realms of uncertainty, sometimes to the realms of fable.

If you read in the scholarly controversies of that age, you will observe the slowly growing tension, the tension between the scholar and the conservative which has remained with the Christian Church from that day to this. You are beginning to find persons for whom the words 'critical approach' represent sanity and the only fruitful avenue to truth or even apologetic. You are beginning to find other persons for whom the noun *critic* is coming to represent a person who is potentially dangerous to the faith and who is possibly arrogant in spirit because he necessarily pretends to be more enlightened than the great Christian thinkers of the past. Some of the stories which 'the critics' question were more strongly attested in tradition than certain doctrines which were commonly accepted by the Catholic Church but which did not rest upon scripture. If Tillemont could question the ox and the ass, why (it was asked) might he not question the stories about our Lady's parents, which impinged more nearly upon Catholic doctrine?

The sands of historical apologetic were beginning to shift. Did it happen? Was there an ox in the stable? Was the Greek view of original sin so uniform and explicit as Bossuet assumed? Critical study always creates in the popular mind the air of uncertainty: and in the early years of the eighteenth century this air of uncertainty was perhaps increased by the assaults upon the critics. For the critics could be shown to disagree, and to disagree frequently: and it was in the interests of their assailants to display their disagreements.

In 1713 the discalced Carmelite Honoré de Sainte-Marie published a volume entitled *Reflexions on the rules and use of criticism*. It was translated into Spanish and Italian, and was believed by many competent conservatives to provide the soundest antidote to what they regarded as the excesses of the critics.

In the first place, argued Honoré, the critics who appear to be working with sound and systematic methods are really working on a basis of arbitrary and subjective opinion. Take the greatest of them all, Mabillon. Mabillon is confronted with a mass of monastic charters coming from the early Middle Ages and all posing as genuine. Mabillon claims to be able to show that many of these charters can be rejected as later forgeries. How does he know that they are spurious? He replies that they are incompatible with the genuine charters. But how does he know which charters are genuine in order to find the criterion on which he judges other charters to be spurious? Mabillon replies that ancient charters carry a stamp of truth which is manifest to a practised antiquary, as manifest as gold is to an experienced goldsmith. By assiduously reading ancient documents one forms little by little a kind of taste which enables one to discriminate true documents from false. And this, argued Honoré, is in the last resort an appeal to the subjective, to *taste*. There can never under such conditions be any guarantee that the taste has been rightly formed upon authentic documents. This subjective element which Mabillon applied to charters is applied by other critics over the whole range of ancient documents. Tillemont and Baillet and Ruinart reject numerous acts of the early martyrs because they claim to find them incompatible with the criterion which they have formed upon reading acts which they regard as indisputably genuine, like martyrdoms of Polycarp or Justin Martyr. And this judgment upon which acts are genuine is almost entirely a subjective judgment.[1]

If this arbitrary quality applies to a judgment upon documents, it applies *a fortiori* to some of the motives which lead them to reject documents as spurious. For example: the critics hold the principle that where a document recounts stories of miracles which sound incredible and fabulous, the document is likely to be written later and to be supposititious. They are far from denying that miracles occur: they accept as genuine numerous documents in which miracles are related. We are back again at the purely arbitrary—a patristic writer recounts a miracle and M. Baillet thinks it credible, another writer recounts a miracle and M. Baillet thinks it incredible; and there is no regular criterion for distinguishing the two documents except the mere taste of the scholar. If the possibility of miracles is allowed—and all these critics do allow it—the healing of a sick man by St Felix of Nola is not more credible, because more easily paralleled, than the transportation of the holy house from Nazareth to Loretto, a miracle in which Honoré believed.

This dependence upon personal taste is the explanation for the astonishing disagreements and contradictions between scholars working in good faith upon precisely the same set of documents. Honoré did with the critics what Bossuet had done with the disagreements of the Protestants—seized them and banged them together. And this mutual disagreement is paralleled by an internal uneasiness within each of the critics about the respect which is due to tradition. Plutarch reports that a traveller on a vessel near the gulf of Corinth heard a voice saying 'Great Pan is dead'. Eusebius tells us that this happened at the time of our Lord's death. Tillemont accepts the story.[1] Yet Tillemont rejects the story that St Paul preached in Spain, though the fact is attested by many of the most eminent among the Fathers. Dupin accepts, on the authority of the Fathers, that the Epistle to Barnabas is by Barnabas. Yet he maintains against a unanimous consensus of Fathers that the apostles did not write the apostles' creed. Honoré's case is made out. He is saying to the historical critics of 1719 what Liddon was to say to the Biblical critics of 1866—if you go so far, you must go further and jettison doctrines which you will see cannot be jettisoned. Both Honoré and Liddon supposed that the *reductio ad absurdum* would bring the critics to a sound mind.

The critics' cardinal assumption in discriminating documents is that language or customs which are found in one age are not found in an earlier age. Suppose that there is only one mention of extreme unction for some centuries. The critics conclude that the document containing this single mention is a fabricated document from the later age. It would be scholarly, said Honoré, to recognize the possibility that this single mention is early evidence for the existence of extreme unction. Underlying

5

all their conclusions is a failure to recognize adequately the evidential force of the tradition of the Church. If we suppose that the tradition of the Church has remained unchanging, we are not surprised at earlier language condemning a heresy which has not yet arisen. If we are to denounce as spurious all those documents which condemn a heresy but were written before it arose, we should have to reject every single ante-Nicene document to which St Athanasius appealed in his justification of the *homoousios*. It is not surprising that you find the doctrines of the fourth century in documents of the second century: the surprising thing would be not to find them.

Therefore the critics are working upon a theory of a church changing its practices and even doctrines as it advances through history. This theory, argued Honoré, impinges directly upon the doctrine of tradition: and it is impossible to claim that the investigations of the critics deal only with historical details and do not affect Catholic truth.

Neither Mabillon nor Tillemont possessed any *theory* of change. If they had been challenged about their doctrine of tradition, they would doubtless have put forward a doctrine indistinguishable or almost indistinguishable from the doctrine of their friend Bossuet. But in practical research they were seeking to 'place' documents —spurious documents, anonymous documents, undated documents—into a chronology, a historical setting. And consequently they were keenly looking for phrases suitable to a particular date, for doctrinal language, for examples of practices which were datable with probability from other sources. When Cardinal Baronius had published his *Annals*, he had betrayed no sign, throughout those massive volumes, that doctrine possessed a history. Underlying the profounder work of Tillemont, Dupin, Baillet, Mabillon, was no theory of change: but there was a practical, working, recognition of change, a recognition which increased the sense of confusion among the apologists reared upon the idea of absolute immutability.

The defenders of traditional apologetic appeared, in the years succeeding 1685, to be driven towards more and more eccentric theories to account for historical change. Some of these theories may be thought trivial and even absurd. But they are worth noticing because they disclose and illustrate the predicament of apologetic.

Bartholomew Germon was for many years one of the editors of the leading Jesuit journal in Paris and without question a learned man. He was known as the principal assailant of Mabillon's famous work *De Re Diplomatica*. In 1713 he published a work of some interest as representing a line of apologetic not so far away from that of Hardouin. The documents written by the Fathers now, admittedly, contain many errors and heresies. It is exceedingly probable that they have been corrupted by heretics in the course of their transmission to us. This must be true, for example, of the *Shepherd* of Hermas. For the primitive Church appears to have debated for a long time whether to include Hermas in the canon of the New Testament; and it is incredible that they should seriously have considered the question if the text of Hermas was the text which we now possess. Probably Novatianists or Montanists, or some other sect which refused to admit penitence after baptism, were responsible for the tampering. We can trace this tampering in certain apocryphal documents like the long recension of the Ignatian epistles or the Clementine Recognitions. Scholarly authorities have believed that Clement of Alexandria would not be held in such respect by the Church unless he had suffered interpolation. St Augustine himself thought there had been tampering with Cyprian. We learn from a medieval writer that Arnald 'the Albigensian' corrupted the lesser works of Augustine, Jerome, Isidore and Bernard. Germon's real point was not to seek to prove that in any document where the language was incompatible with later usage interpolation must have occurred, though he does seem to claim that people who believe this ought not to be blamed. He readily

67

allowed that the Fathers were but men, that they often disagreed among themselves, that individual Fathers were often wrong, that they wrote loosely because heresies had not yet arisen or because they were working with an inadequate vocabulary. But he was contending that it is only by recognizing these faults that we can see the true tradition of the Church and not try to make the true tradition square with erroneous language which appears in primitive documents. And to opponents who accused him of weakening all authority by rendering the authority of the Fathers uncertain, he replied that it is only if we recognize adulteration that the true tradition of the Church will stand out clear and impregnable.[1]

The Vatican librarian utilized an argument destined to a longer and more prosperous history. Emanuel a Schelstrate was an ardent and learned defender against the Gallican writers of the high antiquity of the papal primacy. From 1678 he had been arguing that the apparent silences and vacillations in the primitive material are to be accounted for by the discipline whereby the early Church refused to communicate to catechumens or the heathen the knowledge of its deepest mysteries.

The sixteenth century, in its confident appeal to unwritten tradition, had of course mentioned the refusal of the primitive Christians to throw their pearls before swine: and the existence of what since the Protestant Daillé was called the *arcana fidei* was well-known. Daillé had regarded the *arcana* as a disciplinary measure of the fourth and fifth centuries and had not attributed it to the most primitive period. Nor did Catholic writers often use it as a doctrinal argument. Even in the appeal to immutability, as presented against the Protestants by Nicole and Arnauld and Bossuet, it played no part.

Schelstrate turned it into an apologetic weapon. Criticized by a hostile Lutheran, he published at Rome in 1685 its most coherent statement, *De Disciplina Arcani*. Christ, in committing the gospel to the apostles, had instituted the discipline. It explained everything—the uncertain language of the ante-Nicenes upon the Trinity, the absence from the primitive documents of the doctrines and rites connected with the seven sacraments. We need not enter into the details of the theory. In Schelstrate it was not quite in the crude and simple form in which it appeared in some of his disciples. It bred no confidence in the Gallican writers, and it embarrassed some of the non-Gallican writers because Schelstrate had partly built up his theory with the aid of Dionysius the Areopagite and the Isidorian decretals, both of which he regarded as genuine. Nevertheless with a certain school of writers Schelstrate was regarded as an authority of importance even until the last quarter of the nineteenth century.[1] The reason why it was so successful, more successful in the long run than the theories of sounder writers in that age, is significant. It played something of the part to be played later by a theory of development, in allowing the historical critic to recognize openly that the language for some doctrine or the incidence of some practice does not appear until late in the history of the Church. Like the theory of development, it enabled the research worker to pursue his researches into changing ecclesiastical history while continuing to retain his conviction of an essential immutability.

Honoré de Saint-Marie himself preferred to put his trust in 'liturgical tradition'. It is certain that the Church has been conservative of her liturgical formulas. It is possible that the Church may be protected from error in putting forward historical facts as well as doctrinal formulas in the liturgy. We should therefore accept upon the continuous tradition of the Church what the Church has proposed to us, particularly in its Breviary and other liturgical forms. 'It is more reasonable, as well as more pious, to receive with simplicity the historical facts which the Church puts before us, than to try to examine them according to a criticism which is too severe and too punctilious.'[2]

Here then are three lines of argument, each of which betrays in a different way the predicament of apologetic in the face, not so much of Bayle and Voltaire and the coming age of scepticism, but of the rising tide of profound historical and Catholic scholarship. If there is one characteristic which they display it is what might be called anti-intellectualism. No doubt this is the historical side of the trend towards philosophical distrust of reason which we find in Huet and d'Olivet.[1] But it is also a sign of efforts to escape the dogmatic impasse into which modern and critical scholarship is driving the normal theory of tradition—efforts which may in some writers appear frantic. If you are not a Gallican (and the next hundred years was to wound Gallicanism sorely), you are perforce abandoning, little by little, the fortress in which you have been entrenched for the last 200 years and more, and must seek new and better standing-ground.

Isaac Berruyer was a Jesuit who possessed one of the ablest apologetic minds among French Catholics of the middle eighteenth century, the most difficult of all years for apologetic writers. In three parts, printed respectively in 1728, 1753, and 1758, he had written a *History of the People of God* which was (in effect) the Bible put into a modern French paraphrase. He did not minimize the modernity of his style: and since he possessed a brilliant and imaginative mind, he brought the simple Biblical narratives home to his readers with a new force. Modern paraphrases were shocking enough in themselves, and all parts of this 'Bible to be read as literature' were condemned by various authorities, the second part being burnt by the public hangman at Paris in 1755. His taste was not always as sober as his pen was effective, and he disturbed the French public in the same way that Milman was later to disturb the English public by calling Abraham a sheikh. But there was other suspect matter in the book apart from style and taste. The dogmatic theologians suspected the Christology, the Jansenists the attitude to grace, the Gallicans the doctrine of authority and the Roman see. And it was discovered that Berruyer had been a pupil of Hardouin.

Berruyer denied that he shared Hardouin's theory of a fabricated antiquity:[1] he believed that the theory was an extravaganza. He thought that because Hardouin had been erroneous in historical judgment the public should not blind themselves to his services in other directions, in exegesis, in disclosure of the perils of philosophy in relation to the Christian revelation. It was true that he hardly used non-Biblical antiquity in his narrative of Jewish and apostolic history. This was partly due to his ill-health which at times kept him confined to an arm-chair and prevented him from reading widely. But in the later stages of the *History of the People of God* one particular question was beginning to worry Berruyer, a question not unrelated to what Hardouin had taught—the question of faith and Christian certitude. And at his death he left in manuscript a book called *Reflexions on faith* which was published by his friends in 1762 (and put on the Index in 1764). This book attempted to tackle the problem which was to become the ultimate theological problem of the nineteenth-century Church, Catholic or Protestant—the problem of the relation between Christian certainty and the inevitable failure of historical inquiry ever to produce results which are more than probable results.

What, asked Berruyer, are the 'immediate and decisive reasons' for the individual articles of faith which the Church proposes to the believer? The traditional answer would be the infallible promise to the Church, which rests upon the monuments of antiquity and the evidence of scripture. Berruyer thought that Hardouin, whatever his absurdities, had shown that even the most hallowed kind of evidence may be regarded as only probable. The Church cannot be proposing to us the *homoousios* because the Council of Nicaea decreed it, since we have no certain and final knowledge that the Council of Nicaea was held—we have only probable historical evidence for the Council or its decision. We need only establish, by moral motives of credibility, the existence of a society charged with preserving and transmitting the revelation: and once this is established, all other historical evidences, even perhaps scriptural evidences, may be put aside that we may listen to the living voice of the authority established by God. The ground of certainty cannot be an appeal to historical tradition, a Gallican proclamation of the doctrines of the Fathers. How do we judge what is the consensus of the Fathers? To ask such a question is to deliver ourselves to uncertainty and to probability, to hold the faith as the judgment of a discursive reason and not as assent to a divinely revealed truth. The ground of certainty, therefore, can only be the infallible teaching of the present Church. For example, wrote Berruyer,

> God has not willed that in the matter of belief the decisive reasoning of the Catholic should run thus:
>> Jesus Christ has said in his Gospel, Take eat, this is my body. Therefore the Body of Jesus Christ is really present in the Eucharist.
> God has substituted for this way of reasoning another which is more adapted to meet all doubts: 'The Church of Jesus Christ teaches me that the Body of Jesus Christ is really present in the Eucharist: Therefore the words of Jesus Christ must be adequate to the meaning of the reality.'

Therefore the Church has no need of proof-texts to prove her doctrines. Theologians and controversialists should be encouraged to go on adducing texts. But texts of scripture do not warrant proof of doctrine—at least if they do it is only accidentally and not intentionally. It is in consequence of our presuppositions that we take these texts as authorizing doctrines which are already in our minds apart from the texts. 'I do not like,' says Berruyer, 'I do not like catechisms overloaded with proof-texts. Tell me simply—these are the truths which the Church guards and propounds to me.... Tell me nothing more.' Rest on antiquity and one is confronted with a crowd of thorny and interminable critical discussions—to appeal to the Fathers is to appeal to criticism. 'The thing proved', said Berruyer, 'is altogether more certain than the proof that is given.' Proof texts and historical evidences are more like ornaments and wreaths of flowers with which one crowns dogmas in theological treatises. 'If I must base my belief on these historical facts, I shall often be reduced to distinctions and subtleties and definitions so that I may reconcile them all with the faith, the far surer faith of the Church of Rome who teaches and guides me.'

And so no evidence drawn from the past can ever control the present. The present is supreme, and historical records irrelevant. The puzzle over immutability has been postulated into nothingness.

These men—Berruyer, Germon and their friends—were a little, untypical minority amid the apologetic of France in the eighteenth century; their thought unbalanced by the strain of fighting on a double front, against the Jansenist to the right and the Encyclopaedist to the left. And yet it is clear that criticism has introduced new concerns into apologetic. The quest has already begun—the quest to remove Christian doctrine from the sphere of historical investigation—the quest which was to trouble the Hegelians and the British idealists and so much of Protestant thought during the nineteenth century, and which was to reappear in an acute form within the Roman Church with Loisy and Tyrrell early in the twentieth century.

Berruyer had been led towards his fideism by his deductions from Hardouin's eccentricities, reinforced by the new powers, first of Catholic historical criticism, and then of French Deist infidelity. It is the least overlaid example of a movement running through anti-Gallican apologetic in the years after 1700. It is a sign that the theory of immutability found in Bossuet, and the apologetic based upon it, was gently subsiding rather than collapsing, like a house whose foundations have been built in shifting soil. And no alternative explanation had yet appeared.

# CHAPTER IV

# PROGRESS IN RELIGION

The Protestants began their assaults upon the ancient Christian Fathers as a counter-attack upon the cogent apologetic of the Gallican school. When Pierre Jurieu, the refugee minister in Holland, replied to Bossuet's *History of the Variations* by selecting Petau's statements about the unorthodoxy of the ante-Nicene Fathers, his motive was the traditional motive, the motive of Daillé's *De Usu Patrum*—the need to show the Gallicans, and in this case the arch-Gallican Bossuet, that the authority of the Fathers was neither absolute nor infallible. Jurieu was no Latitudinarian. He was one of the last defenders of Calvinism in a generation when Calvinism seemed to be dying. He still believed, like his Reformed predecessors, that in all that was important, in 'substance', Protestant doctrines and practices were justified by an appeal to the primitive Church as subsidiary to the appeal to scripture.

The writers of the left wing, the Barbeyracs and the Whitbys, the thinkers on the fringe of Deism, even an Anglican bishop like Hoadly, could not appeal to the primitive Church with the same confidence as their Protestant predecessors. Latitudinarian is a vague term, often used to cover the widest variety of thought: and even among the left wing of the Latitudinarians we find enough diversity to imperil generalizations about them. If it is true, as Whiston once grumbled, that the second-hand price of patristic texts had sunk to a level discreditable to the clergy of the Church of England, some of those whom history has agreed to call Latitudinarians studied and respected the ancient Church. At the opposite extreme were others who were outspoken in their avowal that appeal to the primitive Church was erroneous. Why? The early Christians were ignorant, uninstructed, and benighted. How shall they be a guide to us?

In December 1748 Dr Conyers Middleton, Fellow of Trinity College, Cambridge, published a celebrated book—*A Free Inquiry into the miraculous powers which are supposed to have subsisted in the Christian Church from the earliest ages, through several successive centuries.*[1] Middleton aimed to prove that the accounts of miracles outside the New Testament were untrustworthy. Many students have written of this able book as though Middleton's concealed intention was to discredit miracles altogether, the miracles of the New Testament by implication: and it cannot be doubted that the book marks an important stage in that process by which the inerrancy of the Bible must inevitably, sooner or later, be questioned. But this view of *A Free Inquiry* mistakes Middleton's purpose. He was not trying to discredit the supernatural: he was trying to discredit the authority of the primitive Church, which (for that age in its concern for 'evidences') rested in part upon the miraculous powers which its members were reported to have exercised. Middleton believed that in order to smash the authority of the primitive Church he must prove that God had not worked miraculous signs in the primitive Church.

Certainly *A Free Inquiry* promulgated the defects of the primitive Church and of the Fathers more forcibly than they had yet been asserted by any Christian writer. The stories of miracles could only (he held) be conscious forgeries, lies. The trick was an easier trick to win than the critics, in admiring his ability, have supposed. Middleton used the technique which an eminent authority has ascribed to Lytton Strachey—he selected all the most absurd passages from a mass of ancient literature, printed them side by side, and then conscientiously refrained from laughing. To recount, without comment, Theodoret's narrative of St Simeon Stylites on his pillar is enough for Middleton to discredit the character and good faith of Theodoret. The Fathers were superstitious, prejudiced, possessed of an enthusiastic zeal for every doctrine which a wild imagination could graft upon Christianity, scrupling no art or means by which they might propagate their belief, using jugglers and ventriloquists and itinerant wonder-workers, believing in necromancers, conjurers and familiar spirits. Was there another age of church history in which so many spurious books were forged by Christians? Upon a rash Archdeacon of Sudbury, who warned his clergy, absurdly, of the 'conspiracy' of the Jesuits to claim that all ancient literature was spurious, Middleton poured his mockery and contempt. Not only was the Jesuit theory believed by none, not even the Jesuits, but the claim of the Archdeacon that this alleged conspiracy was a menace to all Protestants was a preposterous misunderstanding. If Hardouin had been right nothing but gain could have accrued to the Protestant churches. As Hardouin cheerfully jettisoned the Fathers to protect Roman Catholic orthodoxy, Conyers Middleton, with an equal fervour and an equal want of historical sense, jettisoned the Fathers to protect the duty of Protestant common sense to interpret the scriptures.[1]

What had happened, when reduced to its simplest form, was that the Latitudinarians could no longer appeal to the primitive Church in confidence that it would support their contentions. They claimed to be the true successors of the Reformation. But no longer could they stand up, as Jewel had stood up at St Paul's Cross, and appeal with confidence to the first six centuries. If a dispute between Latitudinarian theology and conservative theology could be settled by an appeal to the primitive Church, there could be little doubt which primitive doctrine and practice would favour. Middleton, abandoning the entire Protestant tradition, handed over the primitive Church, lock, stock and barrel, to the Roman Catholic Church. The Fathers believed in relics, monkery, prayers for the dead, celibacy, fasting, holy oil, the sign of the cross, the superstitious use of pictures and images and of the consecrated elements. On the road between the Protestant claim to antiquity, and the view of Newman's *Essay on Development* that if Ambrose or Athanasius had returned to Oxford in 1845 there could be no doubt which church they would 'mistake' for their own, Middleton's book is a land-mark.

It is therefore assumed by the main stream of English thought in the eighteenth century, whether or not it would rightly have been classed as Latitudinarian, that theology has progressed, or, as they would rather have put it, 'improved'. 'My religion', said Sir Robert Walpole to Queen Caroline when she tried to persuade him to read Butler's *Analogy*, 'is fixed: I do not want to change or improve it.' Many of the divines of the eighteenth century did not share this old-fashioned attitude to the course of religious thought. They looked to find better theology: and with better theology a fuller understanding of the once-given revelation.

The arrival of the 'age of reason' during the last quarter of the seventeenth century had thrown into disrepute every form of authority except the Bible. Whether in natural philosophy or in metaphysical philosophy or in classics and literature or in patristic study the battle of the ancients and moderns was joined, and the moderns were winning. The cosmology of hierarchies ('The Great Chain of Being') was losing ground before the cosmology of progress. Newton had shown that the world bore the marks of reasonable design: Locke had shown the simplicity and con-trivance of the mental processes which appropriated and understood that design. The new-found confidence in reason as the test of truth questioned any form of 'tradition', any mere acceptance of alleged truths which rested upon transmission from ancestors. And theology therefore needed restatement. Locke, in the preface to his *Reasonableness of Christianity*, professed his intention of going directly to the Bible because all the 'systems of divinity' now failed to satisfy. We cannot any longer, in this new and wider world, speak in the language which contented our fathers. Theology must be 'improved' if it is to be intelligible.

If theology is to be improved, it must be based no longer upon authority, upon abstract formulas derived from outmoded philosophical formulas. It must be based upon observation and experience. Butler's *Analogy* is the high example of the new theology of the eighteenth century, the effort to repose Christian truth upon an empirical basis of natural observation. Since Newton the study of nature had become, not only the strongest rational argument upon the side of religious truth, but in some sense 'revelatory'. To Locke 'Reason is natural Revelation, whereby the eternal Father of light and fountain of all knowledge communicated to mankind that portion of truth which He has laid within the reach of their natural faculties'. In the design of the universe Berkeley discerned a standing and continuous revelation.

The idea of progress in theology (among the more advanced thinkers only), was partly derived from the analogy with the rising idea of progress in secular thought: partly from the general analogy with the natural sciences whose 'improvements' could not be denied. Aware that knowledge of every natural kind was increasing, Christian thinkers sometimes asked whether we might not expect a similar increase in knowledge of what was above nature. We have invented the mariners' compass: we have made advances in agriculture and bee-keeping: we have improved gunpowder, which (wrote John Edwards in 1699) gives us 'a more thrifty and frugal way of killing our enemies': we have discovered that the blood circulates: we have discerned the laws of gravity: we have made vast improvements in chemistry, in the quality of organs, in the mechanism of clocks. Jeroboam needed an army of 800,000 *chosen* (!) men, Xerxes brought two millions into Greece. Now there is no need of these vast armies, 'a tempest of bombs and granadoes will dispatch the business more easily than a shower of arrows'. 'And shall Divinity', asked John Edwards, after cataloguing these beneficent discoveries, 'shall Divinity, which is the great Art of Arts, remain unimproved?'[1]

It was not common to find the analogy made so crisply as this: and there were many who followed Joseph Glanvill in arguing that here no analogy was possible—that while natural knowledge could increase *ad infinitum* knowledge of the revelation could not increase since it had been given once for all. But scholarship was improving. What Mabillon and Tillemont were on the continent, Bentley and Bingham and others were in the history of English scholarship. Better texts, better linguistic apparatus, better knowledge of antiquity—the possibility of a more accurate understanding of the text or context of the New Testament could not be denied. It was an easy passage from the idea of improvement in scholarship to the idea of an improved understanding of the revelation.

*For the age they lived in*, Cranmer and Ridley and Latimer, even Luther and Calvin, were burning and shining lights. But the age they lived in was 'comparatively dark'. Who is the best commentator upon St Paul? The Latitudinarians to a man have no doubt—it is John Locke, and with Locke's assistance we may put aside all other aids, whether patristic or reformed. If you need an aid to Locke, one eminent preacher recommended you to go to a few books, notably Bossuet's *History of the Variations of the Protestant Churches*, which will enable you to understand the nature and the inevitable mutability of dogmatic opinions.[1] I do not think that Bossuet would have been surprised to find himself labelled as a text-book for the use of Protestant theologians in their effort to understand the nature of dogma. One part of the *History of the Variations* was devoted to showing implicitly that a recognition of the possibility of variation was one of the variations towards which Protestantism was tending. Professor John Hey, Norrisian Professor of Divinity in the University of Cambridge in the last quarter of the century, in a paragraph attempting to recommend the Fathers with all the warmth which he could muster, could not get beyond this tepid praise:

Be it that Mr Locke has best explained St Paul's Epistles; his explanation may not supersede all attention to remarks of the ancients on particular passages: were anyone about to see whether Mr Locke could not be improved upon, I apprehend he should consult the ancients occasionally; though possibly they may afford greater help on other parts of Scripture than on those which Mr Locke has explained.[2]

Tractarian authors often appeared to claim that they discovered the discrepancy between Latitudinarian Christianity and a patristic or reformed Christianity. They could not point it out more candidly than did the Latitudinarians themselves. Indeed a not unimportant part of the Latitudinarian effort was devoted to justifying their departures. Modern scholars have sometimes written as though the controversy over clerical or university subscription to the Thirty-nine Articles was concerned only with preventing the Church of England from sliding into Arianism. But one of the most important features of that controversy was the effort to prevent formulas, devised in an age believed to be less well-instructed, from hindering modern 'improvements'. Are we to tie the ordinand at his ordination to a particular form of theology which will exclude his subsequent intellectual development? So the opponents of subscription argued. Those Latitudinarians who defended subscription argued that we must maintain the Thirty-nine Articles, however inadequate we think them as theological expressions, because any other hypothetical formulas would cabin and confine us more. The Articles, by their very antiquity, have achieved a latitude of meaning which everyone has agreed to accept, and no one now understands them all in their literal and original sense. If we frame new articles, we shall all have to understand them in the literal and contemporary sense, and thus shall lose our liberty of opinion, the most precious possession of the Church of England. Hence the defenders of subscription were the first to concentrate upon a problem momentous for the theory of tradition—static doctrinal formulas do not always, whatever the appearances, maintain doctrine in a static condition. People's minds grow and develop and we are therefore bound to understand historical formulas in a sense slightly different from the sense in which our ancestors understood them. For the first time in Christian history they were asking questions about the relation of an always changing vocabulary to the ideas and doctrines which the language is seeking to represent.[1]

The Latitudinarian thinkers thus painted an impressionistic picture of the course of Christian doctrinal history. First, there was the delivery of the revelation, which is enshrined in the scriptures. This, and this alone, is immutable. Then the primitive Church attempted to express the revelation, with greater or less success, in a series of creeds or doctrinal formulas, which are authoritative in so far as they express scripture and are faulty in proportion as they adopt the methods of allegory or of an outworn philosophy. Then began the slow corruption of doctrine through the medieval centuries, a view which the Latitudinarians shared with their Protestant predecessors. Then came the Reformation, which excised the gangrene and purified the spiritual body: but it could be seen, in perspective, that the reformers had continued to share some of the mistakes of the medieval thinkers. Now, at last, with new knowledge and better critical equipment and less mystical philosophies and a stern dose of common sense, we had come to understand the scriptures better than the Reformers, far better than the schoolmen who hardly understood them at all, better even than the primitive Church. Most of the Latitudinarians agreed that we could not hold a candle to the primitive Church in moral endeavour: it was only knowledge that was in question. What was needed was a combination of primitive endeavour with modern and informed direction of the endeavour. The line dividing moral endeavour from enthusiasm is narrow: and the Latitudinarian tributes to the primitive moral endeavours are rather theoretical than practical. They bowed low before primitive purity as a utopian, generalized, unspecific condition. Bind them to concrete instances of primitive purity and they would think some of them zealotry.

The revelation, then, was still immutable. For the revelation was the propositions enshrined in scripture. Tradition consists in the passing of the same book from generation to generation. But Christian doctrine was not part of the revelation. Christian doctrine consisted in successive human attempts, from age to age, to express, in modern terms and perhaps with the aid of modern philosophies, the nature of this scriptural revelation. These doctrinal expressions had not been 'improving' at a uniform rate. As in the sciences, and the rise and fall of civilizations, doctrinal knowledge improves by fits and starts—now a step up the staircase and now a slip back, and then another step. You are not to think that this means that we are proud of our achievements. The dwarf can see farther than the giant if he is sitting upon the shoulders of the giant. We are using all the experience of the centuries, able to follow the debates and arguments of all the Christian sages. It is not surprising that we can see farther, because we have all their equipment as well as our own.

With this theory most of the lesser Latitudinarian thinkers were content. It found one of its most interesting, able and attractive expressions in those Bampton lectures delivered in 1832 by Dr Hampden of Oxford University, the lectures which were to act so explosively in the early years of the Oxford Movement.

In one other way the notion of progress in civilization contributed to the notion of progress in theology. In 1730, though no one quite believed in the 'progress of society' as so many during the nineteenth century were to believe in it, they were honest or sanguine enough to believe their own education to be more widespread and their manners more refined, than at any previous time in the history of mankind. There was some evidence, partly from European history and partly from recently acquired knowledge of primitive people in Asia or Africa or America, that there was a relation between the acceptance of the gospel and a growth towards a higher morality: not only that acceptance of the Christian gospel led towards higher morality, but that growth towards higher morality prepared a society to accept the Christian gospel. If then there is a relation between better moral habits and an increased capacity to receive divine communication, it is probable that the present generation is more capable of understanding that communication than any previous generation. So argued Edmund Law, archdeacon and later Bishop of Carlisle, the most outspoken and coherent theorist of this school.[1]

The idea of moral progress need not carry with it the idea of progressive revelation. But the Latitudinarians were so accustomed to think in moral terms that their theologians often conceived 'revelation' as equivalent, or almost equivalent, to the bestowal by God of ethical rules for the conduct of human life: after a succession of 'revelations' to Noah and to Moses and to the prophets, which have given to men rules of conduct ever more adapted to that stage of social living to which men could then attain, the unique revelation in the New Testament disclosed the best and the final way of life. If then they were also showing that, thanks to the New Testament, moral and social behaviour had improved (not steadily but by fits and starts) over the centuries, it was clear that the full meaning and relations of the moral precepts enjoined by the New Testament might only appear under new moral and social circumstances. 'Shall virtue be so revealed that man shall have no occasion to study it? That is against all our ideas of the government of the world. Besides, all the dispensations of grace are progressive, why not the improvements of natural virtue?'[2]

It is progress in theology, or progress in doctrinal understanding of an immutable revelation which the Latitudinarians were propounding, not 'progressive revelation'. Newman claimed Butler's *Analogy* in support of his theory of development; and critics like James Mozley charged him with blurring Butler's thought for his own purposes. It is true that in Butler himself, and in most of the main English churchmen of the eighteenth century, the division between an immutable revelation and a progressive understanding of that revelation in the light of better scholarship or new circumstances is perfectly plain. But there are rare moments when this idea seems to lead easily towards the idea of progressive revelation. If Locke and Berkeley were right in seeing nature and design as 'revelatory', they were approaching the modern distinction between 'general revelation' and 'special revelation', where the special revelation is conceived as certain unique events of history and the general revelation conceived as progressive, since the knowledge of nature is patently growing year by year, and is thereby affecting the way in which we regard the unique historical events. The divines of the eighteenth century refrained from any expressions of this kind: partly because they distrusted any statement which appeared to minimize the absolute and sole authority in religion of the Bible; and partly because they were advocates of what might be called 'scholarly Pelagianism'. They always, or almost always, conceived the increase in theological understanding as exactly parallel to the increase in scientific understanding, an increase won by sound and scholarly endeavour.

> As it is owned [wrote Bishop Butler] the whole scheme of scripture is not yet understood; so if it ever comes to be understood, before the restitution of all things, and without miraculous interpositions; it must be in the same way as natural knowledge is come at: by the continuance and progress of learning and of liberty; and by particular persons attending, comparing and pursuing, intimations scattered up and down it, which are overlooked and disregarded by the generality of the world. For this is the way in which all improvements are made; by thoughtful men's tracing on obscure hints, as it were, dropped us by nature accidentally, or which seem to come into our minds by chance. Nor is it at all incredible, that a book, which has been so long in the possession of mankind, should contain many truths as yet undiscovered. For, all the same phenomena, and the same faculties of investigation, from which such great discoveries in natural knowledge have been made in the present and last age, were equally in the possession of mankind, several thousand years before. And possibly it might be intended that events, as they come to pass, shall open and ascertain the meaning of several parts of scripture.[1]

The conclusion and the argument are framed with the caution habitual to Butler. Revelation is given and unchanging. But there may be progress in the understanding of the revelation: a progress analogical to that which is evident in the slow development in knowledge of nature. In both nature and super-nature God gave data: and then he gave us equipment whereby we might little by little comprehend them.

This is no doctrine of a progressive revelation. But not much is needed to turn it into a doctrine of progressive revelation. And how nearly it could approach to 'progressive revelation', not only in Julius Hare and Frederick Denison Maurice, who are the true Victorian successors of Butler and his Georgian fellows, but even in the eighteenth century, is proved by the case of the Deist Tindal.

In 1730 Tindal had used with destructive assurance an argument found among many of the Deists. If God is just and loving, he must have given to every man the chance of salvation, an equal chance of salvation. Why then did the Messiah come so late in human history? Why were so many generations allowed to be born and live and suffer and die in ignorance of that which gave meaning to their living and suffering and dying? Revelation must, therefore, be implanted in every man by virtue of his nature, revelation is coextensive with natural religion. To postulate a subsequent and special revelation in history is to postulate injustice in God. Christianity is as old as creation.

To much Latitudinarian theology this declaration was not so unattractive: for they were already portraying the Christian revelation as the republication of the law of nature. But Tindal needed an answer: he received a great many, some of which were profound enough to have redeemed permanently the Christian thought of the eighteenth century from the charge of superficiality. One of the answers must approach the notion of 'progressive revelation'. For without this notion Tindal could hardly be answered at all.

For many opponents of Tindal, like Bishop Sherlock, it was enough to demonstrate a progressive revelation in the Old Testament. God, in revealing, must take into account the capacities of those who were to receive his word. We do not feed children upon caviare, nor try to stuff adult knowledge into their little and sorely tried heads. We begin with simple truths and lead them onwards. The life of a society bears a resemblance to the life of a child.[1] A society needs to attain to a certain state of culture, of manners, before it is capable of receiving the deepest moral truths. You must begin with a simple code, a series of *Do nots* like the ten commandments, and only with the growth of the people's knowledge and obedience can they begin to understand the deeper springs of action, the investigation of motives, the furthest implications of the law of love.

Perhaps all the defenders of Christianity against Deism would have preferred to restrain the idea of progressive revelations to the Old Testament. (The plural *revelations* is correct. They think not so much of a God continuously revealing more of himself, but of a series of revelations to chosen and receptive individuals—Abraham, Moses, prophets.) Most of them did restrain the idea. All, without exception, were agreed that a unique and in some sense final revelation had come into history with the gospel. None of these thinkers approached Lessing or the theory that the Christian gospel is itself an interim revelation on the road to something yet higher in store for the human race.

But some apologists—Edmund Law and William Worthington openly, Butler in side-glances—answered Tindal by appealing to 'progress in theology', not only in the Old Testament, but since the New. It is a sign how akin are the eighteenth-century notion of theological progress and the nineteenth-century notion of progressive revelation. For, as a riposte to Tindal, an assertion that theology has improved is useless and irrelevant. The only answer that will do is an assertion that God has revealed more of himself: not that *our* ways are gradual, but that *His* ways are gradual.

Newman, the advocate of Bishop Butler, trained on Butler's thought, reverencing the *Analogy*, using the argument of the *Analogy* as the typical argument of his life—was he influenced in this area of thought by Butler? Was there, in the genesis of the theory of development, some little heritage of Protestant thought in the eighteenth century, some relic of Butler? In framing ideas Newman could not help but express himself with one eye on Bishop Butler. The inheritance from Butler conditioned (as he said in the *Apologia*) his whole outlook on faith and reason: and we shall see that his theology of faith and reason conditioned the expression of his theory of development; and without that theology of faith and reason the *Essay on Development* would not have been cast into its published form. That Butler entered indirectly into the *Essay* is not here in question: no one doubts it. I wish now to ask a narrower question: whether the idea of progress in theology, so characteristic of the Latitudinarian thinkers and allowed by Butler in one decisive passage and some subsidiary passages, helped to prepare Newman's mind for an idea of development.

The question would be answered easily, in the negative—did not Newman himself, in the *Essay*, lay partial claim to Butler as a theologian of development and represent himself as the authentic follower of Butler's train of thought.

It ought to be easy to answer the question in the negative, because even about the *Essay on Development* hangs an aroma which is curiously and characteristically Tractarian: the book, though an un-Tractarian book, could only have been written by a man who had been a Tractarian. The Tractarian movement, in its doctrine of authority, was directly assailing the Latitudinarian theories like progress in theology. The Tractarians wished to re-establish the Vincentian Canon which the Latitudinarians had jettisoned or neglected; to appeal to a stable tradition of doctrine which could be found in antiquity, not (as in Berruyer) by faith or postulation, but (as in Bossuet) by genuine historical inquiry. Newman's *Lectures on the Prophetical Office of the Church*, which appeared in 1837, framed the most coherent, lucid and cogent argument for the Tractarian point of view.

The Tractarians wished to assert that the Latitudinarian view of doctrine could be seen, both theoretically and empirically, to surrender the Christian revelation into the moulding hands of unredeemed reason; to turn doctrine into that modicum within the revelation which the educated modern man felt himself rationally able to accept; to emasculate preaching and evangelism by turning faith into probabilities, a matter of opinion. Against this let us declare the faith of the ancient and undivided Church, demand obedience to its doctrine and its practice, preach the word once delivered to the saints, stand firm upon the canon *quod ubique quod semper quod ab omnibus* which condemns the 'popular Protestants' on the one side because they have subtracted from the ancient creed, and the Roman Catholics upon the other because they have added to the ancient creed, reform anew the Church of England where it has for a little time slipped from this canon in its practice though not in its formularies or its liturgy.... The primacy of the ancient Church, and the stability of its teaching and practice—these are the basis of the Tractarian theory of authority, shared at once by Newman, by Pusey and by Keble.

Yet, even in the middle years of the 1830's, the stability of Keble and Pusey was different from the stability of Newman. After Newman had joined the Church of Rome, he looked back upon his Anglican career with no feeling of break, but with a sense of continuity. It always seemed to him that his change in 1845 relentlessly issued from those trains of thought which he had pursued while he was an Anglican. Something had 'developed' in his own mind which, nevertheless, had not lost its inner intellectual unity and identity during its course. Perhaps the element of moral dynamism in Newman's character and thought, that element which he canonized in Thomas Scott's motto 'Growth the only evidence of life', conditioned his own introspection and his personal interpretation of his religious course. But whether this conviction, or sensation, of continuity was well-founded or not, at least one difference separated Newman from Pusey and Keble—he was more powerfully influenced than they by Butler's *Analogy*.

The decisive text of Butler appeared in two different places in Newman's publications on development, once in the University Sermon of 2 February 1843, his first utterance upon the subject, and once in the *Essay on Development* itself. Both instances claimed the general support of Butler for Newman's case: and to both instances he added an appended statement that Butler's meaning was not quite the same as his own. These appended statements give clues to the discrepancy which Newman himself perceived between Butler's thought and his own, in spite of the general support on which he believed himself to rest. In 1843, he expressed the difference thus: 'Butler is speaking of the *discovery* of *new* truths in passages of Scripture, and the text speaks of a *further insight* into the *primitive* and *received* sense of scripture passages, gained by meditating upon them, and bringing out their one idea more completely.' Newman must have thought he could see a difference between 'the discovery of new truths in ancient texts' and 'further insight into ancient truths'. He must have thought so because he underlined the word *new*, as though by calling a development a *further insight* he prevented it from being new. It is not plain how these proceedings, which Newman evidently regarded as diverse, might differ. Nevertheless, he was also expressing here two genuine divergences from Butler. First, Butler's 'revelation' was the Bible and the Bible only. Newman's 'revelation' (in accordance with Tractarian doctrine) was the Bible as understood by the ancient Church. Secondly, for Butler the agent of development was the reason, the informed and scholarly reason of the academic. For Newman the agent of development was the reason and more than the reason, the reason plus the conscience or moral insight: in Newman's expression is something more 'religious' and less purely intellectual.

This second is the truly significant divergence. If the development is the development of scholarly research, then the parallel or analogy with the development of the natural sciences is established. To Butler this analogy is essential: it is the very ground on which he expects progress in theology. But if the development is not only a scholarly development but is in part due to obedience, to moral insight, then there is no parallel or analogy—or at least a less exact parallel—with the development of the natural sciences.

It might be said that this does not affect the crucial fact, reiterated by Newman, that both men were teaching the possibility or probability of the development of Christian doctrine. But how momentous this difference could become appeared in the appended statement which he added to the quotation from Butler in the *Essay* of 1845: 'Butler was not contemplating the case of new articles of faith, or developments imperative on our acceptance, but he surely bears witness to the probability of developments in Christian doctrine considered in themselves.' Butler, it was confessed here by Newman, was not thinking of such progress in theology which attained in the end to be imposed as articles of faith, articles necessary for salvation.

For Butler 'development' means progress in theology. For Newman 'development' means progress in theology until the results become binding upon the belief of Christians.

Why are these results made obligatory upon the belief of Christians? Is it that all instructed Christians can perceive that these results are the true and correct results? But according to Newman's ideas it is not possible for everyone to perceive that these results are the true and correct results. For these results (according to Newman) have been appropriated by conscience as much as by reason. One man's conscience cannot communicate with another man's conscience in such a way as to convince. Therefore the results do not become obligatory because all instructed Christians can perceive that they are true and correct. Wherefore then do they become obligatory? It can only be

because they have (subsequently to the 'revelation') acquired a
new status derived from an infallible judgment which asserts
them to be the true and correct results. If development is partly
by moral insight and not only intellectual, and if that development can become obligatory, then the power which declares it to
be true is equivalent to a revealer.

By his lower view of the power of reason, Newman had thus
discarded, or partially discarded, the analogy with scientific
development. All the evolutionary philosophies of religion in the
nineteenth century placed the analogy with science as the key to
their approach to religious thought: and in the next chapter we
shall find grave reasons for reserve about the view that Newman's
idea of development was closely related to the evolutionary
philosophies of his contemporaries. His belief that truth is apprehended not only by reason but by conscience-and-reason has
already separated him from the Latitudinarian view of progress
in theology, and consequently from their liberal successors of the
next century.

But if he had eschewed the analogy between theology and
natural science, he tried to maintain the analogy with nature—in
a loose way, but still an analogy which he claimed to derive from
Butler. Nature develops, and must develop to be nature: therefore there is a probability that Christian doctrine develops. 'The
general analogy of the world, physical and moral, confirms this
conclusion, as we are reminded by the great authority....'[1]
Since the author of Nature is the author of Grace, it is probable
that his workings will be on the same principles in both spheres.
Nature develops: Ergo....

Thus, eschewing the analogy with the rational development of
knowledge, he fastened upon the analogy with the organic and
unrational development of nature. He could find more than one
text of Butler to justify this analogy—

The whole natural world and government of it is a scheme or system;
not a fixed, but a progressive one; a scheme in which the operation

of various means takes up a great length of time before the ends they tend to can be attained. The change of seasons, the ripening of the fruits of the earth, the very history of a flower...and so is human life. Thus vegetable bodies, and those of animals, though possibly formed at once, yet grow up by degrees to a mature state....[1]

And Newman is not mistaken. Butler was indeed using the analogy of organic growth to prove that since God works by gradual means in nature, it is no objection to his goodness (the shadow of the Deist Tindal again slants across the page of the *Analogy*) that he should work by gradual means in the realm of grace.

Newman gave one concrete instance of what he meant: a most un-Butlerish instance. 'Preservation is involved in the idea of creation.' God created a world and needed to sustain it: by analogy, it seems, he created a creed 'once for all in the beginning, yet blesses its growth still, and dispenses its increase'.

It might be argued that empirically we can know nothing about a creation, meaning an act of creation. We observe a manifold of nature existing and from its evidences of design infer the possibility or probability of a designer. James Mozley argued therefore that here Newman was not arguing from analogy: for to argue from creation and preservation is not to argue from nature to revelation but from revelation to revelation, and an inference from revelation to revelation is no analogy, and is not turned into an analogy by the mere assertion that the reasoning is analogical.[2] But though Butler would not have used this line of reasoning, it is not altogether foreign to his method. For while the basis of his argument rested upon the analogy between nature on the one side and natural and revealed religion upon the other, he did not always stick consistently to the main theme. He was sometimes ready to allow, though with a congenital habit of caution, the analogy between natural religion and revealed. Because he could assume among his readers a belief in God, in the future life, in creation, he could have used this kind of analogy in his argument for revealed religion. For example, against the improbability of miracles, he contended primarily that our ignorance of the constitution of nature prevents us from determining general laws about the possible; but, secondly, that at the origin of the world or of mankind 'there was a power exerted, totally different from the present course of nature'; and, though he admitted that such a power cannot properly be called 'miraculous', he felt able to claim that such a supposition removed the *a priori* improbability, on the ground of generally observed laws of nature, from the fact of miracle.[1] The argument was only possible to one who could assume his readers to accept the notions of natural religion. And Newman might claim the same liberty. He was not being quite so unfaithful to Butler as Mozley supposed in introducing an analogy from 'creation and preservation'.

But Newman claimed Butler for his case on a wider ground than this. The whole course of nature, physical and moral, suggests to us a progressive development. Butler had inferred from the observation of the world—from the ripening of fruit, from the growth of an animal, from human growth in knowledge and experience, from the course of moral discipline—that the scheme of God's government was not 'fixed' but 'progressive'. And since Butler was seeking to argue, by probability upon probability, that the total scheme of providence may be affirmed (though not observed) to be a unity, that the principles upon which He acts in the realm of grace may be supposed to be similar to those upon which He acts in the realm of nature, Newman claimed this general analogy to establish an *a priori* probability for a development in revelation.

The use of the argument was not illegitimate. But Butler could not have used it. For the basis of all Butler's theory is the proposition that we have no right to expect, from *a priori* reasoning, how God will act. From observing nature we discern a partial scheme or pattern which appears to be a part of a wider scheme or pattern which transcends our observation. Nature does not fulfil the conditions which, on *a priori* principles, we should expect. Therefore we have no grounds for demanding that God's action, in natural religion or revelation, should conform to the expectations of our reasoning faculty. If a revelation is supposed to have been given, we are no judges of the kind of revelation which it ought to be, the mode or modes by which it shall be communicated, whether the revelation will be given once for all or will be continuous. According to Butler's rational foundation, it is impossible for us to lay down conditions about the revelation, and in his Tractarian days Newman had wholeheartedly accepted the verdict. But now, in 1845, he argued that since the revelation was patently given with 'gaps', that it was not given as a complete scheme or system, but as hints here and suggestions there, we could infer from analogy an *a priori* probability that these 'gaps' were intended to be filled, that these hints and suggestions were meant to be expanded. In this view he was directly contradicting Butler. According to Butler's reasoning, the existence of 'gaps' established no probability of any kind that those 'gaps' could be expected to be filled.

Newman, with half his mind, knew that Butler here did not support him. He tried to claim that Butler's reasoning 'does not here apply', or that analogy, if thus applied, would 'overthrow' the notion of revelation altogether. His efforts to show this do not convince. Butler simply and negatively urged that if a revelation is supposed we are no judges of its communication: it might be a developing revelation or an undeveloping revelation, the analogy from nature does not enable us to decide between the possibilities. Inasmuch as Newman was seeking to infer, from the existence of a particular sort of revelation, the probability that it must be supposed to be developing, he was neither reasoning from Butler's premises nor from Butler's analogy with nature.

It will be clear, when we come to examine the main lines of Newman's theory of development, that the theory did not arise in his mind because he was familiar with the ideas of religious and theological progress which Butler shared with many in the eighteenth century. His own theory was discrepant from the notions of religious progress found in Butler or (still more) in Edmund Law. He knew that he was writing for Anglican readers, that he needed a bridge over the chasm which divided his new thought on development from their habitual way of thinking. In Butler, whom nearly all Anglicans revered as a philosopher, he found language which partially and fragmentarily supported his effort to establish an *a priori* probability of development. But he was utilizing Butler's thought, not basing his reasoning on Butler's principles.

Yet the analogy with nature might be thought, by a later generation, to push into the foreground an idea which to Butler himself had been casual. To the scientists and philosophers of Butler's world, nature seemed like a beautifully designed and arranged mechanism. The scientists and philosophers of the 1840's were beginning to see nature as an organism, were beginning to use words like 'development' or 'evolution' to describe her processes. An analogy with nature might have different consequences for a generation whose world was not the world of Bishop Butler.

# CHAPTER V

# NEWMAN AND THE
# PHILOSOPHY OF EVOLUTION

Once it used to be loosely and superficially argued that Newman's theory of development was the application to religion of the general philosophy of movement which was conquering western thought at the end of the eighteenth and beginning of the nineteenth century: that body of thought of which the first signs are perhaps in Leibniz and the culmination in Hegel and then Darwin. Everything was to be understood in terms of process or 'evolution' as the word was coming to be used in those days before the biologists had captured it and given it a new and colourful tinge. Newman, it was argued, sought to convince himself that the Church of Rome had not corrupted the gospel although she appeared to have changed or added to her teaching; he found conviction by falling back upon the contemporary principles which the Tractarians had set out to resist: he accepted, in a general and vague sense, the notions of process and evolution, and applied them to the continuity and history of the Catholic Church. Where Catholic theologians had believed that the Church, to be inerrant, must always have taught explicitly or implicitly what she now taught, Newman argued that immutability was a sign of lifelessness, if indeed it was not an imaginary idea which could have no relation to reality in the circumstances of developing history. 'What he does', wrote his ablest Anglican critic and close friend James Mozley, conscientiously refraining from the note of exclamation, 'what he does is to assert the old ultra-liberal theory of Christianity, and to join the Church of Rome.' A less reputable critic used language still stronger: 'It is German infidelity communicated in the music and perfume of

St Peter's: it is Strauss in the garment and rope of the Franciscan...
Mr Newman is travelling to Germany by way of Italy.' The
view persisted into this century. Even John Oman lent to it the
weight of his authority.[1]

In 1933, Professor F. L. Cross challenged the common interpretation in an article in the *Church Quarterly Review*.[2] Was it
probable that the arch-critic of liberalism should have 'borrowed
...from a liberal source'? We find that his method of presenting
his case is not a piece of academic theorizing but is directed to
solving a particular problem, a 'concrete theological dilemma'.
He had believed the Church of England represented the Church
of antiquity more faithfully than did the Church of Rome. In the
face of Anglican reaction against his contentions and in face of
Wiseman's arguments, he was now losing that belief. To show
that the contemporary Church of Rome was the true representative of the Church of antiquity, he must show that growth of some
sort was inherent in the gospel and the Christian society. Recant-
ing some of the conclusions he had framed in his early study of
the Arians of the fourth century, he came to believe that the faith
of Nicaea and the *homoousios* were themselves developments
upon earlier Trinitarian theory, developments in such a sense that
it could be said that the Church of antiquity herself bore the marks
of inner growth in the history of her own thought and life. Hence
the promulgation of the theory of development had nothing in
common with evolutionary, immanentist, progressive, German
liberal theories.

Professor Cross's article caused needed readjustment: and with
various modifications his case has been accepted by all[3] the main
students of Newman since 1933. One simple fact is almost
enough, by itself, to dispel the idea. Newman never believed in
progress. From the window of his sanctuaries at Oriel, Littlemore and the Oratory, he looked out upon the world and, seeing
revolution, avarice, moral degradation, atheistic speculation and
sacrilege, believed that St Augustine was right in thinking every

kingdom of the earth to be founded on robbery. No one succumbed less to the idolatry of material discovery or to the
enchantments of scholarly and scientific research. He believed in
religious progress as little as he believed in secular progress, and
that was not at all. While in the mind of every contemporary
liberal the idea of religious development was as inevitably contained in the idea of progress as a core is contained in a ripening
apple or a heart in a growing child, Newman saw not even a link
between the two ideas, still less a co-inherence.

But the contemporary philosophy of development cannot be
dismissed so cavalierly. Several highly intelligent contemporaries,
Roman Catholic as well as Anglican, believed that in proclaiming
his theory he had adopted that philosophy. And this should be no
matter of surprise. He had adopted a word for his theory, the
word *development*, which was typical of the contemporary philosophies of history or religion or science. He was writing in an
academic environment where that word carried a not-so-distant
whiff from the continental cauldrons which had brewed it. It
was a word redolent of other words like 'tendency', 'trend,'
'influences', 'process', 'leading idea', 'interaction of ideas', words
which at their worst damaged English thinking temporarily by
insinuating imprecise jargon into the vocabulary, and at their best
enriched permanently the sympathies and understanding of English
historical study.

To adopt a word is not to adopt a philosophy which that word
has often represented, though it may be to communicate ideas
the more easily to persons who habitually think in those terms.
St John could receive the word *logos* and impose on it his own
pattern while using it as a bridge to communicate his thought to
those who used and understood that language. But this was not
Newman's intention. He was not writing his *Essay* for liberals,
he was writing it to satisfy his own mind, to convince his friends
and disciples and public that he was taking no unconsidered step
in his change of allegiance. He did not need the word *development*

as a bridge; for the people to whom he wished to communicate his thought repudiated evolutionary philosophy as warmly and decisively as himself. He needed the word as a form of explanation to himself, an answer to the problem which had been puzzling his mind, a key which would solve the perplexity that the canon *quod ubique quod semper quod ab omnibus*, as he had affirmed it in the *Lectures on the Prophetical Office of the Church* of 1837, had failed him as a test of the Church's dogmatic authority.

The word was becoming characteristic of the new and advanced school of historians. And Newman was a historian. Lord Acton believed that Newman, if he had cared deeply for scholarship, would have been one of the eminent historians of the nineteenth century, since he was naturally endowed with a historical sympathy. He had written nothing but the *Arians of the Fourth Century* and a number of essays and articles, theological and not historical by intention. But in his own field, the Fathers, he had worked over and over the sources, and was acquiring some of the insights for which the new German school of history was contending. More, he had to use German historians as aids to his studies. Though he had long ago been given a German grammar by an Anglican friend, who wished to persuade him to learn German, he had never made time or opportunity, and he could not read German. But Heeren and Gieseler were two German historians of the newer school whose principal works had been translated into English: and in Gieseler's *Text-book of Church History*, of which an English translation was published in 1836, he found a reference-book written in 'a reckless and arbitrary tone such as cannot be surpassed by the most dogmatical schoolman' and yet 'most able and useful'.[1] He was familiar, too, with the works of the Frenchman Guizot, and several of the historical writings of the liberal Anglicans Thirlwall and Milman, who had absorbed and moderately expressed the principles of the German school descending from Niebuhr. Newman criticized Thirlwall gently, perhaps because he was the historian of Greece and not of the

Church, perhaps because he was now a bishop of the Church of England. Milman's *History of Christianity* he criticized stringently in print, in his long review in the *British Critic* of 1841, singling out for attack the notion that Christianity was 'an idea which had developed itself' in response to circumstances, the notion which verbally at least he was to insert into the *Essay on Development*. Though he repudiated the historical methods and principles which he thus found in the Germans and the liberal Anglicans, it is undeniable that (by 1845, even by 1839) his mind had been influenced by their methods and insights. He had long been accustomed to use phrases like 'the march of the whole of educated Europe', 'the current of the age which cannot be stopped', 'the principles which will develop themselves', 'the equable and orderly march and natural succession of views', 'a certain continuous advance and determinate path which belong to the history of a doctrine, policy or institution'. The theologian in Newman vehemently distrusted the new school of historians, the historian in him could not help learning from them.

In January 1844 a writer in the *Edinburgh Review* (John Stuart Mill incognito) inserted into a critique of Michelet a warm and friendly welcome to the new historians and a plea that English minds might adopt their highest principles. There were three stages of historical writing. The first consisted in judging the past by present feelings and notions, to refer all ages and forms of human life to the standard of the age in which the historian lives. Whatever cannot be translated into the language of his own time is meaningless to him. He cannot imagine anything different from his own experience. If he finds *rex* applied to Clovis, he immediately starts writing about 'the French monarchy'. If he passes judgments upon persons or episodes of the past, he is moved by his personal attitude to contemporary controversy— the Tory condemns Pericles, the Liberal Caesar, and the man who does not like John Wesley will regard John Knox as nothing but 'a coarse-minded fanatic'.

The second stage consisted in seeking, so far as possible, to regard the past age not with a modern, but with a contemporary eye: to perceive with an act of imaginative and poetic sympathy which shall yet not outrun the documents. And the third stage, dependent upon the second, consists not only in writing history, but in constructing a science of history: to see history as a series of phenomena, produced by causes and susceptible of 'explanation'. 'All history is conceived as a successive chain of cause and effect; or (by an apter metaphor) as a gradually unrolling web, in which every fresh part that comes into view is a prolongation of the part previously unrolled, whether we can trace the separate threads from the one to the other or not.' Some law or process is to be discerned and discovered, the principles along which a society changes from one state into another.

Newman disapproved of the notorious principles of the *Edinburgh Review* and doubtless did not read the article. But his friend and disciple W. G. Ward read and marked it: and in the celebrated book of 1844 for which he was degraded from his degree, *The Ideal of a Christian Church*, he held up as a virtue of his ideal Church the consciousness of its own historical process; he applied to the history of the Christian Church the thought which the Edinburgh Reviewer had proclaimed as a general law: it would be part of his ideal that we should be enabled 'to have brought before our eyes a successive picture of the past ages of the Church, viewed as a Catholic would view them, and glowing with life and reality; to have made clear and transparent, in the record of past facts, the essential and all-important distinctions of character, which have separated the heretic from the orthodox; to witness, as if present at successive periods, the gradual and orderly development of Christian doctrine...'.[1]

'I am satisfied', a Cambridge ecclesiastical historian had written a few years earlier, 'that in Church history, as in every other subject, there is "nothing new under the sun", and hence much service might be rendered to sobriety by showing that the errors and sins of the human mind touching religion are of necessity the same in every age.' By 1844 the breezes of Oxford were puffing away these ancient cobwebs of historical writing. That Newman's theory of development was not a liberal theory, in the sense of contemporary evolutionary philosophy, is certain. But that his expression of it was influenced by the continental school of history whose influence was rising all around him is to my mind equally certain.[1]

W. G. Ward was to be a link between Newman and one other exponent of a quasi-evolutionary philosophy, Johann Adam Möhler of the University of Tübingen.

In Germany the flourishing life of the universities and the repute of the philosophers was bound to influence the thinkers of the Roman Catholic Church. Roman Catholic teachers had to seek to commend their faith to a public growing increasingly aware of the problems of modern theology and increasingly sharing the assumptions and viewpoints of Protestant theologians and philosophers. The influence of the Enlightenment had led some Catholic thinkers far from traditionalist Tridentine thought. Some of their clergy had attended the lectures of eminent Protestant critics like Paulus: the theology of the Catholic faculties at Freiburg-im-Breisgau and at Bonn was impregnated with liberal and critical principles. The German manifestation of the Romantic movement had caused a revival of interest in the Catholic Middle Ages and had brought a series of eminent converts to the Roman Church. And the new life and new confidence thus acquired began to stimulate theological study. While at Mainz the Catholic teaching was becoming ever more Ultramontane, for the most part the theology of the leading Catholic teachers in Germany was liberal, forward in historical criticism, distrustful of scholasticism and traditional means of apologetic, often Gallican or quasi-Gallican in ecclesiology. Sometimes they were directly or indirectly influenced by Kantian or Hegelian idealism, or by the theology of Schleiermacher.

The state of Württemberg, of old a Protestant stronghold, had lately acquired territories in Upper Suabia where the population was almost solidly Catholic. The Government, confronted by a divided kingdom, tried to treat the two churches as equal in law: and this policy, in a state in which Protestant teaching was flourishing at the university, necessarily encouraged higher education for Catholics. In 1812 a Catholic theological faculty was constituted in the Catholic area at Ellwangen: in 1817 this was transferred to the University of Tübingen and incorporated as a faculty of theology there. At Tübingen the young Catholic professors found themselves face to face with established Protestant theologians. The consequent debate, which at first was free from acrimony, forced the Catholics to present their faith in terms which the Protestants could respect. It seemed above all essential to meet the Protestant criticism that Catholic authority nullified genuine research by ordering the research worker to produce a determined answer. Through all the Catholic theologians of Tübingen we can see this criticism underlying their apologetic: it was necessary to claim liberty of inquiry. And if they claimed liberty of inquiry, they must also allow (at least in part) that some of the Protestants' historical conclusions upon the growth of Catholic dogma were accurate. The new Catholic apologetic must therefore seek some way of reconciling Catholic dogma with a theory of historical movement. Perhaps for the first time Catholic theologians were having to frame a doctrine of authority and tradition which allowed the partial justice of Protestant historical criticism while it denied any theological deductions which the Protestants sought to draw from it.[1]

The Catholics of Tübingen not only claimed liberty of inquiry: they enjoyed a wide liberty of thought. The relations between the papacy and the Catholics of Germany were delicate. While the papacy was weak during the late eighteenth century and the age of revolution, Febronian and Josephist ideals had become influential: a strong body of German Catholic opinion wished to limit the authority of the papacy over German Catholics. Josephist doctrine was powerful in Württemberg. Werkmeister, the Catholic preacher at the court of Stuttgart, had claimed for the sovereign the right to alter those elements in the Catholic liturgy which were inappropriate to modern times and had demanded mass in the vernacular. The Ellwangen theologians, in common with many other Catholic thinkers of Germany, criticized relics, pilgrimages, indulgences, extreme Mariolatry; some of them disliked the rule of celibacy for the clergy; some of them sympathized (at first) with the programme of Wessenberg, the vicar-general of the diocese of Constance, who was propagating, during the years of the faculty at Ellwangen, his plea for a German national Church independent of Rome. The ecclesiastical ground in Germany was not sufficiently firm for the authorities to tread heavily upon religious speculation by loyal Catholics. Nor were the authorities so minded. It would have been impolitic for authority to offer a handle to the enemy by repressing Catholic scholars who were claiming liberty of inquiry. And above all the scholastic philosophy, though it was beginning to revive, was not yet self-confident enough to fight vigorously against Catholic apologetic based on non-scholastic or anti-scholastic assumptions.[1]

It would have been easy for the school of Tübingen to follow the vacillations of other German theological faculties and be content with a minimizing of Catholicism in face of the liberal critics of the day—the old policy of the later Enlightenment. Certainly they at first advocated many changes. Hirscher,[2] one of the founders of the school, asked in his first published work of 1821 for the suppression of private masses, the giving of the chalice to the laity, and mass in the vernacular. The work was placed on the Index in 1823 (and was not the last work of Hirscher to find its way into the Index)—yet Hirscher's pupil Johann Adam Möhler was continuing to advocate some of this programme in 1823-5.

Tübingen was saved from a merely minimizing and negative approach by its first theological leader, Johann Sebastian Drey, who from the foundation in 1817 held the chairs of dogmatic theology, apologetics, and encyclopaedic theology.

From his earliest publications Drey began to use the idealistic philosophy of the day as a weapon of Catholic apologetic. He had read Kant, Fichte, Schelling: he was soon to be affected by the theology of feeling and experience taught by Schleiermacher. Under these influences he sought to explain the outer phenomena of Catholic doctrine and organization in terms of the living spirit within the community. The Catholic theologians, he held, had followed the Protestants in turning authority into the dead hand of the past. Protestantism had come to base itself upon a historical exegesis of the documents contained in the Bible. The Catholic theologians had likewise turned the scriptures and the Fathers and the Councils into a dead hand of the past, and had failed to preserve a sufficient sense of the living organism which underlay these documents and decisions.[1] He applied this theory courageously to a particular case—the history of sacramental confession. Catholicism is in essence unchanging, its dogmas are immutable. But we must expect rites, ceremonies, organization to change from age to age in accordance with the needs of succeeding generations. The Lord did not intend the Church to be rigid and ossified, but able to adapt herself to every man and every civilization. In this way the essential truth creating the practice of confession is unchanging. But the form has changed from age to age, has grown with the Church from public to private, and has finally issued in the regulations of canon law.

In 1819 Drey published his *Introduction to the Study of Theology*.[2] He sought to analyse the various fields of theological study and their coherence. His assumptions and conclusions are in a general way consistent with modern Catholicism, though he did not discuss particular Catholic dogmas. The approach was critical and differed from the traditional approach of apologetic—it could almost be a Protestant theologian using the methods of modern German thought but arriving at conclusions different from the conclusions of other Protestants. In the course of the *Introduction* Drey shows the influence both of a modified form of historico-philosophical idealism and of a modified form of Schleiermacher's theology of religion as feeling or religious consciousness.[1]

Religion to Drey is the religious consciousness of God and the feelings evoked by that consciousness. It is the task of theology to explain this consciousness and these feelings. The Church is the living body of religious persons and therefore the life of the Church is the true basis of all theological knowledge, for it provides the material on which all theologizing must be based. The life of the Church is for the theologian what the life of the State is for the political theorist or the animal organism for the biologist. This is why each separate Church provides its own theology—an explanation of its own life. Hence the work of historical theology must precede systematic and dogmatic theology. We must discover the life, practices, worship, morals and teaching of the Church before we can advance to scientific theology. 'In the nature of things the teacher or writer in the Church must emphasize the element of theoretical knowledge, but the living element in the Church is not this knowledge, but practical religiosity.'[2]

This study of Christian life must be the study of the total life of the Church. We can theoretically distinguish the history of the Church in its origin from the history of the Church since its Biblical foundation. Yet the study of Christianity is a unity: and there is a sense in which the study of the development and expansion of Christianity is as momentous and necessary as the study of the Bible—this at least is the Catholic view.

Thus observing the Church historically, we must take the higher idea of history as the 'Strife and Weaving' of a single Principle, a Spirit, which breaks through the spirit of each age. All the phenomena of history must be interpreted thus, and Christianity among them. Hence the history of Christianity may be divided into two elements—an 'inner history' of that which is peculiar to Christianity itself, and an 'outer history' of phenomena arising from the conflict of Christianity with the world. The inner history is really the history of its teaching—the history of a system of ideas and their development—a system of ideas which is ever trying to 'unroll itself' upon the spirit of men with an authority which is of the essence of Christianity itself.

We should not exclude outer influences—like contemporary philosophy—in studying this unrolling of Christian teaching. It is commonly asserted that the use of a particular philosophy in the explanation of Christian theology is a sign of 'corruption'. Yet it is inevitable that if Christianity is to be unfolded to the spirit of men it should be affected by the ideas of the age in which it is being unfolded. It is the duty of theology to trace such influences and it will expect them. Nor will it necessarily regard them as corruption. What matters is whether the philosophical ideas are in the spirit of Christianity and in harmony with it. Only if they are not in harmony with it can corruption arise. The explanation of Christian teaching in such a way is not corruption but the essential task of theology.

Not every explanation or modification of doctrine, whether mediated through historical reflection on the Bible, or mediated through philosophical speculation, is in the spirit of Christianity. The individuals who are the agents in such modification can err. The spirit of Christianity and of its doctrines is always in the wholeness of the Church; and the universal Church cuts off the modification contrary to its spirit as an individual innovation. Hence come schisms: and the study of heresies and schisms belongs to theology because they have all made the Church more conscious of her true self.

The Christian Church can only subsist by means of a constitution. In part it has had a constitution since its beginning, in part it has formed one for itself in the course of time. The constitution implies those arrangements of the organic body of the community whereby it secures the authoritative development of its doctrine and its inner life and holds off external influences which hamper that development. It is the task of Church authority to watch over the development of doctrine and the contemporary shape of the Creed, to ensure the true process of development.

This is the outline of Drey's theory. The language is strange and unusual; in spite of the phrases reminiscent of the idealist philosophers and of Schleiermacher, it would be possible to state the central thought in a manner not so remote from traditional apologetic. There was a revelation: this revelation has been unfolded in the historical life of the Church: ecclesiastical authority, which speaks for the infallible Church, has ensured the rightness of the development and the cutting-off of the developments when they prove to be erroneous corruptions. What is new in the theory is the expectation of a kind of *inevitability* about development, a point in which the direct idealistic influence is perhaps most marked. His characteristic attitude to the Church is that she is a living body, an organism. Organisms must grow if they are to be themselves. The revelation has been from the first explicated and will continue to be explicated, for such explication is a necessary part of growth.

In 1819 Drey founded as the organ of his school that periodical destined to a distinguished history—the *Theologische Quartalschrift* of Tübingen. The earlier years of the periodical were marked by the spirit of Roman Catholic liberalism: and its object was the restatement of Catholicism with the aid of the new historical and critical and philosophical instruments. Its spirit was more devout and Catholic, less rationalist, than the work of some theologians of the school of Bonn or Freiburg. And this was the strength of the school: it was able to accept many of the methods of Protestant theology while remaining faithful to the Tridentine tradition. In the first volume a series of articles set out some of Drey's leading ideas.[1]

Drey's attitude is typical of the whole Catholic school of Tübingen in those early days. It was a vague approach, perhaps: as the school matured, it clarified its theory and modified or abandoned those elements in the theory or expression of it which patently conflicted with traditional ideas of authority. Drey himself came to regret the vagueness of his *Introduction*. Drey's greatest pupil Möhler likewise began with a romantic but imprecise warmth and ended in a theology which was coherent. Yet neither Drey nor Möhler[1] abandoned the basic idea, the idea of the Church as an inner organism, growing and so expressing itself in concrete forms.

The most celebrated performance of this earlier, romantic, idealistic phase of the Tübingen Catholics was Möhler's *Unity in the Church*,[2] published in 1825. Here he portrayed the Church as an organism of which the Holy Spirit is the principle of life. This life, or love-in-the-community, which is the essence of Catholicism, creates faith and is the source of truth. Interior faith is the root of exterior faith, which is assent to dogmas. Though interior faith is communicated with the help of words, it precedes any external expression, any dogma. 'Jesus Christ before speaking carried his doctrine in his own soul: Peter was persuaded by God's influence about the worth of Jesus Christ before he replied to Jesus' question.' The principle of life exists in Christians before they frame or comprehend the doctrine. Hence the Church is not based upon scripture, for the Spirit existed before the letter. Whoever understands the living Spirit will understand the letter which is the expression of it. Möhler, at this stage of his thought, seems invariably to put dogma into the category of those external propositions which represent the unchanging idea or substance or principle: and his doctrine of development consisted in maintaining that the idea, the principle, was unchanging while the external expression of it might vary according to external circumstances, philosophies, heresies, and pastoral needs. 'Christianity does not consist in expressions, in forms, in phrases. It is an interior life, a holy force: and all its dogmas have validity only in so far as they express the substance which is presupposed....' As a doctrine of development, rather than a doctrine of tradition, Möhler made his theory no clearer than Drey. The test of such a theory is its application to concrete historical occasions; the test is not whether a general and inexact notion of development is put forward as an umbrella or excuse for the delivery of historical investigation that changes have occurred, but *what* and *which* expressions or practices are admitted to be innovations and in what sense they are admitted to be innovations. None of the Tübingen scholars attempted this kind of precision. Möhler's theory of development is perfectly consistent both with the view that development consists only in clarified expression and with a less conservative view—the absence of concrete illustration does not allow the reader to determine what is intended.

In 1827 the German Protestants were using of the Tübingen Catholics the portentous verb *schleiermacherianisieren*. But the school, like so many theological schools of Europe between 1828 and 1835, moved steadily to the right. Drey and Möhler both came to regret the vagueness and laxity of their earlier thought; Möhler came (by 1834) to dub his book on *Unity* 'youthful folly'. In Möhler's case the move was hastened by a long and acrimonious controversy with his Protestant colleague Ferdinand Christian Baur, and by his desire to draw a sharp line between Baur's evolutionary and Hegelian historicism and his own theories of tradition. Hardening his opinions in a traditional direction, he published in 1832 the *Symbolik*, a direct attack upon Protestantism by an examination of the Protestant formularies and comparison of them with the latest productions of German Protestant thought. In the earliest edition of *Symbolik* the old romantic strain, though less manifest than in *Unity*, is still visible. In successive editions he moved still further away from the doctrine of his early years. The faint suggestion of *Unity* that dogma is of secondary importance has vanished from *Symbolik*.[1] Baur, paying Möhler the backhanded compliment of being a new hope for ecumenical discussion because Catholic theology, like Protestant, was becoming subject to the influence of Schleiermacher, forced Möhler to distinguish his own theory from any Hegelian or quasi-Hegelian theory which taught that truth was becoming known through a process, and to assert ever more strenuously that development could only be a development of a truth which was given and always known.

Did Newman know anything of, or adopt anything from, Möhler?

He mentioned Möhler in the *Essay* of 1845, in a passing phrase which proves that he had not read him—'The view on which this essay has been written has at all times, perhaps, been implicitly adopted by theologians, and, I believe, has recently been illustrated by several distinguished writers of the continent, such as de Maistre and Möhler.'[1] That Newman could not have read German was not a final bar to his reading Möhler. *Unity* had been translated into French in 1839, *Symbolik* into English in 1843. But the phrase of the essay, 'I believe', pleads ignorance, is equivalent to a denial of first-hand knowledge and a claim to be based upon hearsay.

A theologian who was seeking to attribute a doctrinal theory to the Roman Catholic Church might reasonably be expected to take some precautions to discover whether anyone else had taught the same before him. Not so Newman. He was a man of exceptional independence of mind. Though he frequently pillaged in secondary as well as original sources, his mind possessed an intrinsic integrity. The unfriendly have argued that the original genius of Newman's mind consisted in an infinite capacity for not reading important books. It would be truer to say that his mind, unresting and powerful, was so constituted that he must impose his own pattern on all his material. The arguments and the conclusions in all his writing carry a first-hand atmosphere, a freshness which comes only to one who has assimilated and digested his authorities and thought through his subject. He had been educated at Oxford, and partly by Whately, who more than any other philosopher of the century believed creative thinking to arise from reasoned meditation upon a few books but great books, and neglected the desire to be 'up to date' with contemporary and probably ephemeral scholarship. It was a neglect which Acton regretted. The air of freshness which Newman succeeded in imparting to every subject that his pen handled was one of the secrets, both of the power which he always exercised over his disciples, and of the suspicion which conservatives always bestowed upon him, whether those conservatives were Anglican as in the earlier half of his life or Roman Catholic as in the later.

He had heard, then, that an idea of development was to be found in Möhler. Yet, half-unconvinced of the value of reading books written by other people if those other people were modern, he took no steps to inform himself directly of the content, merits, or present standing of the theory. And if any further proof were wanting that he did not know Möhler, it is to be found in that astonishing juxtaposition of names 'several distinguished writers of the continent, such as de Maistre and Möhler'. De Maistre, the political theorist of an ecclesiastical reaction after the Battle of Waterloo, the papal version of Metternichism, had possessed many remarkable qualities but being a theologian was not one of them: and if he had in *Du Pape* made loose statements which loose-thinking Englishmen turned into a theory of doctrinal development, he could not be whispered in the same sentence as Möhler by anyone who had perused them. Well might the Anglican Milman ask 'Have those who quote de Maistre and Möhler together...read both?'[1]

Yet Acton's papers in the University Library at Cambridge show that Acton decisively believed that *somehow* Möhler had influenced Newman even though Newman could not, or did not, read Möhler. Acton's opinion on the matter is worth weighing: for he was one of the very few people who knew both sides of the question. He knew Newman personally and had worked with him: he was the most intimate friend and pupil of Döllinger, who had learnt much from Möhler's work: he was himself interested in the genesis of the idea of development and had studied Möhler and Baur. Knowing both parties to the question as probably no one else did, he was convinced that Möhler had influenced Newman. He was not sure how it had happened, but that it had happened he was in no doubt at all. In his notes and cards you can see him casting around for some theory which will fit the facts. And he succeeded in unearthing, and noting among his private papers, two spectacular items of information.

In the 1830's and 1840's the leading theologian of the Roman schools was the Jesuit professor at the Collegio Romano, Giovanni Perrone. A man without profundity or deep learning, but with a precise common sense which rendered his expositions models of clear reasoning, he had published a text-book which was already being widely used in Roman Catholic seminaries, *Praelectiones Theologicae*. In his 1835 edition he had ignored the problem presented by the history of dogma. But he then encountered Newman's *Lectures on the Prophetical Office of the Church* and felt the thrust of that well-argued attack upon Rome for disregarding history and for changing the dogmas of antiquity. To meet this attack, to 'stop the mouth' of his adversaries as he put it, Perrone in his new edition of 1843 sent his readers to Möhler's *Symbolik*. Acton therefore guessed that Newman's own attack as an Anglican had forced Perrone to bring Möhler to Newman's attention: and so the Tractarian reassertion of immutability, of Bull, Bossuet and the Vincentian Canon, had forced Roman theology into allowing the possibility of development which Newman was to expound so fruitfully.

This clever guess has the unexpectedness of the neatest form of research. It is like the inquiry how the Red Indians learnt to scalp the white settlers, which proved that the Red Indians had learnt the habit from the white settlers. It is nothing but a guess. And against it, there is no scrap of evidence that Newman was reading, or was influenced by, Perrone at this time. An undergraduate of

Pembroke College and a pupil of Newman, Renouf, denied the probability that Newman read Perrone at this time—but the claim by an undergraduate to know the reading of his tutor may reasonably be thought over-confident.[1]

Acton's second piece of information came from Renouf himself. Later in his life, Renouf claimed that while he was an undergraduate (that is, between 1840 and 1842) he had told Newman that he would find precedent for these theories in de Maistre and Möhler.[2] Renouf became a scholar and not likely to make such a claim without some basis in memory. The claim is uncheckable, and is difficult to accept, for a reason which will appear.

Among the high Tractarians in the England of 1835 to 1845 the reputation of Möhler was steadily rising.

Dr Nicholas Wiseman had set out on the course which was to mark his whole career, the effort to give English Roman Catholics, and through them other Englishmen, a wider horizon over the Roman Catholic Church than they now possessed. Himself a scholar, and aware of the new theological currents flowing from Tübingen, he began to draw the attention of the English to the German Catholics and especially to Möhler. He had met Möhler, and while remaining critical of his liberalism, admired his patristic learning. As early as 1834 he had sent a message to Newman through a friend to persuade him to read Möhler on St Athanasius.[3] In the *Dublin Review* he began to bring German Catholic scholarship before his readers.

The time was ripe. The English high churchmen were becoming interested in German Catholic scholarship. They were being shocked by rationalism in Germany, by the progress of Biblical criticism, by extreme publications like Strauss's life of Jesus. Because so few of them could read German, they judged German theology by rumour and hearsay which inevitably report what will startle and alarm. Thirlwall had written that the knowledge of German now seemed to expose the theologian to the same suspicion of heresy as attached, some centuries before, to the knowledge of Greek. The eccentric Rector of Lincoln College, Dr Tatham, had preached in St Mary's, Oxford, a sermon lasting two and a half hours, in which he expressed the hope that all the German critics would sink to the bottom of the North Sea.

Even when allowance is made for gossip and exaggeration, it was patent to any observer that theologians who had abandoned belief in the literal inspiration of the Bible, and had sometimes abandoned belief in miracles as well, continued to hold teaching posts in the Protestant churches of Germany.

The English judgment upon these facts is cardinal for the understanding of Tractarian ecclesiology. The Caroline divines, holding that episcopacy was the rightful ministry of the Church, felt bound to make room in their ecclesiology for the continental reformed churches which still represented, with whatever reservations, the great age of the Reformation. Reformed continental Protestantism now seemed to be abandoning the Christian faith as it had always been understood; and so far as Tractarian ecclesiology was concerned, the Protestant churches of the continent could be dismissed. But how had this happened? There could only be one answer—rationalism must have been 'implicit' in the teaching of Luther and the original reformers. Though it was difficult to fit Luther into the category of 'rationalist', the solution was found in the surprising theory that Luther had taught the free right of private judgment, and that the right of private judgment leads inevitably to the prevailing rationalism. Already Hugh James Rose had warned Anglicans of the ancestry of this rationalism: and the growing Tractarian conviction of the truth of this theory was summarized in a book of 1844 by Dewar, the British chaplain at Hamburg;[1] Dewar began his account of German Protestantism with Luther, and while admitting that not all or even the majority of Lutherans were rationalist held that the Lutheran principle was bound to end in Strauss, Feuerbach, and Bruno Bauer. This English view was materially assisted by the

German Protestant theologians themselves. To gain a hearing in Germany for a new system of theology it must be shown to be consistent with the theology of Luther and the German Reformation; and therefore critics like Bretschneider or theologians like Schleiermacher claimed that their theology was indeed the logical outcome of Lutheran thought.

In this state of mind among the Anglicans, the *Symbolik* began to be known, mainly from hearsay, as an important work. In it a German Catholic theologian had considered the dogmatic formulas of the Reformation, examined their weaknesses, shown what the deductions from them must be. The younger generation of German clergy was being trained by the *Symbolik* in dogmatic theology—so Döllinger claimed to Gladstone.[1] Here was a book which might well interest Tractarians.

Already in 1842 the *Christian Remembrancer* was writing of 'the celebrated Möhler' and 'the great author of the *Symbolik*': and early in 1843 it took the opportunity of a review of Manning's work *The Unity of the Church* to review Möhler's *Unity* in parallel and to provide a short biography of Möhler.[2] In 1842 appeared an English translation of Möhler's life of St Anselm; and in 1843 a two-volume translation of the *Symbolik* itself, under the misleading title of *Symbolism* and prefaced by a long and laudatory memoir of the author.

Where there was interest in Möhler, there was also bound to be interest in *Unity in the Church*. This was never during this period to be translated into English, because the leading English Catholics, the only likely translators, were suspicious of its phrases. But it was the caustic, energetic and provocative W. G. Ward who took the significant step of isolating the doctrine of development in Möhler and applying it to the Tractarian controversy. In the late summer of 1841 Ward received a copy of the French translation of *Unity in the Church*. He immediately perceived the importance of it. An article in *The British Critic* for October 1841 (on *Arnold's Sermons*) recommended the work, gave copious extracts from it, and professed adherence to the general principle of development. In a number of passages printed in the *British Critic* during 1842 and 1843 Ward returned to the theory in its application to the dogma of the Catholic Church.[1] In Möhler the principle of development was only one facet of a wider philosophical approach. Ward was at this stage seizing upon the one facet for a particular purpose of controversy. Already in 1842 the conservative Tractarians were beginning to discern perilous possibilities in the theory. William Palmer of Worcester College, that loyal, sturdy and sententious Tractarian, felt impelled to add a note, critical of the theory, to the third edition of his work *On the Church*, published in 1842. Ward did not treat the subject critically or extensively. But it became a normal assumption with him, and runs through the book of 1844 which turned all Oxford against him, *The Ideal of a Christian Church*. Ward compensated for a certain lack of theological solidity by the trenchancy and piquancy of his pen. By 1844 he was roundly asserting, 'My difficulty in defending this doctrine of development arises from my inability to conceive how anyone can have, for a single day, pursued a course of moral and religious action, and yet deny it.'[2] Thus interest in Möhler was steadily rising as the controversy over Romanism in the Tractarian party became more clamorous. Thirlwall, by now Bishop of St David's, was one of the few Englishmen to have read Möhler's *Unity*: and in September 1845, a week or two before Newman finished writing his *Essay*, Thirlwall delivered a charge to his clergy in which he recognized the value and truth of much in Möhler, and yet warned them against the theory of development as 'characteristic' of the Romanizing party among the Tractarians.

That Newman read these various articles and Palmer's ripostes is sufficiently proved by the form of the sentence in which he referred to Möhler in the *Essay*: 'several distinguished writers of the continent, such as de Maistre and Möhler'. For the odd juxtaposition was not due to Newman. He found it in the controversy between the *British Critic* and William Palmer. Palmer habitually coupled the names of de Maistre and Möhler before Newman had written a line upon the subject of development.[1] Plainly Newman had not been unmoved by the publicity which Ward and Palmer were giving to the theory. When he preached his sermon on development on 2 February 1843, he was not starting an idea of which his hearers had not heard. He was taking sides in a public and hotly debated controversy.

The library at Littlemore contained French translations of Möhler's *Unity*, of the *Symbolik* and of the *Athanasius*. These were certainly for use. For in the Bodleian Library are the papers of Mark Pattison, an intimate disciple of Newman from 1842 to 1846, and during those years often near the point of joining the Roman Catholic Church. Those papers show that the idea of development was playing a not insignificant part in Pattison's internal struggle. On a visit to Littlemore in October 1843 he studied Möhler's *Unity*: in 1844 and 1845 he was working lethargically and spasmodically at the *Symbolik*. At various times he discussed tradition and development with Newman himself and with others in Newman's circle.[2]

The question may now reappear—was Newman influenced by Möhler? The answer, of course, is still No. The line of thought, the expression of ideas, the use of analogies, the form and argument were Newman's, original to him, individual, stamped with the impress of that unusual cast of mind. By the courtesy of the Oratorian Fathers I have been enabled to peruse the note-books and drafts with which Newman, from March 1844, prepared to write the *Essay*. In those note-books you can see the hares which he starts, the scents which he came to see were false, the analogies which he brought into the open to eye critically and discard, a process reminiscent of a dog worrying at an old glove. There are his authorities and the ideas which they suggested to him— and apart from Guizot and Gieseler (historians touched by the modern spirit) they are patristic authorities. He was not reading Möhler, nor Wiseman, nor Perrone, nor even Petau. He was reading Justin Martyr, Athanasius, Tertullian, Ambrose, Lactantius, Cyril.[1]

And yet the theory of development—coming not from Newman's mind but from across the seas—was in the atmosphere which surrounded Newman at Littlemore. Wiseman had succeeded, partly by direct communication and partly by the agency of the *Dublin Review*, in lifting Tractarian eyes to German Catholic theology in general and to Möhler in particular. Then W. G. Ward had seized upon and isolated the single element of development in Möhler's total scheme of thought, and in the exaggerated form which Möhler had later abandoned, and had thrust the whole question into public debate. It was discussed by Newman's friends, studied by his pupils, controverted by his enemies.

There is therefore that fragment of a relationship between liberal German philosophy and Newman's theory. Newman ascribed to an eminent Catholic theologian a theory of development like his own: not realizing that this theory was derived from an earlier work which its author had himself come to regret, which was now regarded as disreputable by many Roman Catholic theologians, and which was influenced by the philosophical theories of development in contemporary German Protestantism.

# CHAPTER VI

# WARD

As late as 1841 Newman was still declaring, with Bossuet, Bull, Pusey, and Keble, that novelty in doctrine was heresy. On 2 February 1843 he preached his last university sermon, an hour and a half in delivery, his first public utterance upon the question, and in the published version headed 'the theory of developments in religious doctrine'.[1] The language of the sermon, though suspect to the Tractarian leaders, was sufficiently unspecific, and Tractarians like Palmer tried to distinguish between the false theory of development which they were associating with Ward and the ideas of Newman. But the *Essay* of 1845 made plain the swing of Newman's mind. Between the stance of the Tractarians and the stance of the *Essay* there is no mediating posture. The doctrine of authority in the one directly contradicts the doctrine of authority in the other.

Between 1841 and the spring of 1843 Newman's mind therefore crossed the Rubicon. In response to the assaults upon Tract 90 or to the charges of divers bishops, or to the 'calamity' of the Jerusalem bishopric, or to the cogency of Wiseman's arguments about the doctrine of schism in the Fathers, he had lost his confidence in the Tractarian doctrine of authority, and with it his assurance of the Catholicity of the Church of England. He had applied the test of antiquity to the teaching and practice of the Church of England, he had pressed her to measure herself against antiquity, and the Church of England was refusing, and refusing vociferously, to be measured into the bed which he designed. Knowing of old that the *via media* was a 'paper religion' which had existed in a few great minds of the seventeenth century and in a few of his contemporaries and disciples, he had hoped to lead the whole Church to accept the pattern of Catholic antiquity which his patristic studies presented to him. And in the pit of disrepute and self-distrust into which episcopal judgments and popular opinion threw him in 1841 and 1842, he sensed, perhaps more with his heart than with his head, the repudiation by his Church of the principles for which he had contended. The effort to justify Anglicanism by the Vincentian Canon seemed to have collapsed.

If his principles were sound, some existing Church there must be, and that Church was neither the Protestant bodies nor the Church of England which was proving herself to be a Protestant body. Only one other claimant (in Newman's eyes) existed. But though the inference was patent, immediately patent, he was hindered by an apparently unscalable barrier from making that inference. He was condemning the Church of England because it failed to satisfy the test of the Vincentian Canon, the test of faithfulness to antiquity. Subjected to the same test precisely, the Church of Rome failed likewise. He could hardly leave the Church of England because she had departed from antiquity and join a church which his historical knowledge proved to have been guilty of the same offence. If the Vincentian Canon was the motive for walking out of the porch of one church, it could not be the motive for walking into the porch of another. If the Vincentian Canon were discarded, his arguments against Rome were worthless—but equally worthless were his arguments against the Latitudinarians. Between the authority of the Church and agnosticism he could see no standing ground: and for him the authority of the Church was null apart from that authority of antiquity which the Vincentian Canon had so laconically summarized.

The passage to the idea of development therefore looks like a leap, an intellectual venture to a doctrine which has no continuity nor connection with his earlier doctrine. Not surprisingly, scholars have cast about to find an external impulse or impetus which pushed him into the leap between 1841 and 1843. I have already examined what little can be said in favour of the view that the liberal philosophy of movement provided this impetus:

it was part of the environment and helped to condition the expression and the vocabulary, but no more. Some scholars have appealed to Petau. Petau had become notorious to a circle of English readers wider than that select band who had trudged conscientiously through Bishop Bull's Latin refutation. For he had been pilloried in one of those scathingly unjust and delightful footnotes which Gibbon had appended to his history: 'To arraign the faith of the ante-Nicene Fathers was the object, or at least has been the effect, of the stupendous work of Petavius on the Trinity; nor has the deep impression been erased by the learned defence of Bishop Bull.' Frank Newman, John Henry's unsympathetic brother, asserts in his deplorable book of reminiscences that this footnote first drew his brother's attention to Petau. Though Frank's memory was not trustworthy the detail is possibly authentic. But Newman could not avoid reading Petau in his studies. As soon as he began to investigate the Arian controversy and the Fathers, he needed both Petau and Bull as reference books.

It has therefore been suggested that, once Newman had been roused by Anglican clamour to the defects of the Vincentian Canon, he felt the force in Petau's historical studies and saw that Christian doctrine did not begin to change only in the fifth century, that the Church of the first five centuries, so far from being a monolithic block of immovable orthodoxy, bore upon its surface the marks of shaping and chiselling.[1]

But I do not think that Petau provided any kind of impetus, nor that anyone who worked through Newman's notes in preparation for his *Essay* could judge this probable. The proposition 'Here is a Roman Catholic theologian, indeed a Jesuit, who admits changes of doctrine in the early Church, therefore a theory of development is possible' never crossed the threshold of Newman's mind. Marvellous though it is, he was not concerned with, and did not inquire, whether Roman Catholic theologians had ever taught a doctrine of development. If his theory were true, it would be accepted by the true Church—that was enough for him. The order of ideas does not seem to have been 'Petau's historical researches are good—therefore doctrine began to change before the fifth century', but the contrary, 'doctrine began to change before the fifth century—therefore Petau's historical researches are more cogent, and Bull's less cogent, than I supposed'.

Newman himself was aware of no external impulse. He was aware, instead, of a continuity, a train of thought unfolding itself in his mind. Just how he had clambered across the chasm from the Tractarian theory to the theory of development he could not later determine with logical precision. This did not perturb him— 'For myself, it was not logic which carried me on; as well might one say that the quicksilver in the barometer changes the weather. It is the concrete being that reasons; pass a number of years, and I find myself in a new place; how? the whole man moves; paper logic is but the record of it.'[1] In a sermon of this time of change he compared the thinker to a mountaineer, who climbs a cliff with narrow and sloping holds, and, looking back from the summit down the precipice, can see no trace of the route by which he has ascended. But though he could not plainly discern the logic of his change, he believed that the chasm was not a chasm, he believed *ex animo* in a continuity between his Tractarian principles and his new principles. No doubt we should make allowances for psychological aspects of his mind, the passionate devotion to 'consistency', and the element of self-justification which faintly entered into most of what he published between 1840 and 1878. We should also make allowances for the inescapable temptation, after 1845, to prove to the surviving Tractarians that his own course was the true and right issue of their principles. But when these allowances have been made, and when we remember that the *Essay* itself undertook to refute the main positions adopted in the *Lectures on the Prophetical Office of the Church* and others among his earlier works, Newman's own sense of continuity remains. His notes, as he prepared for the *Essay*, prove that mentally he set it in a context of his earlier work: the sermon of 2 February 1843 on development was published as the last of his series of university sermons, beginning as early as 1826, upon faith and reason: that sermon was formulated in a way which made it, unlike the *Essay*, not intolerable (however unwelcome) to the sturdiest of conservative Tractarians like William Palmer. It was the consciousness of a continuity with his Anglican principles which gave the *Essay* its peculiar and unique aroma, which lifted it out of the stream of all traditional Roman Catholic theology, which made it almost impossible for Giovanni Perrone and the contemporary Roman theologians to understand, and which incidentally provided it with such argumentative cogency as it possessed.

Newman learnt from Bishop Butler much of lasting power in his mental principles. But he also learnt one form of argument which harmed him both as a controversialist and as a Christian thinker. Butler's apology for revelation can easily be caricatured by the unsympathetic in these terms: you find it difficult to believe the Christian revelation—yet there are many truths of nature and natural religion which you already believe and which nevertheless are equally difficult to believe. This type of argument, put a little more pointedly and specifically, became almost a habit with Newman, especially in the middle stages of his life. On grounds of reason you are refusing to believe truth *A*, yet the difficulties are just as formidable about truth *B* which you already accept. You find it difficult to see that the doctrine of apostolic succession, which you reject, has scriptural foundation, yet the divinity of the Holy Spirit, which you accept, has equally little scriptural foundation. You refuse to believe the doctrine of the immaculate conception, yet the doctrine of original sin is equally difficult to believe. Though he suffered an occasional qualm about its use, and once called it 'the kill-or-cure remedy', he intended it to prove, against rationalists, liberals, and Latitudinarians, that reason is no safe guide to what in the revelation is to be accepted or rejected.

The argument, though learnt from Butler, is not quite Butler's. For Newman pressed it in a different context. Butler could base himself upon confident assumptions of natural religion, assumptions which rested upon external observation and the verification of the sciences—the probability in the universe of intelligence, construction, design, order, harmony. In his mind there was no contrast between divine truth and human truth: the analogy of religious truth with nature was not mere guess nor act of blind faith, but rested upon probabilities claimed to be derived from verifiable evidence. By the middle of the nineteenth century this suggested synthesis between reason and faith, revelation and science, appeared to be collapsing: partly because the scientists were beginning to query the truth of accepted affirmations of the accepted revelation, and partly because the practical and moral earnestness of religious men had led them to question the religious value of argument and evidences. In the divide between the religious philosophers of evidence characteristic of the eighteenth century, and the theologians of the nineteenth century who in appealing to faith and the revelation discounted or minimized external evidences, proofs, and philosophy of religion, Newman stands (with the greater part of his mind) in the second category. It may be true that he had learnt from Butler that probability is the guide of life. But Newman, at the Tractarian stage of his thinking, suspected the probabilities which external evidence offered to the mind. It was 'antecedent probability' rather than probability which, he believed, conditioned the understanding of the external evidence. You receive impressions through your senses and they are but phenomena and your reason cannot arrange them confidently. But you acquire (through 'faith', or conscience, or moral growth) an 'antecedent probability', a cast of mind, an outlook upon the evidence which enables you to perceive the pattern in it. He had not read Kant (though he had read S. T. Coleridge). But Hume's philosophical scepticism was a more potent force in the background of his mind than perhaps he was ever aware. He never believed the argument from design to be cogent to anyone who did not already possess 'faith'. He was not resting upon 'blind faith', for the external evidence needed subsequently to corroborate the antecedent probability. But without the antecedent probability, the evidence tells you nothing reliable.

If the synthesis between science and religion is probable, Butler's type of argument is powerful. But if the synthesis is believed to be either impossible or not worth seeking, the argument loses all ultimate cogency and becomes a mere *argumentum ad hominem* with perilous potentialities. This is why James Mozley accused Newman of irresponsibility in its use, why Acton thought that Newman's reasoning diminished the validity of belief to those who did not think as he did, why Thirlwall judged his mind to be 'essentially sceptical and sophistical', and why Huxley said he could compile a 'Primer of Infidelity' from three of Newman's works.[1] The use of the argument harmed the balance of Newman's thinking because its practical enforcement included a sceptical display of the difficulties inherent in the doctrine accepted, and was therefore calculated to impress Newman himself as well as others with the scantiness of the evidence and the force of the sceptical arguments. Yet he was not trying to frighten his readers into authority by conjuring a bogy of scepticism. To him it was no bogy. He was seeing his brother Frank, had seen his friend Blanco White, move away towards Unitarianism. Discovering no external assurance that history was guided by the hand of God,[2] he looked out upon society and saw suffering, disease, squalor, misery, men falling away from Christianity and not returning, the long procession of the world, its Babel of languages, the astrologers of Chaldaea and the chariots of Egypt, and he shrank away with a sensitive horror. This bogy of scepticism was no bogy; it was his personal terror, the dead hand which scrabbled at him in the night when his faith was sleeping.

In 1838 he wrote a *Tract for the Times* (Tract 85) which carried the sceptical side of his thought to the limit. One epoch of Newman's thought gives a measure of apparent justification to Thirl-wall's charge of 'sophistry'. In Tract 85, written in 1838; in *The Catholicity of the Anglican Church*, contemplated in 1839, published in 1840; in Tract 90, published in 1841—there is an appearance of special pleading, of plausibility, of speciousness. The reader admires and disbelieves the argument simultaneously. It is a symptom of the incipient uneasiness of Newman's mind. But if by the charge of sophistry is meant that he was dishonest, or that the arguments were in any sense external to him, that he was using expedients rather than arguments, that he did not believe them with his whole mind, nothing could be less well-founded. Of no one is it truer than of Newman that a man's thought is himself. He believed confidently in his own reasoning. And if some of the reasoning looks to others like sophistry, that is not because New-man was a sophist, but because the *Via Media* as he had conceived it, which a few years before had appeared as a broad, well-paved, and bustling highway, seemed now to be turning itself into a rocky and scrambling ridge with a precipice in the mists on either hand.

Tract 85 put forward, with an unusually frank avowal of trepidation, the classical argument—if you reject the system of the Church you will end in atheism: or (put a little more crudely) the evidence is so strong against the Bible and Christianity that only the infallible authority of the Church can enable you to believe it. The 'popular Protestants' cannot with consistency object to the Tractarians that they believe more without an adequate scriptural foundation, unless they themselves cease to believe so much as they do believe. If they deny the apostolic succession because they do not find it in scripture, then they must deny the divinity of the Holy Spirit, the necessity of infant bap-tism, the observance of Sunday, the inspiration of scripture, all of which are in scripture as little, or as obscurely, as the doctrine of apostolic succession. And he selected many of the passages from the Bible which suggested that this was not true or a revelation from God—there are two stories of the Creation in the book of

Genesis,[1] the book of Chronicles appears to contradict the book of Kings, Deuteronomy appears to contradict Exodus: the observer thinks it at first sight incredible that Abraham should have denied his wife twice and Isaac once, that a whale should have swallowed Jonah or the apostles found a coin in a fish's mouth: the Synoptists appear to contradict the fourth Gospel, there are two discrepant accounts of the death of Judas Iscariot, if you did not know the scripture was inspired you would think the feeding of the four thousand and the feeding of the five thousand were two different accounts of the same event, and that several texts of St Luke were only a corrupt version of the Sermon on the Mount in St Matthew....This argument purported to show that acceptance of the canon depended upon accepting the authority of the ancient church—remove that authority and the internal evidence of the scriptures is inadequate for, or even contrary to, the idea of their inspiration. In short you can only believe the infallibility of the Bible if you believe the infallibility of the ancient church: and if you believe the infallibility of the ancient church you must also believe in the other truths of dogma which at present you reject. Revelation must be plain to all or it is not revelation. Therefore the revelation is plainly in scripture, or plainly in the ancient church's exposition of the obscure texts of scripture, or plainly not in scripture (but in tradition). The revelation is not plainly in scripture, or all men would agree what it taught and they do not. Therefore the revelation is either in the obscure texts of scripture as expounded and explained by the ancients—or it is not in scripture but tradition—we have to choose between 'the Church system' and 'Romanism'. There is a third possibility—that no revelation has been given. Newman admitted, in a phrase which struck into W. G. Ward's mind, that the chances on a revelation were possibly three to two in favour. But we must act on the probable revelation and prove it in love and life. Why must we act? Because our 'feelings' tell us, because our 'instincts', our high-ideals, our consciousness of the barrenness of the negative, our quest for 'happiness', drive us onward to act and to prove. To whom else shall we go?

In his notes as he prepared to write the *Essay on Development*, he remarked that the *Essay* ought to be read with Tract 85. The Tract showed negatively the perils and weakness of liberalism, the *Essay* persuaded positively to the Church claiming the infallibility which was the safeguard against liberalism.[1] He did not further explain why or how the Tract and the *Essay* were linked in his mind. Did he mean 'Since Christianity can only be maintained if there exists a church with an infallible claim upon us, historical investigation of antiquity is merely a variety of private judgment, can have no control over our present views and is therefore irrelevant: and hence we only need some explanation how that Church is right in proposing her teaching as immutable in spite of the historical evidence to the contrary: and this explanation I am providing in the theory of development'? If Newman meant something like this when he wrote that note among his papers, he was throwing history over the bulwarks like Berruyer a century before him and Tyrrell half a century after him.

Lord Acton believed this to be the general intention of the *Essay*. Acton once wrote that for Newman the theory of development was a way over history, that it enabled him to disregard history, that by it he overcame 'masses of difficulties', 'emancipated' himself from history, allowed the voice of the present church to 'supersede the study of the past'.[2] Nor was Acton the only student to believe that this was Newman's aim. The same inference was drawn, though from his Tractarian teaching upon faith and reason, by W. G. Ward.

Logical as Newman never was; prosaic as Newman was poetic; downright and immoderate in his speculative gusto as in his conversation and laughter; a keen student of Mill and Carlyle and later of Kant, conscious of the power of the new 'infidelity' and its advantages over the shallower Tindals and Voltaires of the last century; aware at once of the skill of his intellect and its

129

apparent incompetence to assist his moral life ('I have the intellect of an archangel, and the habits of an eating, walking and sleeping rhinoceros'); reacting against the mixture of radical utilitarianism and Arnoldian liberalism which for three years and more he had tossed discontentedly from horn to horn in himself and others—Ward attended the lectures of 1838 which formed Tract 85 and found in them the rational (or anti-rational) seal of his conversion. His utilitarian penchant had convinced him that the natural theology of the eighteenth century was dying, his speculative power had driven him to argue that no metaphysical arguments or external evidence could bring to the 'impartial' mind demonstration, perhaps not even probability, of the simplest metaphysical truth, of the existence of God or design. The pure intellect —rather, the mere intellect—working upon external evidence, dissolved, destroyed, led into trackless labyrinths. And yet he knew, he claimed, with a perception as immediate as that of himself, that goodness is real, that man has a conscience, that conscience is unintelligible unless it be referred to a purpose beyond itself, that it knows its goal to be 'sanctity', that the knowledge of this goal implies both the possibility of moral growth and the existence of a 'given' standard wherein sanctity is judged and clarified and expounded.... Already perhaps, when he succumbed to Newman's power, he had almost totally disjoined the reason from the conscience. Reason led to darkness, conscience to light.

From this quagmire Newman's moral authority and doctrine of faith rescued him. Faith, it seemed to Ward that Newman was saying, is not the issue of argument, proof, external evidence, balancing of probabilities, not the final stage in a series of intellectual inferences. Faith is a loving response to God speaking. We know that truth is a mighty harmony, that this world is God's world, that at last we shall see the unity of all things. But in this life the evidence of the senses and of the visible sometimes seems to conflict with God's word; and if his word and his outward world seem to convey different messages, are at variance in the information which they bring, it is ours—it is our duty—to trust the revealed word for a space, and meanwhile to search amid the perishable shadows of Time for the footsteps and the resting-places of the Eternal.

But, if external experience, so far from leading us towards revealed truth, appears to conflict with it—how do we know the word which we trust to be God's word? We know it (Newman seemed to Ward to say) by an inner and personal certainty. 'Religious men have, in their own religiousness, an evidence of the truth of their religion. That religion is true which has power, and so far as it has power: nothing but what is Divine can reach the heart....'[1] The conscience of man knows that it must: it knows that it cannot. And that which comes and with gentle touch heals the limping feet, is truth. In Newman's *University Sermons* Ward could find plenty to sustain and deepen his belief in the supremacy of conscience over reason, perhaps even the antithesis between conscience and reason. Newman more than once had taken Hume's satirical conclusion and baptized it—'Our most holy Religion is founded on Faith, not on Reason'. To reason upon spiritual and moral truths without spiritual and moral experience is like a blind man professing to lecture upon light and colour. 'It is as absurd to argue men, as to torture them, into believing'; in scripture the act of faith depends upon no previous act of reason, faith is 'rightly' said to be 'against Reason, to triumph over Reason', to be 'illogical'; no intellectual act is necessary for right faith besides itself. And when critics assailed these contentions on the ground that they justified superstition, bigotry or Islam equally with Christian faith, Newman had replied that faith is preserved in the truth by a right state of heart, by holiness, by dutifulness—we believe because we love, we know the shepherd's voice because we are his sheep and we follow not robbers and strangers because we know not the voice of strangers. Evidence is not the groundwork of faith but its reward.[2]

Newman's thought possessed another side. But that other side Ward hardly saw, for it met neither his moral need nor his fear of the sceptical power of 'mere reason'. Claiming that he was but clarifying and systematizing Newman's doctrine, he launched his own philosophy of faith. It should be read in his articles in the *British Critic* from 1841 to 1843, as well as in *The Ideal of a Christian Church* of 1844, for in the articles he could make his point in several different contexts. A streak of slickness, of plausibility, entered into much of Ward's writing, and this vice was encouraged by the pressure of controversies in which he so zestfully engaged. The *Ideal*, a book as ill-arranged and ungainly as its author's person, is one of those clever books which proves that the line between being highly articulate and being wearisome is narrow. It is therefore too easy to underestimate the philosophical vigour and penetration of Ward's mind. Gladstone, judging his theory only by the *Ideal*, called it 'as frail a bark as ever carried sail'.[1] Yet, shorn of excrescences and paradoxes, it might have floated for longer than Gladstone expected. It must be remembered that Ward was 32 years old when he published the *Ideal*, and that his critical faculty was as yet more highly developed than his constructive power.

Obedience to conscience, said Ward, is not one method of attaining metaphysical truth: it is the only method. Newman was teaching that if you try Christian principle, you will come to confirm it in experience and to perceive its truth. Ward taught that if you act upon your conscience—upon what you perceive at the moment to be true—you will progress until you arrive at Christian principle. He was relying upon a quasi-Kantian contention which Newman would have repudiated, that the intellect provides knowledge only of phenomena, the conscience of realities. He rejected the probability from external evidence even that God is good or personal. As the conscience is well-disciplined, it 'discriminates and appropriates moral and religious truth of whatever kind, and disposes the mind to listen to this external message rather than that; while each new truth thus brought before it from without, in proportion as it is deeply received and made the subject of religious action and contemplation, elicits a deep and hitherto unknown harmony from within, which is the full warrant and sufficient evidence of that truth'. Conscience receives moral guidance from outside, first from parents in childhood, then from schoolmasters, finally from the philosophical or religious systems which are presented to adults—and so far as it sees it must act. The conscience does not know that the propositions offered to it from outside are truthful—for conscience may be wrong, the sense of obligation may need enlightening. But so far as he sees, the conscientious person must act. And in acting conscientiously, he comes to discern how truthful or how untruthful are the propositions offered. A simple uneducated person has the duty of acting in accordance with the teaching of that church (if any) in which he has been educated: and perhaps he may continue all his life in that way. But when other truth is presented to him which Ward regards as higher truth—suppose that he has been educated in a Unitarian community and then is presented with further truth by a Presbyterian missionary—he is enabled to distinguish between what is true of the old and what is untrue, and what claims the new has upon him—not by philosophical or historical inquiry into the rival merits of the two religious systems, a task of which he is incapable, but by a continued conscientious life according to the principles which he discerns—by discovering that he is no longer able to live conscientiously according to his old beliefs, and is forced therefore out of them into the new. And what is true of the simple uneducated person is true universally. It is not only that the intellect of the most eminent philosopher is liable to partiality, confusion, prejudice. It is that this class of moral facts is outside the normal investigations of the mere intellect, since the intellect can investigate phenomena alone.

The moral experience therefore not only expects that the conditions of moral progress (which the individual cannot discover for himself) shall be given. If any 'revelation' is acted upon as true, moral power and therefore moral progress is the issue. But it must be a revelation presented from outside to the conscience. If the intellect travels round looking for revelations to decide between their various claims, the intellect becomes the arbiter: being the arbiter means being neutral: and being neutral excludes all possibility of understanding the revelation since *ex hypothesi* the revelation can only be understood by being obeyed. Faith, therefore, is acting in implicit belief upon propositions whose probable and external evidence is insufficient to warrant belief, and expecting, by the act of believing, to find evidence which shall confirm or disprove the propositions.

It will be observed that Ward needed to assume that a particular kind of moral quality, or sanctity, was the highest and to suppose that a belief in this form of sanctity as the highest would be self-evident to anyone before whose conscience the ideal was brought. He held that sanctity consisted in monastic and ascetic sanctity and this alone: he seems hardly at this stage of his thinking to have conceived the possibility of a diversity in vocation. He held also, as a matter partly of personal experience and partly of historical inquiry, that this sanctity was to be found only among persons who believed a particular system of dogmas, namely those offered by the Roman Catholic Church or by those Anglicans who taught likewise. Therefore a relentless conclusion about those dogmas needed to be drawn. No test of external evidence—not the test of scripture, nor the test of inquiry into the history of dogma—was a reliable test upon the truth of those dogmas. The only test possible was whether the dogmas had elicited the type of sanctity which he saw to be the highest. Saints are the sources from which moral and religious truth flow upon the world. And therefore if saints have believed a doctrine, this is enough. We cannot test it by our intellect, for by the circumstance that we are not saints we have excluded the possibility that we may understand the doctrine. We cannot test it by scholarly study of scripture or antiquity, since these are irrelevant. And therefore 'From the circumstance that some doctrine, wholly foreign to our moral experience, appears to us to have literally no foundation whatever, either in reason or in scripture, not even the faintest probability arises that it may not be true.'[1]

With this formidable thesis Ward inevitably threw historical investigation overboard. Historical inquiry is but one form of external evidence, one form of 'impartial' reasoning upon empirical data: and all 'impartial' reasoning upon empirical data is irrelevant to the investigation which system or delivery claiming to be a revelation is in truth the *perfect* revelation—not the *authentic* revelation, for every external delivery which the conscientious mind accepts partakes in greater or less degree of the nature of a revelation and is therefore in its measure authentic. The only three systems of thought which he denied could be revealing, even partially, were first, atheism, on the ground that no man could act conscientiously over a period and remain an atheist; second, liberalism, because it urged the soul to decide after scholarly investigations into scripture or history and therefore encouraged men to transform themselves from disciples into judges; and third, the doctrine of justification by faith alone, because in teaching that right faith led to right living it directly assailed Ward's principle that right living led to right faith.

Ward relished boisterous and explosive language until it became a vice. But stripped of the extremism, the overstatements, the paradoxical methods of expression, his theory must be allowed to have found some place for external evidence and consequently for history. New facts are presented to the conscience which lead to an extended range of moral apprehension. The external world does present a strong probability of design and of a personal God *to the conscientious person*. External evidences lead men towards Christianity, they are the occasions (not the causes) of conversion —for a man who is argued into Christianity can as easily be argued out of it, and therefore argument cannot cause conversion. Further, until the middle of 1843 Ward still believed that in the unhappy conditions, the 'degraded state' of Christian disunity, some element of historical inquiry was an unfortunate necessity in receiving the external revelation offered to the conscience. After the middle of 1843 he was sufficiently convinced of the infallibility of the Church of Rome to be able to exclude even this element of 'impartial' history. History was now useful, within the acceptance of the revelation, partly because it impressed more deeply upon the mind of the Catholic inquirer the nature and profundity of the truths which the Church puts before him: still more because it displayed sanctity in all its lovely and stirring diversity. The *Acta Sanctorum* became the highest purpose and utility of historical inquiry. History was not undertaken in the direct pursuit of truth: it was undertaken as an instrument of moral progress, which was the condition of truth's apprehension. It was not undertaken in the pursuit of religious truth because it could not attain religious truth—

Our view of facts springs really from our view of doctrine, not the reverse; we read history by the light of our principles, in vain do we seek for principles by the study of history....Let others, if they will, lay their whole stress on the petty and interminable warfare of details, the hostile array of fact against fact, date against date, text against text, father against father: be it our task to throw ourselves boldly on men's higher and spiritual nature; and to represent the one Ancient Truth, in those varied forms of attraction and beauty, which may elicit the hidden sympathies, and draw towards themselves the aspirations, wandering as it were in search of an object, of those whom we address. Such a course springs, we must again and again repeat, from no distrust whatever in the real testimony of external facts, but from the conviction that those, whom we should most desire to attract, will be led really by far higher considerations....[1]

With this theory it might be thought that Ward needed no idea of development, since the only purpose of a doctrine of development is to reconcile the notion of an immutable revelation with the uncomfortable findings of historians, and he had excluded the possibility that those findings might be uncomfortable. Ward, confident in the teaching power of the present Church, felt free to allow whatever might (within limits) be discovered by historical research: partly he needed the idea as a subsidiary weakening of the case of his Anglican opponents like Palmer with their constant appeal to the Vincentian Canon: partly he was under the influence of Möhler's *Unity* and its romantic desire to set forth the harmony and beauty of the progress of Christian truth. But though the theory runs through his articles and his book, it is a subsidiary argument: and if the teaching Church had declared to Ward without reserve that doctrine had never changed, Ward's philosophical and dogmatic fortress would not have been weakened. For he had removed it from any sphere where argument could weaken it.

To defend his system Ward constantly appealed to Newman, constantly quoted him, constantly referred to him in terms of high praise: he claimed only to be expounding Newman's philosophy of faith. And of the first articles in the *British Critic*, of the earlier statements of the theory, Newman approved. In February 1843, when revising his *University Sermons* for the press, he added a footnote at p. 242 to express his general approval of the theory contained in the articles and his hope that Ward would publish some systematic expression of them. He had been embarrassed by the reiterated 'puffing' which he received in the *British Critic*, and was a little more perturbed by the way in which Ward in the *Ideal* claimed him as his master. No doubt he was also right, when he wrote the *Apologia* in 1864, in remembering that Ward's syllogistic habits of mind were 'uncongenial' to him and was not simply reading back into the 1840's his vehement distrust of Ward during the 1860's. But both his public silence and his private letters show that he disapproved neither Ward's general line nor the road by which he was seeking a philosophy of conscience. He had looked forward to the appearance of the *Ideal*, and told Dalgairns that it was the 'great thing we have to look for now'.[1]

But the *Ideal* dissatisfied him. Dalgairns found him reading it at Littlemore soon after it appeared. Newman, being asked his opinion, shook his head and said 'It won't do': and he sent a message that he could not approve the statement in the *Ideal* of the sources of religious knowledge.

It is not surprising that he felt it to be erroneous. Newman's philosophy of faith gave Ward many hints and phrases, pegs on which he might hang his theory of conscience. But the attitude of the two thinkers to external evidence differed. And the different attitudes to evidence issued, not only in different philosophies of faith, but in a different attitude to history. A single contrast in argument points and illustrates the divergence between the two minds. Newman claimed that the existence of developments in doctrine (proved by history) formed an antecedent probability for the existence of an infallible authority. Ward claimed that the existence of an infallible authority (proved by conscience) formed an antecedent probability for the existence of developments in doctrine. Take the idea of development out of Ward and you leave his philosophy where it was before. Not so with Newman. If the infallible Church had suddenly declared that doctrine had never developed, had condemned the theory of development, Ward's reasons for becoming a Roman Catholic would have remained as cogent as before, Newman's argumentative reasons for becoming a Roman Catholic would have perished. Ward possessed a theory of development *although* impartial historical inquiry could not find religious truth: Newman possessed a theory of development *because* impartial historical inquiry could, in its measure, find truth.

Acton said that the theory emancipated Newman from history. I will confess that the first time I read the *Essay* I thought the verdict was true. I think so no longer.

# CHAPTER VII

# NEWMAN'S THEORY

The *Essay on the Development of Christian Doctrine*, published finally in November 1845, contains two distinct but interdependent lines of thought—the one historical, the other doctrinal: two sections, separable by the unraveller yet interwoven like the strands of a sisal rope. The bulk of the book forms a historical inquiry into the primitive and patristic Church: when in March 1844 Newman took the note-book into which he was to set many fragments and passing ideas to assist his mind in writing the *Essay*, he wrote boldly at the front, *Write it historically*. And anyone who has read the *Essay* knows that historical illustrations proliferate on nearly every page. Historical investigation suggests to us a problem, an intellectual paradox, a difficulty which demands some theory to explain it. And so the doctrinal hypothesis was proffered to account for this difficulty.

For prolonged historical investigation into the ancient Church proved that none of the present bodies, claiming to be churches, precisely resembled the ancient Church. Newman did not argue that the Protestant bodies were not true images of the ancient Church. He assumed it, regarded it as a matter which needed no proof, since the Protestant had discarded so much which the church of antiquity valued, from fasting to the real presence. If any proof were needed that Protestantism is not 'historical Christianity', we may observe that the Protestants have jettisoned a thousand years of Christian history, the history of the Middle Ages; that England has long neglected, and continues to neglect, the study of ecclesiastical history so that perhaps the only English writer 'who has any claim to be considered an ecclesiastical historian is the infidel Gibbon'. 'Whatever be historical Christianity, it is not Protestantism. If ever there were a safe truth, it is this.'

'Whatever be historical Christianity...'—the typically loose use of words was not denying that the Protestants existed in history and claimed to be Christians. Newman was merely denying that the authentic lineaments of the ancient Church were now to be found among Protestant churches. If an external and non-Christian observer be postulated, he would have observed in the ancient Church certain marks, characteristics, features, which he would not discern in looking at the modern Protestant bodies. History shows you a portrait with a face—a face with dim outlines hazily seen in misty light. You look round the room and you see other faces, modern faces. In the shadowy light you cannot make out the precise lines of the figure in the portrait. But though the light is dim, you can yet see enough to be sure that it is not a portrait of any of the persons in the room—with one possible exception.

Yet if the dim portrait is enough to prove the negative, it is probably not enough to demonstrate the positive. Newman does not argue the discrepancy between the ancient Church and the modern Roman Catholic Church. Though he offered many illustrations of the discrepancy in the course of the *Essay*, they do not form a coherent argument so much as illustrate an assumption running through the book. Rome has (apparently) added to what the ancient Church taught whereas the Protestants have (apparently) subtracted from it. But in both the image of the ancient Church has been blurred.

Newman rejected with decision the only theory which, though accepting the verdict that history shows discrepancy, sought to assert the discrepancy to be apparent and not real—Schelstrate's theory of the *Disciplina Arcani*. This theory, wrote Newman, 'is no key to the whole difficulty, as we find it, for an obvious reason; the variations continue beyond the time when it is conceivable that the discipline was in force'.[1] And to anyone who asked why this theory should now be impossible when it was possible 150 years ago, Newman pointed simply to the discovery of the forgeries. The 'state of things' is not as it was when an appeal lay to the pseudo-Dionysius, or to the primitive Decretals, or to St Dionysius' answers to St Paul, or to the *Coena Domini* of St Cyprian.

Thus history proves—so conclusively that there is no need seriously to argue the point—discrepancy between ancient Christianity and any variety, every variety, of modern Christianity.

He did not suppose that all variations were relevant to his argument. He would not have been perturbed by the knowledge that liturgies or some forms of organization have changed through the centuries. A society is bound to 'develop'—that was not in question between himself and his opponents, for the Protestants admitted it as freely as he. The question is of doctrine. And Newman was convinced that historical investigation proves growth and variety in Christian teaching, in doctrine, of such importance that the Vincentian Canon *quod ubique quod semper quod ab omnibus*, on which both the Church of England with their Bishop Bull and the Church of Rome with their Bishop Bossuet had been standing, is inadequate as a present guide to, or test of, true and authentic Christianity. The Vincentian Canon, he wrote, 'true as it must be considered in the abstract, is hardly available now or effective of any satisfactory result. The solution it offers is as difficult as the original problem.'

The dim portrait, therefore, is enough to show that no modern church is an exact image or representation of the ancient Church, even in its teaching about the revelation. But, though this negative has, however reluctantly, to be accepted, there is one modern face in the room wherein one can see the wrinkles and the lines, the slant of the head and the angle of the shoulders and the glance of eyes, which remind the observer of the face in the portrait. One modern face, though it differs from the face in the portrait, strikes the observer as bearing the same family likeness, as being possibly even the same person at a later epoch of his maturity. Much of the historical material in the *Essay* is directed to displaying this resemblance; a resemblance canonized in the celebrated conclusion

> Did St Athanasius or St Ambrose come suddenly to life, it cannot be doubted what communion they would mistake for their own.... Were the two saints...to travel until they reached another fair city, seated among groves, green meadows, and calm streams, the holy brothers would turn from many a high aisle and solemn cloister which they found there, and ask the way to some small chapel where mass was said in the populous alley or forlorn suburb....[1]

Christianity was accused of being superstitious in ancient times: the Roman Catholic Church, but not the Protestant churches, is accused of being superstitious now. The ancient Church held poverty in admiration, was hated by the non-Christian as proselytizing, anti-social, revolutionary, intolerant, and associated with intrigue, bore the reputation of a secret society, was the natural enemy of non-Christian governments, was despised by the intellectuals and feared by the populace, was spread over the known world, was reproached as 'credulous, weak-minded, and poor-spirited'. These superficial resemblances were important to Newman partly because they genuinely illustrated that similarity between the slant of the head in the portrait and in the modern face, and partly because they arose from a continuity and persistence of identical principles. The ancient Church allegorized the scriptures: it was dogmatic and polemical, fled from heresy as St John leapt from his bath at Cerinthus' approach, believed intellectual error to be sin and not mere error, repudiated the view that truth and falsehood in religion are but matters of opinion, adhered strenuously to the sacramental principle, fasted with rigidity, venerated outward forms of worship like the sign of the cross, held the mystical virtue of unity and the law of obedience to ecclesiastical authority....

In the mind of any careful reader two queries will rise. First, whatever in the argument is an argument for the western church, is perhaps equally strong as an argument for the eastern church. Newman hardly mentioned the Eastern Orthodox Church in the *Essay*, except in two casual references to her stagnation and infertility. As he knew little enough about the Middle Ages, he knew little enough about Byzantium, having derived his knowledge of it, almost exclusively, from Gibbon. And it is well known that since Gibbon depended for guidance upon Tillemont, and since Tillemont did not carry his history into the Byzantine epoch, Gibbon's history of later Byzantium is more admirable for its manner than its matter. Secondly, this argument from resemblance of impression, or from identity of principle, is a curious and a surprising form of the Vincentian Canon that Christianity is always the same. The argument is that though history shows none of the modern churches to be identical with the ancient Church, history also shows one of the modern churches to be more nearly identical than any other.

This feature of the *Essay* is momentous, and was not sufficiently understood by its contemporary antagonists. The classical objection of the non-Catholic critics, and indeed some of the Catholic critics, was the simple retort—if you allow development at all, how shall you confine development to certain developments? Are not Luther and Calvin and Locke and Hoadly and Wesley and Schleiermacher and Strauss as much 'developments' as St Thomas Aquinas and Duns Scotus? Newman provided certain tests for distinguishing between developments, tests which convinced no one and which he himself once admitted to be incapable of performing their ostensible purpose. But the existence of these alleged 'tests' blinded some critics, and at times (perhaps) even Newman himself, to the basis upon which they rested. To the classical retort Newman possessed an answer of a kind, an answer which did not repose upon his tests but upon which his tests reposed. Among many developments claiming to be the authentic developments of primitive Christianity, you must choose that structure of development which comes nearest, in resemblance, to the ancient and undivided Church. Then, when you have found the face which is *most* like the face in the portrait, you must ask yourself, how is it, that in spite of these resemblances the face bears such important marks of difference from the portrait?

The argument is not 'History shows that change has occurred: therefore we must adopt mutability instead of immutability as a general principle'. The argument is 'The less mutability has occurred the truer is the modern church: but since history shows that *some* mutability has occurred, even in the least mutable of churches, we need a theory...'. In short, we need what Newman called 'a hypothesis to account for a difficulty'.

Like all his Anglican work, the *Essay* was still based, for its ultimate justification, upon a historical inquiry into the ancient Church.

Acton and other critics probably believed the *Essay* to be a file which sawed away the shackles of historical evidence because at one stage of his argument Newman almost pleaded guilty to the indictment.

How dim are the outlines of the face in the portrait?

In his introduction, Newman claimed that 'bold outlines, which cannot be disregarded', rise out of the records of the past to prove that historical Christianity is not Protestantism. But though the outlines are bold to prove the negative, they are too fragmentary 'to imprint upon our minds the living image of Christianity'. If history be (alone) our teacher, we cannot pass beyond a 'half-knowledge' of Christianity.

In any field of history where 'facts are scarce', the facts are not intelligible unless a pattern is imposed upon them: facts do not create the pattern which can enable the historical mind to understand them. When Niebuhr was examining the early history of Rome and Thirlwall was sorting the legends of Greek mythology, they could discriminate and sift a more or less solid substratum of fact. To explain these scattered data intelligibly to our minds, they needed to suggest a theoretical pattern into which the facts might rationally fit: and this theoretical pattern could not be constructed out of the facts alone (though the existence of the fragmentary evidence is necessary to the construction) but must also be affected by probabilities arising from the later and better-known development of the Greek states or the Roman republic, and sometimes by the experience, the cast of mind, and perhaps the prejudice, of the historian who is constructing the pattern. Where 'facts are scarce' this is the ordinary method of historical study: and however liable to abuse and to bias, however delicate and doubtful in execution, it is the only fruitful means of historical inquiry.

In studying the first three hundred years of Christian history, the historian encounters an array of undigested and often incompatible facts. *Some* pattern he must frame if he is to make this array intelligible to himself or to anyone else: anti-Christian writers cannot dispense with general hypotheses any more than Christian writers. In framing an intelligible pattern, the Christian historian has two props which are external to the immediate historical information. The first is the 'antecedent probability' arising from his acceptance of a revelation: for example, Newman argues a general, rational, probability that if a revelation has been given an infallible interpreter has been given with it. The second is the existence of a body of later information—from the Church of the fourth, fifth or later centuries—which must needs be considered if a truthful pattern is to be discerned. As Thirlwall needed a knowledge of later Greece to understand or discriminate among the sparse information of the mythological age, so the historian cannot reasonably expect to understand primitive Christian history without seeing it in the light of later Christian history. Newman took as his example what he calls 'Popedom'. In the first three centuries after Christ we find a number of 'scanty' hints and 'faint' scraps of information about the Roman see—texts about St Peter in the New Testament which are 'more or less obscure and needing a comment', suggestions drawn from Clement or

Ignatius, Polycarp, Cyprian, Irenaeus and others. On the one side these notices are as numerous and clear as primitive notices in favour of the real presence or of original sin: on the other side they are not self-explanatory. Judging the earlier by the later, we find more emphatic assertions of papal power during the fourth and fifth centuries, and later still an exercise of still wider authority. Examining the rational probabilities, apart from all historical evidence, we find reason to suppose 'an absolute need' of monarchical power in the Church and consequently a warrant for expecting it to be provided. In the light of this general probability, and of the later history of the papacy, we are justified in understanding the hints and scraps of the early centuries as unformulated but implicit recognitions of an authority which in subsequent centuries and circumstances was to receive open and definite expression.[1]

Newman had utilized the basis of the argument eight years before, in the *Lectures on the Prophetical Office of the Church* (and it reappeared in Tract 85), to account for the gaps in the primitive evidence which seemed to militate against the Tractarian appeal to antiquity. 'Understand the earlier in the light of the later.' Though the argument had been used in a measure by the Gallicans of the seventeenth century, something about Newman's expression did not please his critics, on the ground that the theory allows a historian to juggle with the evidence according to his whim: and when the Newman of 1845 assented, though with unspecified reservations, to an earlier verdict by the Newman of 1837 that Roman Catholic teaching, by resting all upon the present authority of the Church, removed the need for any appeal to antiquity,[2] he lent support to the belief that, like Ward, he was elevating doctrine beyond the sphere of historical inquiry.

But Newman at least allowed that in a 'secondary sense', historical information was necessary—necessary to illustrate and corroborate where it could not prove. These hypothetical patterns which historians construct need to rest upon facts as well as account for them. The parallels which he adduced from secular historians like Thirlwall show that he wished to apply later evidence to an earlier epoch, not as an old-fashioned argument *de praescriptione* ('The Church has always believed the same and she believed *x* in the fifth century, therefore she believed *x* in the third'), but as a genuine use according to the strict canons of historical scholarship.[1] The argument was futile unless the full flower of developed doctrine was 'anticipated' by a bud which you could see—by scraps of indubitable information.

What is meant by words like *explain* and *understand* in sentences like 'we can understand the third century only in the light of the fifth'? You find in the third century isolated phrases, doctrinal teaching couched in language whereof the meaning is not self-evident. What did the authors of the third century mean? They were seeking to express their feelings, their response to, or impression of, the once-given revelation, and they must therefore be supposed to have intended what was expressed by a later and systematic statement of that revelation. You find no other *system* of thought, into which these isolated expressions fit, except the later Catholic system. By diligent collation, by the methods of a Daillé or a Jurieu, you might list a series of heretical-sounding propositions, of 'stray heterodox expressions', from the early Christian fathers: but you cannot make these propositions into a consistent and harmonious body of thought—'they are "a rope of sand"...not a *catena*; each stands by itself, with an independence, or an irrelevancy, which precludes the chance of assimilation or coalition'.[2] What then can history do?

It can prove that 'historical Christianity is not Protestantism'. It cannot prove positively that 'historical Christianity is Roman Catholicism': partly because the information is lacking, and partly because all historical study must be content with 'moral' proof by probabilities, but chiefly because history *can* prove discrepancy between primitive Christianity and Roman Catholicism. Yet history can provide enough information to illustrate a theory which is admittedly framed upon considerations apart from the information, but which can alone (so Newman claimed) provide a pattern wherein the sparse information becomes intelligible. Were the historical information different, the theory would have to be altered or abandoned.

It is not therefore true that Newman's theory (however it might justly be accused of imposing a pattern upon historical data) was guilty of jettisoning history altogether, at least in Newman's intention. Precisely because he felt the historical difficulties to be irreducible, he could not, as he faded out of the Church of England, quietly accept the conventional theories of contemporary apologetic. He needed the idea of development, not because he was no historian, but just in so far as he was one. Morin and Tillemont, Mabillon and Montfaucon, Jortin and Gibbon, even Guizot and Gieseler, had not written in vain. Philosophers have posed a celebrated question to Christian thinkers. 'If Christian teaching rests (at all) upon historical inquiry, might not further historical inquiry disprove it?' Ward answered that it did not so rest and could not thus be disproved. Newman's argument must allow that (theoretically) it could. Observe the extent of that appeal to history which formed the argumentative basis of the *Essay*.

Suppose a revelation, he would say, there is a probability that an infallible authority is given: it is probable that the full Catholic system is the best comment upon the sparse information of early Christian history: it is probable that the sparse information illustrates incipient forms of the developed teaching which is later found. To Newman a combination of probabilities multiplied probability and turned it into a moral certainty. To the Roman theologians, when they came to criticize his theology, this language seemed perilous, as though it removed all certainty from the judgment whether one church was the right church, as though Newman was saying 'the face in the portrait is rather like this face, in spite of differences, and it is highly probable that they are the same, though (on grounds of history and reason) you cannot be

quite certain'. The comparison between early Christian historio-
graphy and the work of secular historians like Thirlwall was
contained in the longest passage omitted by Newman when last he
revised the *Essay* in 1878. Its omission illustrates a marked feature
of that revision—the partial restatement or removal of the appeal
to history, and the consequent weakening of the basis and structure
of the argument.

To account for the discrepancy which history can prove, the
discrepancy between ancient Christianity and modern Roman
Catholicism, we need then a hypothesis. This hypothesis has
made a third force in Catholic theology besides Bossuet's theory of
clearer explanation and the scholastic theory of logical explication.

The proposal takes two forms, two aspects of the same hypothesis, obverse and reverse of the same theory: two analogies,
each of which merges easily and imperceptibly into the other.

(1) The Christian revelation is an *idea* which impressed itself
upon the corporate mind of the Church.

Newman's inconsistent usages of the word *idea* have caused
hours of work to his commentators. In this context *idea* does not
mean the notion which an individual may form of an object, but
the object itself as it is capable of being apprehended in various
notions. An idea will in this sense be more complex and manysided than the individual notions about it, and perhaps never fully
'perceptible' in such notions as human language is capable of
expressing. An idea of importance or complexity can only be
comprehended in all its aspects through a long period of time and
diverse circumstances, which elicit its consequences and its relations. This is what has happened in the development of Christian
doctrine. An 'idea' has been given to the Church: and developments of doctrine are the God-assisted process whereby the
Church comes to comprehend more fully the structure and the
relations of the original revelation, to see round the different
aspects of the one idea which she has been given.

Take a modern analogy, which Newman, if I may judge by the earlier chapters of the *Essay*, would not have repudiated. You may have a broad general idea (almost *ideology*) which influences your life: for example, 'Socialism is the best policy for the country'. The meaning of this general and influential idea is not immediately evident, and its understanding varies between man and man. Though based upon *some* concrete information, it is at first a vague impression, yet an impression which influences a man's behaviour, his vote, his sympathies. Only as this general idea is brought into concrete relationship with particular problems, can it be comprehended in its different aspects—the consequences of nationalization, the union between capital and labour, the meaning of 'classes', the question how when you guarantee employment to everyone you can prevent the value of money from continuously falling—in a series of concrete relations and changing historical circumstances the meaning of the idea is drawn out and understood, you become aware what the original proposition meant throughout its ramifications. You may say that these ramifications are 'implicit'—but not implicit in the logical sense. New knowledge, new awareness, is gained.

The Christian revelation is a more complex 'idea' than this one general proposition. But, in the same way, its various aspects can only be understood in particular, concrete, historical situations and relationships. The Christian meets the Platonist or the Aristotelian, the Arian or the Nestorian, the Gnostic or the Montanist, and, in meeting, apprehends some aspect of the original revelation of which he was not hitherto aware with the top of his mind, but (if aware at all) only as a deep semi-conscious 'feeling' which he had not explained in communicable language. The Church possessed her living idea or ideas; of their relations or consequences she could not be aware until she had tried them out in life, in the world, in the gamut of heresy and the gauntlet of philosophical onslaught.

Truth [Newman quoted the tag] is the daughter of Time.
To live is to change, and to be perfect is to have changed often.

It is sometimes said that the stream is clearest near the spring. Whatever use may fairly be made of this image, it does not apply to the history of a philosophy or sect, which, on the contrary, is more equable, and purer, and stronger, when its bed has become deep, and broad, and full.[1]

(2) The second analogy does not appear, or appears only in passing, in the *Essay*. It should not therefore be disregarded. He had used it in the sermon of 2 February 1843 in which he had first declared to the world his meditation upon the idea of development: and when his *Essay* was attacked by eminent theologians in Rome, it was this second analogy to which he sought to lead them by way of explaining what he intended.

According to Newman, there is a valid analogy between the Church's appropriation of her faith, and the individual Christian's appropriation of his faith. Just as a converted soul grows in the true understanding of the faith which at first he apprehends only in broad outline, so the Church, which at first perceived the content of her faith only in broad outline, grows in the slow understanding of its content.

If we want to know how faith comes to the individual, we must look to the charcoal-burner. The faith of the child was never far from Newman's mind. The illiterate, the peasant, the poor, the busy, can have true faith yet cannot weigh evidence. Faith is a loving assent, a moral assent to the revelation. And this assent may be without rational argument, without preliminary inquiry. It is often a simple and loving reception of an impression made upon the mind: and the investigation of this impression, which we call theological understanding, is later than the impression itself. The mind apprehends God's disclosure of himself with the same direct experience or intuition with which it apprehends physical objects like tables and chairs or the beauty in the serene colours of a Fra Angelico: and then, later, the mind comes with its rationalizing faculty, and examines these proceedings as a scientist tests in his laboratory some hypothetical but still untested flash of genius.[2]

An idea, an experience, an impression, may, like a child's love for its mother, be deeper and bigger than the words, the 'logic', in which the subject of the experience then or later seeks to describe it. A peasant looks at the sky and is able to prophesy the weather accurately, yet would be unable to satisfy the meteorologist that he possesses sufficient reason for his prophecy. And so religion may contain more truth than a theology can describe. 'Mary kept all these sayings and pondered them in her heart.' She received them first: then she reasoned about them. Mary is the type not only of the little child and the peasant, she is the type and model of the theologian and the doctor—and not only of the theologian and doctor, but of the Church herself. The Church first received an impression about which she did not rationalize. And then, in the course of history, she has constructed a theology, doctrines, customs, the offspring of that original impression.

Did he mean that revelation came to the Church in 'experience', impressing 'feelings' upon Christian individuals and congregations? Newman did not eschew the word *feeling*. In one of his earlier manuscript notes upon the theme, he wrote in his diary on 7 April 1843: 'Are not the doctrine of purgatory, saint-worship etc, but the realizations, or vivid representations, of the feelings and ideas which the primitive principles involve? Does any other system secure, contain, those ideas or feelings?' Sometimes he wrote as though the Church appropriated its gospel with such direct intuition that all reasoning was later than the intuition. Once he wrote as though the apprehension of doctrines like the Holy Trinity or the Incarnation or the Real Presence could be appropriated *independently of words*, 'like an impression conveyed through the senses'.[1] He allowed, not only that ideas like these could be conveyed apart from particular propositions used to convey them, but that creeds and dogmas never fully attain to the idea which they seek to represent, and are necessary only because the mind cannot reflect upon its intuitive apprehension except 'piece-meal' and needs to resolve it into a series of aspects and relations. But Newman must not be thought to be a liberal, asserting propositions not to be revelation. Though sometimes, in his careless or luxuriant use of analogies, he sounded as though he thought that all was wordless, that religion was (ultimately) feeling or religious or moral experience, that revelation contained no propositions—he neither believed nor intended to teach that. The 'sacred impression' which can be described as prior to propositions is in part a proposition-bearing impression. That the revelation is not to be contained and encompassed in any doctrinal propositions, that it is directed to the conscience as well as to the mind, he warmly believed: that the revelation could be apart from all propositions was far from his meaning. Much has been given, was given in scripture. The problem is that more than that *much* is now being taught.

This then is the third explanation of the discrepancy between an immutable revelation and doctrinal history. The revelation was given as a unity, as a totality, addressing itself to the hearts and feelings and consciences as well as to the minds of men. It was given partly in the form of propositions. And partly, Christian thinkers have needed to draw out and formulate, not only the intellectual consequences of the given propositions, but the rational expression of what at first they experienced wordlessly and which could only be formulated as their feelings and experiences encountered opposition, error, pagan philosophy, or evangelistic success.

To discover how far this theory departed from any traditional theory of tradition, we need to analyse the nature of the 'additions' which Newman (in common with all Roman Catholic theologians of tradition) imagines to have been made to the rule of faith.

Newman stood altogether with Catholic belief, first, in postulating (against Butler or the Latitudinarians) that doctrinal 'additions' are or can be *de fide* and to be accepted by the faithful with the same faith as they accept the originally explicit deposit; secondly, in asserting (against every probability arising from his general argument and against every sane historical inquiry) that the apostles knew, though *without words*, all the truths which theologians and controversialists have afterwards reduced to formulas; and thirdly, that heresy is always new,[1] though Newman could not hold with Bossuet and his earlier self that every new doctrine is heretical; fourthly, that the 'additions' are always preservative of the original idea—an addition which contradicted or threatened an already established doctrine must be a corruption and a heresy. A true development is 'an addition which illustrates, not obscures, corroborates not corrects, the body of thought from which it proceeds'.[2]

In contrast with the non-scholastic theory of tradition represented by Bossuet, Newman asserted that the Church provides new doctrines, and not simply new definitions or explanations of old doctrines. It is essential to his theory that an idea or an aspect of an idea might be at one time held 'wordlessly' and might subsequently be formulated in words, and it was therefore essential to him to allow that new doctrines (*quoad nos*) had arisen in the history of the Church. This assertion appears in the *Essay* partly as a delivery of historical investigation and partly as an assumption underlying most of the argument. His strenuous attempt to affirm the immutability of Catholic 'principles' like dogmatism and sacramentalism and the supremacy of faith over reason is in part an effort to show how dogmas, while changing, could nevertheless illustrate the unchanging principles from which they arise. But the principal way in which he affirmed this novelty of some doctrines *quoad nos* was to contend that the Church was once *unaware* or *unconscious* of some of the truths which she afterwards defined. Indeed it was the chief purpose of his two analogies—the analogy with the appropriation of a living idea and the analogy of the child's faith—to explain and expound this unawareness. He used a third analogy—the analysis of a poet's mind. In analysing a poem we find whisperings and imaginings beyond what the poet is saying with the surface of his mind, glimpses of which the poet was himself unconscious but which may yet be said to be in some sense part of his mind.

The *Lectures on the Prophetical Office of the Church* had conceived the 'traditional element' in the authority of the Church as a kind of thought or principle deep in the Church's bosom, 'breathing' within her, her 'accustomed and unconscious mode of viewing things', the body of her assumptions rather than any systematic and explicated structure of dogmas.[1] After he had become a Roman Catholic and sought to explain himself in Latin, he called this habitual and unconscious mode of viewing and acting upon truth by the name *intimus sensus*. Within this *intimus sensus* he conceived developments to be due to a process whereby that which was held 'unconsciously' became conscious as it was brought home to the mind of the Church: developments were 'spontaneous, gradual, ethical' in their growth, they were not conscious inferences from premises.[2]

Unlike Bossuet, the scholastic theory of inferences had allowed that a development was not merely a translation into clearer language and had admitted that the Church was in a measure unaware of doctrines later defined, had recognized that there were some doctrines which at an earlier date the Church knew only implicitly—that is, as a little child which knows that 2 plus 2 equals 4 may not yet know that 4 plus 4 equals 8. If Newman's theory could be fitted into the idea of logical explication, there would be nothing new, or startling, about the theory of unconsciousness.

Among the seven 'tests' which Newman half-heartedly alleged for distinguishing true developments from false developments (tests which are rather pegs on which to hang a *historical* thesis than solid supports for a doctrinal explanation), the fifth is termed Logical Sequence.

Newman had disliked logic, or 'mere logic' since the day when he had reacted against the teaching of Whately, whose text-book upon logic he had helped to write. The word *logic* his mind rapidly associated with words like *rationalism*. Individual minds are not moved by logic—it was not by dialectic that it pleased God to save his people: logic is the subsequent record of the movement of the mind, the intellectual effort to arrange or describe a process which transcends logic. 'On a large field', he wrote, 'developments will on the whole be gradual, and orderly, nay, in *logical sequence*. It may be asked whether a development is itself a logical process; and if by this is meant a conscious reasoning from premise to conclusion, of course the answer must be in the negative.'[1] Ideas grow in the mind because they 'remain' in it: the mind meditates upon an idea and slowly perceives more of its reality and its relations. The mind is not inferring anything: it is not even aware what is happening to it. But from time to time circumstances force it to state its view of the idea and so elicit formal statements about it—and logic comes in to analyse these formal statements and their mutual interdependence; and so 'logic is brought in to arrange and inculcate what no science was employed in gaining'.

He did not rule out the possibility of logical inferences in development, and at more than one point in his essay he recognized that they had a part to play.[2] But it was a minor part. For normally explication is not only an explication of a truth of which the Church was once not fully aware, since the explication is itself conditioned by a movement of thought and conscience of which the Church is unaware. Development does not take place by a mere 'mechanism of reasoning'. The Church grows into a truth without any conscious or logical inference: and only after she has grown into it does she look back and perceive the logical implication.

But even then, what is this logical implication which the Church perceives when she looks back? Newman's language, and the historical examples which he offered, prove without a shadow of question that when he talked about the Church perceiving a

ogical sequence, he was not using logic in the sense in which the
ogicians and the mathematicians would use it. Logical sequence
meant a vague but general intellectual coherence. This is so
manifest to the reader of the *Essay* that I will give but one his-
orical illustration of his meaning. 'St Justin or St Irenaeus might
be without any digested ideas of Purgatory or Original Sin, yet
have an intense feeling, which they had not defined or located,
both of the fault of our first nature and the liabilities of our nature
regenerate.'[1] Whatever intellectual connection might be held to be
perceivable between a feeling of the liabilities of our nature
regenerate and a full doctrine of purgatory, it is patent that this
connection cannot be described as a logical connection in any
sense which would satisfy the logicians. The 'logical sequence' of
Newman is not the 'logical implication' of the scholastics, though
the latter might be a part or aspect of the former. It means rather
a subsequent perception of a harmony or congruity or 'natural-
ness' in the way in which ideas have developed.

It is therefore essential to Newman to affirm that new doctrines
have appeared, and not only new in the sense in which a child
who knows that 2 and 2 make 4 does not yet know that 4 and 4
make 8. By his language about the 'idea' and its 'aspects' he
sought to avoid the notion of a continuing revelation. The
original revelation is unique: it was given partly in explicit doctrines, partly in perceptions which were left to be subsequently
drawn out into doctrines, these later doctrines being like the
thoughts of a man who suddenly perceives the truth of a new
proposition, exclaiming 'Yes, I believed that all the time but I did
not know I did because I did not know how to put it like that'.

Another of the 'tests' is crucial for the doctrinal explanation:
the third, entitled 'Power of Assimilation'. This test offers the
reader some of the passages in the *Essay* most unclear and puzzling
to interpret.

The historians have shown that the Christian Church has incorporated many practices and customs which were to be found in

heathenism: incense, vestments, the ring in marriage, tonsure and others. Newman sets forward this fact, admitted by everyone, as an illustration of the 'assimilative' or 'unitive' power of the gospel in the Church, the power which takes what is superstitious or erroneous or neutral and transmutes it to serve the purposes of the Christian community. And as the Church has incorporated practices originally external to herself and transmuted them, so (he appears to argue) she has incorporated doctrines and belief originally external to her own doctrine and yet has transmuted them to serve her own purposes. This might mean one or both of two things. It might mean that doctrines found in the Christian gospel were also found in parallel or anticipation among the religions of non-Christian antiquity. This at least Newman intended: as he talks (among many other illustrations) of the use by the fourth Gospel of 'Gnostic or Platonic words'. But the proposition might also mean that the Christian gospel has in the course of Christian history taken in further truths, to be found among the heathen or the heretic, and incorporated them, transmuted them, dominated them into its own unity of thought. This also Newman means to teach. He compared the growth of an idea to physical growth. A plant grows by incorporating substances external to itself. Christian doctrine has grown by incorporating doctrines 'external' (he did not shrink from the word) to itself and transmuting them. He numbered Christianity among the 'eclectic philosophies' which grow by absorbing elements originally foreign to themselves while preserving their identity.

Does this mean only that the Church has defined doctrine with the assistance of language derived from time to time from the Platonic or Aristotelian philosophies? Newman has frequently been charged with teaching far more than this, with teaching that the Church has from time to time added to the gospel doctrines not originally part of the revelation, and no one can deny that the language of his sixth chapter easily lends itself to this interpretation. But while the language and the meaning are patently remote from the traditional idea of tradition, they are perhaps not quite so remote in intention as in performance. According to Newman's theory it was necessary to assert that *doctrines* which did not form part of the revelation had been added by the Church. But these doctrines were the formulated expressions of an original experience or feeling which did form part of the original revelation; and in this context he was saying no more than when he wrote that external circumstances had assisted the process of doctrinal formulation. In expressing her (partly wordless) feeling or experience, the Church, needing human language, turned to the philosophy of the age to discover the best method of explaining the revealed datum.

Newman is thus brought to a new answer to the old question, why are heretics good for the Church? He cannot say, with Bossuet, that heretics are good for the Church because they call her attention to a problem and so enable her to declare her already known mind upon that problem—because the Church, according to Newman, frequently does not yet know her mind upon the problem. In Newman's theory the heretic is a thinker who makes an effort, but a mistaken or one-sided effort, at a statement of true doctrine, and who thus initiates or continues a doctrinal debate valuable for the Church. History seemed to him to show enough examples of the indecision of popes and councils in the face of doctrinal inquiry to prove that the authorities of the Church were frequently ignorant of the true answer to the problem raised by a heretic, and that this true answer had to be thrashed out, debated, and discovered, before the Church could pronounce her mind on the question. And so Newman could use wholly unprecedented language about the course of doctrinal definition and the inquiries needed before that definition—'The theology of the Church is... a diligent, patient, working out of one doctrine out of many materials. The conduct of Popes, Councils, Fathers, betokens the slow, painful, anxious taking up of new elements into an existing body of belief.'[1] One urgent question here presses upon the student of Newman. Waiving the difficulty of postulating an originally wordless appropriation of such a doctrine as the double procession of the Holy Spirit,[1] we are in difficulties about the language in which these 'new' doctrines are expressed. This language is new language. As language it is not part of the original revelation. Nor is it a restatement of part of the revelation already expressed in propositions. Nor is it logically deducible from the original revelation, since you cannot 'infer' propositions from a wordless experience or feeling or (in Newman's sense) 'idea'. The doctrine then is a statement of part of the revelation not itself a doctrine. Can the doctrine, the language, be said under these circumstances to be 'revealed'? It could only be said to be revealed either by association of ideas or by the contention that the definition by the Church is itself revelation. Traditional theology (Suarez being the chief exception) had refused to allow that the revelation could in any sense be supplemented by further revealed truth. Newman's theory, like that of Suarez, is dependent upon the contention that definition by the Church is 'equivalent' to revelation. If it were established (for example) in Catholic theology that 'revelation ended at the death of the last apostle', Newman's theory could hardly survive without a restatement so drastic as to leave it almost unrecognizable.

The *Essay* was written between March 1844 and September 1845, the greater part in the last few months when he had already resolved to be admitted to the Roman Catholic Church. He had at first no hope that he would finish it by the autumn of 1845: but in the event, still discontented with its style and its matter, he sent it to the press at the end of September. He had intended to publish the *Essay* before he was received. But the actions of Dalgairns and Ambrose St John, the pressure of Stanton and others at Littlemore, the timing of the visit of Father Dominic, led him to seek admission without waiting for publication.

Within four days he became aware of a new problem about his *Essay*. On 11 October Bishop Baggs wrote from Prior Park welcoming him to the Catholic Church. But the Bishop added 'a word of friendly advice' about his forthcoming work. The subject was one 'of great difficulty and delicacy'; he should therefore consult Wiseman or some other experienced divine, lest some of his words might afterwards be misinterpreted. Newman replied that he would burn the book if the bishops wished.[1]

No more than Newman did Wiseman wish the book to be burnt. It was advertised: the whole world knew that a book was on the way: the French Catholics were already asking Wiseman for a French translation. To suppress the book was impossible. Nor did Wiseman wish to suppress it.[2] He perceived how influential it would be with other Oxford men and friends of Newman: and he was big enough to risk the peril that the language of the book, written as it was by one untrained in the technical theology of the Catholic Church, might not in all points be as accurate as his advisers desired.

On 31 October Newman travelled to Oscott for his confirmation by Wiseman on the following day. Newman's shyness made the first interview a trying one: but after dinner on All Saints' Day he had a long talk with Wiseman about his book. Wiseman asked him the nature of the book. Newman described its approach as historical and philosophical rather than theological, and Wiseman said that so long as it was not 'dogmatic, didactic', it could be published. It had been written in a period for which Wiseman was not pastorally responsible. 'The book is a fact: I cannot alter it.' Newman offered to send him the book for revision before it was published, as Bishop Baggs had suggested. Wiseman 'absolutely' declined to see it.

He said [wrote Newman to Hope] that as it professed to be the course of reasoning which I *had* had, it was a *fact* which all his seeing could not alter. There might be error in it, if it so happened, but still, so that I professed (as of course I do) in all things to submit to the

Church, he had nothing to say to it. I have no reason whatever to suppose there is anything at all in it which I should now disclaim, but still he has *not* seen it, and of course speaks *on the chance* of its containing anything.[1]

Six days afterwards Newman, back at Littlemore, received a letter from Wiseman telling him that he had changed his mind and now wished to see the proofs of the *Essay*. One of Wiseman's advisers had said that the book was bound to attract so much attention that it was 'of the utmost importance' that everything in it should be most carefully stated. Wiseman consulted another friend, who agreed. 'I write to say that I will willingly charge myself with this duty, in any manner that will least delay publication.'[2]

Newman immediately wrote to Blanchard, the printer in London, telling him to send the first proofs to Dr Wiseman. But he returned to Wiseman a mild protest. Hope (who in private did not think highly of the book and nicknamed it 'The Extravagant of John', but whom Newman particularly wished to influence) had asserted emphatically ('with much emotion') that if he knew the book had been revised, it would destroy the effect of the book upon himself and others: and on 2 November Newman had given him the assurance, already quoted, that Wiseman had declined to interfere. Newman added a postscript to Wiseman, 'From this specimen I have no doubt, what I was not prepared for, that the news of such a step as your Lordship's friends recommend will produce a great sensation in the Church of England.' Reflection showed him that the postscript was couched in the wrong spirit and he deleted it before copying and sending the letter.

Wiseman did not reply for ten days. On 17 November he wrote to say that he had reconsidered his decision. Revision 'might turn into a fatal blow against the weight of the book'. And Wiseman reiterated his view that 'the work belongs to a period when responsibility could not rest upon me'. He sent back the first proof sheets unread, in order that Newman might be justified in saying in the preface that Wiseman had not in any way interfered. Perhaps however it would be desirable that he should see the conclusion or preface.

Newman at once sent him the preface. On 21 November Wiseman wrote again suggesting minor modifications. The only important addition which he wanted was a formula whereby Newman publicly submitted the *Essay* to the judgment of the Church. 'I should be glad of a sentence added to the effect that you now submit all that you have written to the Church, or that you desire to think on all the matters of which it treats in exact conformity with her doctrine.' Newman added the required sentence, and the *Essay* was published five days later.[1] A week after that the publisher was arranging with Newman for a second impression.

And then could be heard the hum of innumerable bees.

# CHAPTER VIII

# NEWMAN AND ROME

The Anglican critics read the *Essay*, some with anger, some with relief, some with contempt, some with glee, a few (James Mozley *facile princeps*) with serious appraisal, and one (who could be expected to be unexpected—Frederick Denison Maurice) with gratitude that Newman had now abandoned what he believed to be the rigid antiquarianism of the Tractarian doctrine of authority. 'Alas!' cried Henry Hart Milman with satirical despondency, 'Alas, where is Bossuet?'[1]

That Newman read some of these critics is proven. But it must be said at once that none of their criticisms, not even the reluctant but powerful examination to which Mozley subjected the *Essay*, had the least effect upon Newman's mind. There is no scrap of evidence that he later altered a single line in response to any of these early Anglican critics.

But there was another form of criticism, less public and more friendly, to which Newman was sensitive. His own reasons for joining the Church of Rome were important to the peace of his soul: and since the theology of the *Essay* was evidently exerting a favourable influence in removing the objections of some of his friends, he was anxious that the substance of it should be recognized as good Catholic doctrine. On the one side he found much to encourage him—his own hospitable reception at various Catholic colleges, the welcoming letters of English bishops or theologians. Bishop Gillis wrote to Newman in January saying that he had delivered popular lectures on the *Essay* which had aroused widespread interest in Edinburgh, and suggested that he might publish these for the benefit of those who could not be expected to read the *Essay* itself.

But was it the theology of the Catholic Church? There were

Catholic correspondents who wrote to him, sure that in the form in which he expressed himself, it was not. One important theologian, thanking him in the friendliest possible way for the book, and commenting on the good which it would do for Anglicans, ended with a stab of encouragement—'Allow me to say that as you advance in the sweet participation of Catholic Communion, your own mind will happily develop, and you will understand as a man, and think as a man, and speak as a man, of sound and vigorous faith.' These words were not music to Newman's ears. He asked for details. He was sent but six passages, and these he did not think of major importance.[1]

The minds of Roman Catholics in England evidently needed preparing for the thought of the *Essay*. Möhler was the one Catholic theologian of development whose work Newman knew by repute. It seemed desirable that Möhler should be better known in England than he was. In the middle of December Newman proposed to Wiseman that Möhler's *Unity* should be translated into English. More than a year before, Wiseman's *Dublin Review* had reported unfavourably upon the theology of Möhler's *Unity*, and he could not now leave Newman under any illusions.

The last chapter of Möhler's book on Unity [he wrote to Newman] is calculated to obscure the question on which it treats, more than to illustrate it: and I do not think the language employed in it could satisfy Catholic divines in general. If the work be published there must certainly be notes to it....[2]

For the moment the movement of Newman's mind halted. There were other things to do, old friends to influence, a new life to plan, ordination to consider, the journey to Rome to arrange. We hear little argument upon the question for the next six months. A memorandum has survived in Newman's hand, dated 15 July 1846, which looks like a draft for a new preface or statement about the *Essay*. He explains that the book was unfinished: that there were 'very likely mistakes' though he was not at present aware of them, since he 'had to enter upon metaphysical inquiries for which his previous study had not fitted him'. It is clear from the draft that he had not changed his mind, that nothing and no one had yet convinced him that anything in the *Essay* ought to be altered, that he was sticking to his guns. It is also clear that he felt, consciously, that he needed to stick to the guns, that he was under criticism: for he wrote across the top of the draft *Beware of seeming apologetic.*[1]

On 7 September 1846 he sailed from Brighton to Dieppe, passed through Paris where his guide, M. Jules Gondon, undertook the projected French translation of the *Essay*, and arrived in Rome on 28 October. It was now to be decided what the Roman theologians, the men who guided the official theology of the Church, would think of Newman's theories.

At first there was every chance that the encounter would be friendly and successful. Newman was humble. Indeed his humility and gentleness, sometimes under trying conditions, is one of the most edifying features of this visit to Rome. He knew that he had an atmosphere to imbibe, a new vocabulary to understand.

But if he was in the mind to learn rather than teach, he was still earnest to stand by the main planks of his theology. Not only did he now need this for the satisfaction of his own apologia. He had turned to planning a theological school in England which should commend the Catholic faith in modern terms. In this planning of a theological school was implicit a discontent with the prevailing teaching of Roman Catholic theology in England. He wanted the approval of Rome for himself as a theological teacher. And he did not at once see the wide difference between welcoming a kind of doctrinal semi-autobiography from an untrained ex-Anglican, and setting up those doctrines as stamped with a particular approval in the Roman schools. He started moreover with a handicap. He had been nurtured in the Englishman's quondam contempt for scholastic theology. His own approach to theology was historical and philosophical: he had always used the word 'scholastic' in an unfavourable sense. He had realized already that if he were ever to teach theology in the Church he would need to study the scholastic tradition. On 12 May 1846 he began the study of Melchior Cano. But he never took to it easily, and wrote to a friend, jestingly but perhaps a little ruefully, 'We are beginning to read school divinity and make syllogisms. Only fancy my returning to school at my age.' He thought that modern Roman Catholic divines were careful teachers of dogmatic theo- logy but were almost wholly ignorant of historical scholarship. There was a later rumour that W. G. Ward, when lecturing at Old Hall, kicked Perrone's text-book round the room. The fastidious Newman would have found such robust methods distasteful. But he partly agreed. Hope had told him that he would not find *any* theologians at Rome. And Dalgairns, who had preceded him and was receiving his theological training with the French at Langres, wrote to Newman abusing the shallowness and tedium of conventional theology. It was not to be expected that Newman would be able to sympathize with the viewpoint of the Roman theologians without a strenuous exertion of the mind.[1]

In Rome the reigning theologians were three Jesuit professors at the Collegio Romano—the two professors of dogmatic theology Perrone and Passaglia, the professor of canon law Giacomo Mazio. 'There is no doubt', wrote Newman to Dalgairns in December, 'the Jesuits are the only persons here.' Passaglia was a brilliant young man of 34 who had been Perrone's ablest pupil and had recently succeeded to the other chair. Later in life he would leave his order and then his cloth, transform himself into a leading liberal and Cavour's ecclesiastical lieutenant. But in 1846 he was regarded in Rome as the coming theologian, a sparkling lecturer with a reputation for wide patristic learning. Mazio was more canonist than theologian, an attractive and gentle person who had long interested himself in English affairs, had helped to translate Lingard and others into Italian, and was one of the censors of the principal theological journal in Rome, the *Annali delle scienze religiose*. Theologically less acute than the other two, Mazio proved to be more easily dazed at the vagaries of Newman's language.[1]

Between Perrone and Passaglia was beginning to appear the divergence of outlook natural between two such different personalities. Without being a solid student of the schoolmen, Perrone was scholastic in his cast of mind. Passaglia on the contrary was primarily patristic, approved of Petau (and incidentally of Bishop Bull), reckoned little to the authority of either Aristotle or St Thomas Aquinas. A Thomist might have understood Newman more easily—when Newman eventually looked round tradition for support he found his best precedents in the Spanish Thomists of the Counter-Reformation, Suarez and Lugo. But in the Italy of 1846 Thomism—though influential, how should it not be?—was not ruling theological thought. Soon after Newman arrived in Rome he was told by a Jesuit from Propaganda that both Aristotle and St Thomas Aquinas were out of favour in Rome and throughout Italy, that people professed to reverence St Thomas but put him aside. Newman rapidly discerned what he believed to be the reason. St Thomas Aquinas was out of favour because the Dominicans were out of favour. And the Dominicans were out of favour partly because, faithful to St Thomas, their order had been resisting any definition of the doctrine of the immaculate conception, which, it was beginning to be plain, would soon be defined: and partly because they were associated with 'rigorist' or 'probabiliorist' views in moral theology which ran contrary to the prevailing opinion at Rome and to the rising influence of St Alfonso Liguori. This attitude to Thomism, which Newman described to Dalgairns as 'the prevalent depreciation of St Thomas', had important consequences for his discussion with the Roman theologians, and did not ease the work of mutual understanding. But Newman himself was relieved by the circumstance. He disliked (at first) what he heard of Thomist 'rigorism', discouraged Dalgairns' liking for the Dominicans, and said he could not join an order with 'a dominant imperious theology'.[1] No doubt he was seeing the Dominicans partly through Jesuit spectacles, for his chief friends and advisers in Rome were Jesuits. Certainly he found that the three Jesuit professors dominated Roman theology.

Newman was bound to experience difficulty in making himself intelligible to Perrone. For Newman believed that language was always inadequate, he loved analogy and metaphor and parable, he distrusted logic. Perrone preferred crisp, cool, intelligible, syllogistic reasoning, disliked cloudy metaphysics and probable assumptions. After struggling with Newman's Anglican writings, he had judged them to be specimens of muddled thinking, and had published his verdict—*Newman miscet et confundit omnia*. But this wide difference in approach proved in the event less formidable than the difference with Passaglia. Newman at last found it possible to argue with Perrone; in Passaglia he found only a vehement critic, and they never came to understand each other. Apart from the difference in training and mental background, the Roman theologians needed to surmount one obstacle, indefinable perhaps but not trivial. Newman had come into the Roman Catholic Church—had he come on his own terms? His attitude to the *Essay on Development* seemed to suggest that the old arguments which had satisfied for centuries did not satisfy him, that he needed to attribute something new to the Church, a rare and peculiar theory, before he could conscientiously join, that he was weakening the force of the old apologetics and throwing them into the rubbish-heap, that he was leaving the well-paved highway to wander over unmapped ground. For the conservative theologians, whether Roman or English, this unspoken barrier existed. His person they welcomed with warmth and sympathy, his thought perplexed and sometimes frightened them. 'The Roman theologians', wrote Father Ignatius Ryder later, saw Newman to be 'a formidable engine of war on their side, but they were distinctly aware that they did not thoroughly understand the machinery. And so they came to think, some of them, that it might perhaps one day go off of itself or in the wrong direction.'

Sensitive and reserved, Newman was no linguist. The Roman theologians read French, and Newman soon started to hasten the projected French translation of the *Essay* by M. Gondon. But this linguistic barrier had one immediate consequence. The chief commentator upon English affairs in the *Annali delle scienze religiose* was a Scotsman, Dr Alexander Grant, who had been Vice-Rector of the Scots College in Rome since 1841 and succeeded to the Rectorship soon after Newman arrived there. He on his side was reserved, precise, solitary, a man of inflexible character and principles, as is testified both by his friends and by his portrait which, with its prominent chin and severe mouth, now hangs in the library of the Scots College. In the number of the *Annali* for the spring of 1846 Grant promised to review the *Essay* in a future number. Whether this promised review was ever written is not known. It never appeared. And the reason for this failure was later evident. Grant took the most unfavourable view of Newman's work. After he had studied the *Essay*, he concluded that Newman was guilty of 'material heresy', and he did not shrink from saying so to his associates in Rome.[1] That the principal Roman commentator on Tractarian affairs should take this openly critical view was unlucky for Newman. Those who could not read English took their opinions from those who could.

In the eastern states of America Unitarianism was popular, intelligent, well-established. Since the seventeenth century the Unitarians had used the vacillations of the ante-Nicene Fathers as evidence for their criticism of the Trinitarians. As once they had welcomed the admissions of Petau, they now seized upon the admissions of the *Essay on Development* to support their case.

Orestes Brownson had once been a robust Unitarian and a tough radical politician. He had been received into the Roman

Catholic Church in 1844, and had added to his natural vigour and belligerence some of the all-or-nothingness of the newly converted. He suspected the ex-Tractarians in general and Newman in particular because they talked as though their new allegiance was the completion of their Anglicanism. Himself endowed with an assured and companionable lustiness, he thought the English converts 'effeminate' and 'over-delicate'; and a shrewd friend once said that if Newman had not minded a little swearing, Brownson might have been readier to regard his pious face and manners as 'pardonable vices'. Sensitive as only an ex-Unitarian could be to any point scored by his erstwhile colleagues, he determined to controvert and smash the theology of the *Essay on Development*. Brownson was as intelligent as he was massive: but it has been said that humility was the one virtue which he found it impossible to acquire. In July 1846 he published the first of a series of articles in his own periodical, *Brownson's Quarterly Review*. He believed that Newman's thought was frankly heretical; and his bishop, Fitzpatrick of Boston, agreed.[1]

Brownson expounded with a bludgeoning force the traditionalism of Bossuet. The Church asserts the opposite of what Newman asserts. The Church asserts 'that there has been no progress, no increase, no variation of faith; that what she believes and teaches now is precisely what she has always and everywhere believed and taught from the first.... If you believe the Church, you cannot assert developments in your sense of the term: if you do not believe her, you are no Catholic.' Brownson's statements, though he claimed and believed them to rest upon the high authority of Bossuet, differed momentously if surreptitiously from the Gallican theories of the seventeenth century. Gallican divines had appealed to history, confident that a sound and scholarly interpretation of the patristic sources would support them. Brownson, purporting to represent the same tradition of doctrine, was compelled to contend against Newman that sound and scholarly appeals to history were uncatholic, that historical inquiries were forms of private judgment, and that we must receive our history of the primitive Church from the infallible teaching of the present Church.

He did not confine himself to a statement of conservative orthodoxy, but pushed the attack home against Newman's person. It seemed to him astounding that Newman, after his conversion, should not have refrained from publishing this 'essentially anti-Catholic' work and should apparently be unaware of its unsoundness. It seemed strange that Newman had failed to undertake the least inquiry into the authentic teaching of the Church before he joined her. It seemed deplorable that Newman should have come into the Church 'on conditions', not with the simple-hearted surrender of the meek, but under a treaty which stipulated that he should retain his side-arms and march out with honours. It seemed chimerical that he should have laboured 'with a genius, a talent, a learning, a sincerity, an earnestness, which no one can refuse to admire, to develop Protestantism into Catholicity. Vain effort! As well attempt to develop the poisonous sumach into the cedar of Lebanon.'[1] It must therefore be remembered that during the next twelve months the work which was at present one of the two most precious to Newman's heart (the other being the *University Sermons* which were so closely related to it), and on which his status as a Roman Catholic seemed in part to depend, was undergoing able and vigorous sniping from a warrior accustomed to the rules of battle then usual in American journalism. Newman was *intellectually* unperturbed. He thought it odd that a neophyte, hardly a member of the Church for a longer time than himself, should pontificate as the oracle of American orthodoxy. But how keenly he felt Brownson's attacks may be seen from many fragments among his papers.

Before he left England, he had heard brief rumours about Brownson from his friend T. F. Knox in America, and how the chief American Catholic newspaper had written of Newman's 'errors'.[2] He seems to have thought little of the news at the time. But soon after arriving in Rome he was deeply distressed to learn that the controversy in America was known in Rome and had turned into a storm of 'extreme violence'. The American bishops (sharing the views of English critics like Bishop Blomfield, James Mozley, H. H. Milman, Isaac Williams, and *Frazer's Magazine*) 'say it is half Catholicism half infidelity. Of course they know nothing of antiquity or of the state of the case; i.e. [he went on characteristically but erroneously] they are what Knox calls scholastic divines.'[1] He had already been received by Mazio and Passaglia at the Collegio Romano and had discovered that they knew the American news. They admitted the principle of development (so Newman claimed) but told him that, so far as they were able to judge from translated extracts of the *Essay*, he had carried the principle too far.

If Brownson and Grant were his only interpreters, it was plain that he must hurry the French translation. For the next three months, in the intervals of his generally happy and interesting life at Propaganda, Newman sought to hasten the French translation, to harry the deliberate or dallying M. Gondon into getting on with his work. He was encouraged by the preparations for defining the doctrine of the immaculate conception, which he believed could hardly be defined except upon a theory of development like his own. That Perrone was engaged on a book to prove its definability was welcome news. But he had now realized, perhaps for the first time, that to the Roman theologians precision of theological language was important. 'Everything', he told Dalgairns, '*everything* depends on the exactness of the French translation. An incautious rendering of particular phrases may ruin everything.' A week later he heard that some theologians were introducing extracts from his *Essay* into their lectures in order to dissent from them. He complained to Mazio. He protested that if the report were true it would do grievous harm to the Catholic cause in England. Mazio assured him that the report was untrue. But some weeks later he discovered that Passaglia had indeed lectured against him. Passaglia had not mentioned

Newman's name in his lecture, but, being asked at the end of the lecture whether he had been criticizing Newman, replied that he had.[1]

There were three things to be done. One was to buy and read Catholic theology, and henceforth his note-books were sprinkled with little texts culled mainly from the Thomists, particularly Suarez, Lugo, and St Thomas himself. It is typical of Newman in this phase that he appears to have made no strenuous attempt to penetrate to the true mind of his authors. The fragments in the notes rather suggest an anthology of texts made to support a view already formed than any serious historical study. Secondly, he sought to prove his competence in patristic theology by publishing in Latin four long critical notes upon St Athanasius, entitled *Dissertatiunculae Critico-Theologicae* and dedicating them to the Jesuit Rector of Propaganda. The purpose of this ungrateful labour was an open search for theological respectability. The search is a symptom of that simplicity in Newman's character which was so unintelligible to the worldly-wise that they sometimes mistook it for subtlety. Thirdly, he must make Dalgairns push on the lingering French translation.

The French translation was an opportunity to explain himself. From December he was beginning to suggest to Dalgairns various alterations in the wording of the *Essay*. He had discovered, perhaps rather to his surprise, that while the Roman theologians disagreed with his expression of the theory, they objected to the *Essay* above all because it included sceptical language about the capacity of the human reason to attain certainty in matters of faith (especially when those matters of faith were historical). He asked Dalgairns to alter passages which might lead to Roman misunderstanding. He contemplated explaining himself in a new preface but abandoned the idea. 'Though I could not correct my book,' he wrote to Dalgairns, 'yet if you saw any expression etc. which was certainly wrong, you might modify it in the translation, and if you have any remark to make on any other point, let me have it.'[2]

174

On 7 December 1846 Dalgairns wrote from Langres that a French friend had already begun translating some of the *University Sermons*. Since Newman did not respond to the idea, Dalgairns reiterated it, taking the view that a translation of the sermons was the best answer to objections to the *Essay*. Newman accepted the scheme cheerfully, and encouraged Dalgairns to go ahead with his two French translators, M. Gondon for the *Essay*, the Abbé Deferrière ('a young priest full of zeal') for the sermons. The theologians of Rome evidently needed preparing for the thought of the *Essay*. He knew that the theory of development rested in part upon the theory of faith propounded in the later *University Sermons*, and he believed that if Roman minds could see the context they would understand the *Essay* rightly.[1]

Before the translations had progressed far, Dalgairns was forced to report a ludicrous calamity. A French translation of the *Essay*, unauthorised and unwanted, was published by a M. d'Avrigny. Though this buccaneer edition proved the lively interest which the *Essay* had aroused in Catholic France, its translator did not possess the two qualities required to translate competently—he understood neither theology nor the English language. He believed that Mosheim was a Moslem. He omitted the inverted commas when Newman was quoting authors with the aim of refuting them. He thought that 'the faithful departed' were the same people as 'those who have departed from the faith'. From time to time he omitted the word *not*. He declared that Newman had been the editor of *The Times*, because he knew that he had written some *Tracts for the Times*. Yet it was even rumoured in France that the Pope himself had approved the translation.

Dalgairns acted decisively. He wrote to the *Univers* repudiating the book in forcible language.[2]

The vessel of the authorized translations kept running into headwinds. Newman, having decided to translate the *University Sermons* in order to explain the language of the *Essay*, soon discovered that the language of the *University Sermons* needed as much explanation as the language of the *Essay*. More corrections, more clarifications, more patristic authorities, had to be dispatched to Dalgairns. At his end Dalgairns was beginning to realize the possibility of what he called (apologetically) a 'hullabaloo' unless the relations between probability and faith were described more precisely in the French than in the English. And Newman's style and thought did not easily lend themselves to rapid translation into French—

...You cannot conceive the difficulty of putting your John Bull of a style into French. These learned Frenchmen are far too impatient to read a book which leaves any one single premiss of a syllogism to be guessed at by the reader. They chafe and fret at anything which leaves the slightest obscurity. You on the contrary leave many a premiss and pro-syllogism unexpressed. Again, the beauty of French writing lies in the turn of the *sentence* and the flowing of the style; while you express your ideas in energetic, knock-me-down Saxon *words*, each of which is a picture, and cannot possibly be rendered in French. I have in many places made rather a paraphrase than a translation. As for Gondon, he is utterly incapable of fulfilling the task he has undertaken. Whenever there is the semblance of an argument he fails, and especially when the matter is philosophical, he does not understand it and translates like a schoolboy....I should say in justice...that when the matter is simply historical, he manages to translate very well, so that once in the second part he will get on swimmingly. I shall however advise him to suspend operations till our return from Rome.[1]

For the proposed French translation of the *University Sermons*, Newman took the trouble to draft a Latin preface by way of explanation. It was not published until 1937, and then after some measure of diffidence on the part of Newman's executors.[2] The preface tried to show in what sense he understood such words as *probability*, *certainty*, *evidence*. It displays one cause of the difficulty which Newman found in making himself intelligible in Rome, a cause which probably he never realized. Lurking at the back of his mind is the ghostly shadow of Hume. He could see the power in the arguments, he devoted his efforts to resisting the sceptical contentions, he had been brought up in a world wherein anyone with pretensions to philosophical thinking must have meditated upon Hume. To Newman it was no concession to the enemy but a simple and empirically verifiable truth that in the eyes of the world faith and reason seemed to be opposed. 'How does it happen', began his projected preface tactlessly, 'that in the ordinary judgment of mankind faith is contrary to reason, or irrational?' The Roman theologians were accustomed to no such ordinary judgment. The arguments of Hume were discussed in Oxford but were not met in Roman seminaries. In the eyes of Perrone and Passaglia Catholic theology could not be unbalanced by too extreme a response to the arguments of a distant and unknown infidel.

It must not be supposed that when Newman proffered these numerous corrections and modifications to Dalgairns he believed that he was changing his mind under pressure, abandoning his standpoint, or adopting new opinions. He thought that he was clarifying his mind, that is (according to his personal theory of faith and development) he was reaching a more accurate expression of what he had truly believed all the time, though perhaps confusedly. The Roman theologians neither shared nor understood this loose view of the relation between ideas and language. But because Newman held it, he was able to stick to his guns, or to believe himself to be sticking to his guns, throughout his stay in Rome. He could have said, as other converts would have said, that these works had been written while he was an Anglican, that he was no longer an adherent of the theology contained therein, that he had now learnt or was learning truth. He said nothing of the kind. He freely confessed that in details he might have run to extremes, that some language was inaccurate, that he had used *argumenta ad homines* which might be misunderstood. But he was still convinced, and continued to be convinced, that the Roman Church needed his 'philosophical' positions. Only in February 1847 did he at last realize that his hope of founding and leading a new English school of theology was chimerical. In that month he was still writing about the *University Sermons* that after re-reading them he still thought them to be 'as a whole, the best things I have written, and I cannot believe that they are not Catholic, and will not be useful'. He had little sense of breach with his Anglican past (this was partly what rendered his idea of development so unique and personal). He referred to himself not so much in terms of one who has passed from black to white as of one who was a theologian 'lately in another school'. Orestes Brownson, who had rapidly changed from pantheistic Unitarianism to Catholicism, fiercely resented this element in Newman's composition; the element symbolized for Newman himself by the circumstance that the Breviary which he kept by him all his life had been the Breviary of Hurrell Froude; the element which stimulated him to republish his Anglican works during his old age, and which delights the reader of the *Apologia* in the generous portraits of his Anglican friends.

In this personal element, this conviction of self-consistency, he was supported by two immediate reinforcements. He was aware how powerfully the idea of development was still tugging at the heart-strings of some Anglicans. On 18 January 1847, that quaint and talented poet Edward Caswall was received into the Church in Rome after reading through the *Essay* four times. Newman perceived empirical confirmation that his 'philosophical' approach was useful. The second reinforcement was Dr Wiseman. Wiseman was continuing his confidence in Newman. He wrote an encouraging letter urging him not to be perturbed by Brownson's onslaughts ('He is a good man, I believe, but peculiar in his way of viewing things').[1] He continued to hope that Newman might found a theological school, until Newman showed him that the hope was vain. He opened the columns of the *Dublin Review* to defend Newman against Brownson, and enlisted the militant W. G. Ward for the purpose, on the principle that the best defence is attack. From the highest authority in England Newman was receiving comfort to persevere.

This readiness to persevere did not commend itself to the Roman theologians. When Newman complained to the friendly Mazio that Passaglia was lecturing against him, the complaint misfired— Mazio gently defended Passaglia. Mazio and Passaglia had seen that in spite of their criticisms Newman was persistent. They told others that they had tried to discuss it with him and found they could not because he was 'touchy about the book'. Dr Alexander Grant said that the *Essay* was Newman's 'hobby', that he had 'set his mind upon it', and that 'though not at present dogmatically faulty, yet its principles would be condemned by the Church if attention were turned to the subject'. Newman resented Grant's attitude, probably mistaking seclusion for sulkiness and shyness for dislike, and thought his coolness 'quite strange'. He protested to Wiseman, when he heard these Roman complaints, that the charge was unfounded. In early spring the news came of a second explosive article from America. Brownson was shocked that some of the English and American Protestants seemed to be treating an obviously un-Catholic work as Catholic, and was genuinely suffering from the illusion (caused by believing a rumour) that Newman had declared himself to have written the book *ten years* before his reception. Stirred by the echoes of New-man in a book by another ex-Tractarian, and now indignant that Newman had still uttered no public words of retraction, he issued a second manifesto in forcible language—the *Essay* 'deserves to be excluded from every Catholic library for its unorthodox forms of expression, as scandalous, even if not as heretical, erroneous, and rash'.[1]

Newman was now alarmed. In February he had ceased to look forward with any pleasure to the French translations of the *Essay* or the *Sermons*. These had become a worry to him, a new necessity for publicly defending and advocating his theories. He was frightened that one of them might find its way into the Index, and was now hoping that the dilatory M. Gondon would not cease to be dilatory. 'I don't like to begin my career in the Catholic

Church with a condemnation or retractation.'[1] In February he finally gave up the idea of a theological school and turned with decision to the Oratory plan.

There are many persons who can encounter intellectual opposition or even condemnation and cheerfully go their ways. Newman was not one of them. He felt it in his depths. In no one was the thought more the man. Not only the *Apologia* and the *Essay* but nearly everything he wrote has a touch about it of the autobiographical fragment. He always found it difficult to distinguish attacks upon his theology from attacks upon his person. This personal integration was the reason why he suffered such agonies during the later controversies with W. G. Ward and Archbishop Manning, and why he was more pained by the attacks upon the *Grammar of Assent* than would now be thought customary among scholars. As Mazio and Passaglia had discovered, Newman found it impossible to look at his own ideas in the detached and academic spirit of a lecture-room. In this sense, as they had said, he was intellectually 'touchy'. He had devoted his Anglican career and much travail to the proposition that faith was not a bare intellectual assent but a loving and committed response and that conscience was in its measure the guide to truth. That career had not fitted him for discussing detachedly in lecture-rooms.

His low-water mark in Rome, theologically, was the middle of February 1847. In one letter, written in a mood of depression, he seemed to have lost hope for his books. But by the end of February he was recovering. He had failed with Passaglia and Mazio; he had not yet talked seriously with Perrone. He determined, he wrote to Dalgairns, 'to scrape acquaintance with Perrone—whether anything will come of it or not, I don't know'. During the winter he and Ambrose St John had been studying, without enthusiasm, Perrone's course of divinity. They both judged his thought to be 'cut-and-dried', and St John, loyally trying to keep pace with Newman, found Perrone's book 'very dry'. Newman valued the dogmatic course but was contemptuous of Perrone's 'polemics', his ignorance of English affairs and of the Church of England.[1]

On 26 February Newman's diary shows that he called upon Perrone for the first time. In May they met on several occasions.

The new acquaintance was a rapid success. The Roman theologians had never been blind to Newman's earnest spirit. 'I do not know how it is', said Mazio of the *Essay on Development*, 'but so it is, that all these startling things, Mr. Newman brings them round at the end to a good conclusion.'[2] Perrone felt the same. He was ready to take trouble with Newman. In his view of tradition and in his relations with contemporary thought he could find strands which might make a bridge, however rickety, for Newman to pass. On his side Newman, after his winter rebuffs, was a little meeker, a little readier to go half-way. The experience had been salutary. He had come far from that egocentric conversation of November when he had tried to frighten Father Mazio with the bogy that dissent from his books in Roman lecture-rooms would grievously throw back the cause in England. He was now capable of saying 'Give me time to learn: I came to Rome to learn'. He is said to have told a visiting bishop that he was a Protestant when he wrote his essay, that he had no attachment to it, that he was ready to retract any portion of it which authority might require him to retract.[3] Perrone in May met a more teachable Newman than Mazio in November. The acquaintance ripened rapidly, the more rapidly because Dalgairns, who could speak French like the French, arrived in Rome early in May and could interpret Newman's mind. Ambrose St John was soon reporting that Newman had 'struck up quite a close friendship with Perrone. They embrace each other.' Six months later, on St Andrew's Day 1847, even the austere Dr Alexander Grant was ready to invite Father Newman to sing High Mass at the opening of the restored chapel in the Scots College.

Newman had already drafted a number of Latin theses upon faith and reason, with accompanying references to Suarez, Lugo,

Aquinas and others, to show that his theory of faith was capable of being stated in the traditional language of the schools.[1] Sometime during the summer he drafted, for Perrone's comments, Latin theses upon the idea of development. Though the document adds little or nothing to our knowledge of Newman's thought in 1845–7, being a summary of the main ideas of the *Essay*, a summary which is sometimes less cloudy than the original, it is important because it contains Perrone's objections to the thought of the *Essay* and is therefore the only coherent criticism from a Roman theologian at this epoch. Newman did not expect Perrone to provide a constructive or rival statement of his own. He divided each page into two columns, wrote in the left-hand column and (except when he overflowed) left the right-hand column free for Perrone's comments. This procedure, and his introductory letter, prove that he was asking, not for an elaborate statement, but for short notes upon the perils or merits of his language.

Perrone laconically but flatly denied Newman's thesis. Newman's theory depended upon the validity of the analogy between the faith of the individual and the corporate faith of the Church. Perrone absolutely rejected the analogy. In commenting the section upon the faith of the individual, Perrone altogether disregarded the parallels which Newman was seeking to draw. And when Newman asserted that, on occasion, the Church, before a definition, is not *fully* conscious of its mind upon the matter, Perrone simply wrote 'I should not dare to say this'.

The use on the one side, the rejection upon the other, of the analogy with the individual's faith, and consequently the belief in 'awareness' on the one side and 'unawareness' upon the other, carried with it crucial divergences all along the line. Two examples:

(1) How is a definition made?

Perrone thought that, when heresy appears, the local bishops resort to Rome and Rome declares a sentence which makes clear the mind of the Church upon the question. Definition is therefore but a seal of truth, and nothing is new except the sealing. The Church declares its mind, of which it was fully aware before the heresy arose.

Newman thought that, when heresy appears, the mind of the Church has to be *discovered* by meditation, discussion, dialectic, until a definition in accordance with it can be made: and so 'after a difficult childbed, a new dogma is born'. The Church has to reach a recognition of its mind before it can pronounce on the heresy.

Consequently Perrone, like Bossuet, thought a heretic to be an innovator. Newman thought a heretic was a rash and unbalanced inquirer who did not wait for the decision of the Church.

(2) How before a definition is the mind of the Church to be discovered?

In his Latin paper Newman did not resolve the point. He did not attempt to resolve it publicly until his *Rambler* article of 1859, the article with sad consequences for his already ambiguous reputation at Rome. But the implications of his theory, the idea of an *intimus sensus*, the idea that a new dogma is reached after meditation and discussion, seem to demand that by the 'mind of the Church' he must include other churches and even the faithful. The notion of a *magisterium* is 'weaker' in the theory put forward by Newman than in the theory proposed by Perrone.

Newman remained a friend of Perrone and always respected him. But his later history was to show that the critical glosses had not caused him substantially to alter his mind or to abandon his analogy. Perrone had not convinced him because Newman was a historian and Perrone was not. Perrone had no notion of the difficulties created for the older form of the doctrine of tradition by modern historical research. In his Latin paper Newman produced a list of historical instances which (he believed) the old theory could not explain—the validity of heretical baptism,

183

the vacillations of the Fathers about justification, the canon of scripture, the sinlessness of the Virgin Mary, the ante-Nicene language about the Trinity, the doctrine of indulgences, the eucharistic sacrifice. At the end of this list, Perrone serenely commented in his margin 'All these the Church has always held and professed'. How did he know? It was a dogmatic deduction which some inductive evidence from history assailed. Newman, like the Catholics of Tübingen, discerned that the new apologetic must face historical criticism fairly if it was to convince. On the eve of his departure from England, expressing his customary estimate of 'scholastics', he had written to Lord Adare that 'Roman Catholic divines are generally nothing beyond accurate dogmatic teachers—and know little of history or scholarship'.[1] His stay in Rome had raised his judgment upon their dogmatics, but had done nothing to raise his judgment upon their history.

That was why Perrone did not convert him.

# CHAPTER IX

# EPILOGUE

Newman returned to England, to discover with vexation that he still needed to defend himself. The attacks of Brownson had attracted attention: and other, friendlier critics continued to tell him that his doctrine was unsound. He was trying to concentrate upon the building of the Oratory, and for the good of that tender society he wished to avert from it theological suspicion. When seeking to restrain an Oratorian from publishing a book which contained controversial matter, he proffered his own example of silence in the affair of the *Essay*. And to critics he became almost too meek about his work: he would reply (as he had first claimed to Wiseman) that the work was no theological work, it was an external view, a work of philosophy. At the Birmingham Oratory there survives a copy of the *Essay* in which Newman wrote the sentence which marks the low tide of his defence— 'This is the *philosophical* work of a writer who was *not* a *Catholic* and did not pretend to be a theologian, addressed to those who were *not Catholics*.' And in a letter to the *Tablet* of 1852, a letter provoked by Brownson's persistent complaint that in spite of the manifest errors Newman had as yet refused to retract, he confessed publicly that the language in the *Essay* had 'run to the Extreme' of what he thought.[1]

The public utterances of the years between 1847 and 1864, though vague enough, were conservative in their trend and sound, and proved that so far as language was concerned he was trying to use language reconcilable with the views of those who held so vehemently with Bossuet and Perrone. In the *Difficulties of Anglicans* of 1850, in *Discourses on the Scope and Nature of University Education* of 1852, in *Atlantis* in 1858, in the *Apologia* of 1864, he wrote cautiously, not perhaps retracting his theory (though some critics claimed that he had retracted), but expressing the principle so generically and so lacking concrete examples that conservatives could easily accept it. When he was constituting his new Catholic University in Dublin, he held out an olive branch by offering Brownson one of the professorships (that of geography). Brownson did not at first refuse, but the offer was resented by some of Newman's associates, and Brownson was persuaded to withdraw. In 1862 Acton received from Newman a letter which he believed to mark a 'drawing in', in effect a retractation. At least two of the public statements of these years, despite their vagueness, are not easy to reconcile with the *Essay*. The *Apologia* confessed that, though he had not read the *Essay* since its publication, 'I doubt not at all that I made many mistakes in it'.[1]

But once Newman possessed an idea—or rather, as he might have expressed it, once an idea possessed Newman—it was not so easily dispatched. If you take a pencil and paper and analyse every statement about development in the *Apologia*, you find a certain incoherence or self-contradiction, an internal conflict which may be a sign partly of Newman's longing to hold that which is orthodox, that which the Church taught, and yet of his historical and critical conviction that he must not disregard uncomfortable evidence. His note-books show that he continued, though sporadically, to think about the problem. In 1849 he even had a chimerical but passing notion that he would write another book upon the problem if only he could persuade Father Perrone to revise it before it was published. When the definition of the immaculate conception was published in 1854 he collected newspaper cuttings of episcopal addresses which seemed to him to support the principle of development, and Stanton thought it worth retailing to him Roman gossip about the theological differences between Perrone and Passaglia upon the question.[2] But he sought to avoid controversial theology, though he found controversy in plenty. Later in life, in 1866, he sadly pronounced that 'to write theology is like dancing on the tight-rope, some hundred feet above the ground. It is hard to keep from falling, and the fall is great. The questions are so subtle, the distinctions so fine, and critical jealous eyes so many.'[1] For long he kept silence upon the subjects which interested him most.

In 1877 Newman decided at last to revise and republish his *Essay*. After the *Apologia* his personal position was assured and he was no longer a shadowy and half-suspect figure perched on a remote shelf in Birmingham. The events of 1870, and the appeals to the idea of development which various public men had lodged to justify the definition of infallibility, had brought this side of Newman's work back into the public eye. Newman himself had given more balanced statements of the relation between faith and reason, in the *Essay in aid of a Grammar of Assent* in 1870, in his new preface to the republication of his *University Sermons* in 1872, and in his new preface to the republication of *Via Media* in 1877. By 1877 he had republished all his main Anglican works: it seemed natural and appropriate that he should republish the last of them: if, that is, it was an Anglican work.

In the library of the Oratory at Birmingham is the copy of the 1845 edition which he now took into his hands again and read through, read it consecutively for the first time for over thirty years. He took his pencil and made marks against the passages which he disliked: and then pencilled a little note at the beginning —'When now at the end of thirty years I read this anew, I feel there are various statements in it obscure and various that are questionable....'[2] This apparent, preliminary dissatisfaction with the argument leaves almost no trace in the few letters which record the process of revision. To correspondents he allowed that he was dissatisfied with the arrangement, and that the order must be recast; but he continuously claimed, and clearly believed, that he was making no change, or at least no 'substantial' change in the matter and the argument. He did write to Father Coleridge, the editor of the *Month*, asking him whether he had any criticisms to offer upon the language of the *Essay on Development*: and when

Coleridge replied with criticisms about the language on the subject of faith, Newman wrote again—'I have always been aware that some words had to be altered in what I said about faith'. But when he had finished his revising work he wrote to Aubrey de Vere that he had 'done very little to it, except rearranging the portions—which I think an improvement, though it exposes me to the chance of serious mistakes in logic, references, etc. I shall be annoyed if I have made any, for I don't mean to open the book again.'[1] He wrote the preface to the new edition on 2 February 1878, thirty-five years to the day since the delivery of his sermon on development (not a coincidence, I think, for Newman was a man who remembered anniversaries): and in the preface he made the explicit claim that the matter of the book was unaltered.[2]

So far as I know, there is no sign that he was aware of the momentous nature of the step which he was taking. By republishing the book he was claiming for it, quietly but unconsciously, a new and rather more accepted status. It had always been a document of his personal history, an account of his motives for joining the Church in spite of the obstacles presented by his previous theology of *via media*. Now, he removed those parts of the preface which were only intelligible in the light of his personal history. By republishing it he seemed to lend it new status as Catholic theology. In the new preface he allowed that in regard to *historical* judgments he might have conceded too much to the Protestants by way of *argumentum ad hominem*. But doctrinally he showed every sign that he thought it Catholic theology. And the complete absence of strain, absence of any defensive note, can only mean that he was serenely confident in its acceptability as a permissible speculation for a Catholic. By rearranging the book he gave the same impression: for the rearranging of the *Essay* was different in purpose from the clarifying alterations to the *Via Media* and elsewhere among his republications. Many of the revisions which he now adopted were intended to remove a conflict between orthodoxy and the language of the *Essay*.

He conceded in the preface that he might have allowed the Protestants too many concessions of historical fact. It will be retorted that historical fact is the crux. If it is *not* conceded that the papacy is a later development than the episcopate, or if it is still claimed that the Church has always and consciously believed the doctrine of the immaculate conception, then he might as well not have promulgated the doctrine of development. It was facts, brutal historical facts, which clamoured for a theory of explanation, as he had avowed in the *Essay*. Only if you concede the history does the *Essay* matter: and if you start by saying that you only concede the history for the purposes of argument, the *Essay* is puffed away into verbal bubbles. If the papacy is a later development than the episcopate, we need an essay on development. If this cannot be conceded by an orthodox Christian, there is no point in trying to convince him that development has occurred. Newman, it might be said, was almost arguing 'If you believe in development, it will solve your historical problem: but in fact there might be no historical problem—and if so you do not need the theory of development'.

But Newman was fully conscious how the extent of the historical concessions conditioned the nature of the theory. He was asserting, in 1878, that (even if the lowest possible historical concessions are allowed to the Protestants) you cannot account for the historical facts, which every sane and rational man must accept, so long as you cling to the two traditional ways of explaining dogmatic history.

Revising his language in 1877–8, he came nowhere near to changing his language to fit either of the old explanations. He continued to assert a development which was neither translation nor logical inference. The clause in the preface, that the historical concessions might be too many—however gravely it might undermine the appeal to history which was the fortress of the 1845 *Essay*—was therefore doctrinally irrelevant. History, if it did not show all that the Protestants contended, at least showed that development was neither mere translation nor mere logical deduction.[1]

A man who reads a book thirty years after he has written it will dislike some of it and be unable to resist tinkering with numerous sentences. Many, perhaps most, of the changes which Newman introduced in 1878 may be regarded in the light of tinkering: changes which add nothing to the old meaning or water down nothing of the old meaning, sometimes changes (as with all such tinkering) which make no perceptible difference to meaning, style or clarity. The revision of the arrangement makes, as I think, no effective difference in emphasis. In his original manuscript note he had suggested to himself that part of the object of the rearrangement was to lay the stress elsewhere. I do not think that by the mere rearrangement there is any altered stress.[1] Sometimes it is difficult to discern adequate reason for the tinkering. So intricately did he snip with his scissors and paste with his glue that the student who wishes to compare the 1845 edition with the 1878 edition begins to feel as dazed as Father Mazio felt when he first read the *Essay*. Under these conditions it is surprising that only one sentence of the 1845 edition has found its way into two different places of 1878.

A few changes were dictated because in odd places it was patent that the writer of the original essay was still, half-consciously, an Anglican. He excised one or two unfortunate analogies, passages which the recent course of ecclesiastical history had rendered misleading, a passage of temporary interest and now hardly intelligible to the inexpert reader, or historical concessions which he knew to be impermissible to a Roman Catholic. None of these alterations affected the thought of the *Essay*.[2]

The conservative critics, with friendliness or ferocity, had accused Newman—apart from the historical admissions, many of which he was now removing—of a sceptical attitude to human reason, and of admitting antipathy between reason and faith. This charge he had already met in the *Grammar of Assent* and his preface to the *Via Media*, but his revision of the *Essay* carried this rebuttal a stage further by excising or modifying all the more sceptical passages. These modifications carried with them the possibility of a stronger affirmation of the place of logic in theology and therefore in development. In his revision, Newman pushed logic out of the dusty shadows in which it lurks through the 1845 edition. He added new paragraphs asserting the place of reason and of logic in development: but he retained almost all the language which rejected the view that development is only logical inference. The 1878 edition is no more compatible than the 1845 edition with the theories of the logicians. On 5 August 1847 Perrone and Mazio had called on Newman in Rome and during their conversation had drawn his attention to a chief passage about logical explication in St Thomas Aquinas. Newman carefully put the reference in his note-book. But he never used it.[1] The 1878 *Essay* still taught that Christianity was an idea which makes impressions, and that developments are aspects of the original idea slowly elicited: still taught that the Church had been unconscious of truths which she had later defined: still taught (though the fatal phrase of 1845 about additions of doctrine 'external' to it had been removed) that dogma grew by 'incorporation' or 'assimilation'.

The revision showed that from Perrone or from Brownson he had adopted nothing—except perhaps a keener sense of the utility of precise language.[2]

I have tried to describe, and to set in its context within Christian theology, the thought of Newman: the creation of a revised idea of tradition which corresponds within the Roman Catholic Church to those other revisions of the idea of tradition, which the new critical history was forcing upon Christian thinkers. The Roman Church experienced the problem differently, partly because of the apparent need to maintain the idea of infallibility, and partly because, unlike the restatements of the Protestants, the revision was not forced upon her by Biblical criticism. The arrival of historical criticism and a historical sense in European thought transformed the conditions under which theologians were working. And among all their conceptions, the most drastic impact of all hit the accepted theory of authority, and in particular of tradition.

The idea of tradition prevalent in the Roman Catholic Church since the Council of Trent (and indeed since before the Council of Trent) seemed to be rigid and inflexible. In its normal presentation during the eighteenth and early nineteenth century it appeared equally rigid and inflexible. The dominant method of explanation was the explanation associated above all with the name of Bossuet, but in him with all the Gallican school. This method of explanation had once reposed upon, and derived its force from, a particular epoch of critical patristic studies: it had been strong in the seventeenth century because it had appealed freely to history to justify itself as a satisfying account of immutability. And this is why it appeared so rigid in the early nineteenth century: the same method of explanation was being propounded when the historical appeal which once justified it had been transformed by modern historical methods. Nothing looks so ossified in the theology of the nineteenth century as the doctrine of tradition in Newman's critic Orestes Brownson, who was trying to defend an incipient Ultramontanism of the nineteenth century with a theory taken verbally from the seventeenth century, while he disallowed the only historical method which had once sought to justify that theory.

The traditional theory of tradition was less inflexible than it looked. Thomism, out of fashion though it might be in the early nineteenth century, contained ideas of logical explanation: and, since 'logic' is a word which can be used with some breadth (though I fear it should never be used as broadly as Newman tried to use it), this Thomistic mode of explanation concealed under the thinnest of linguistic veils some theories of tradition which amounted to theories of development, which freely admitted historical changes and allowed that the doctrinal definitions of the Church, though new, were equivalent to the revelation.

These more extreme 'logical' explanations—it would be truer to say, these *less* logical forms of the theory of logical explanation —were out of fashion in the early nineteenth century. But as that century wore on, as the needs of Ultramontane apologetic departed more and more from the standards of Gallican apologetic, and as Thomism recovered its influence in the second half of the century, there came a revival of interest in these forms of logical explanation, or at least in explanation with analogies from logic. Where logic ruled, Newman's explanation must be regarded as at least superficial and probably erroneous: for Newman proclaimed the logical explanation to be insufficient, and in so doing admitted the possibility of more drastic change in the history of dogma than Thomism could possibly allow. But the question remains acute for those who still think that logic makes a sufficient explanation: these variations and definitions proved by historical inquiry—in what meaningful sense may it be asserted that these are all implications being logically explicated?

Both the old explanations—clearer language and logical inference—appeared to break down before the new historical sense of the nineteenth century. The Church needed grave caution in accepting the findings of the historians—so much was admitted by every Christian, not only Roman Catholics. Like scientific theories, historical theories were subject to startling revision in the light of later evidence or a more satisfying arrangement of the same evidence: and historical theories were more liable than scientific theories to the corroding influence of prejudice and dogmatism in the mind of the researcher (as Newman was at pains to point out). But to say that historians are frequently wrong, and always prejudiced, always writing from a point of view—this was one thing: to say that historical inquiry must be rejected altogether, that we must never allow it any control, even subsidiary control, in judging the faithfulness of the Church, to say that we must accept religion from the infallible teaching of a present church and dismiss history as the archaeology of private judgment—this is quite another thing. Plenty of Ultramontane apologists took this second line: and not only the proclamations of a good many popular apologists, but even the career of an eminent historian like Pierre Batiffol proves its insidious enchantment in a society afraid of the dissolvent forces of criticism and modernism.

Newman did more than any man to hamper this swing into obscurantism. Many critics have associated him with the anti-historical school, have seen in him the inventor of the supreme dodge to be rid of historical criticism altogether. I have tried to show that this is not an accurate understanding. No doubt a vague, unanalysed, misty appeal to something called 'development' might be utilized by anti-historical apologists seeking to shelter in the arch of a bigger mind than their own. Every thinker suffers from his disciples. Newman of course was no free historical critic. What could the mere intellect do, not only in history but in every intellectual inquiry?—and he glanced restlessly over his shoulder at the ghost of Hume behind him. The moral sense is an instrument for testing and finding truth: and if so, there is no free appeal to history in the sense in which the Baurs and the Harnacks and the Lightfoots understood it. But I have tried to show that, in its measure, there is a genuine appeal to history in his version of the theory of development: and that unless that appeal is recognized the *Essay* is but bubbles. And perhaps this is why Newman—never in any sense Gallican in spite of his Anglican past, always after 1845 a devout disciple of the Pope (though not of the Pope's entourage), even at times an extreme Ultramontane in certain directions—can be said by Acton to have 'blunted the edge of Ultramontanism'.[1]

It has been said that the feat could not have been achieved by a man who was already a Roman Catholic, but only by one who was about to become one, on the ground that liberty of inquiry was needed. This is the kind of speculation which is little profitable and into which I will not enter. But it is certain that, however

Catholic the final result might be, as Father Mazio confessed, he could not have reached that result unless his mind had been open to Butler, to Ward, even to Gieseler. Perhaps a historical consciousness would have entered the Church by some other route—though the issue of the South German historical school, with the departure of the majority into the Old Catholic Church in 1871, does not encourage the idea—but it is certain that Newman and his disciples made a unique contribution to that end. In a way Newman was a prodigy. He was a prodigy because he came to believe in historical development without also believing in liberal philosophies of development. This was what made the *Essay* possible as a contribution to Roman doctrine.

Just as the logicians have to be asked the question how their notion of logical development can be regarded as a meaningful use of the word *logical*, so there is a question still to ask about Newman. Nearly all theologians appear to be agreed that, in accordance with the decree of the Holy Office *Lamentabili* in 1907, it is necessary to maintain that revelation ended with the death of the last apostle. This doctrine of revelation excludes Suarez and Lugo: it probably excludes some parts of the *Essay on Development*. The question then for those who think Newman's theology is Catholic, is this: these new doctrines, of which the Church had a feeling or inkling but of which she was not conscious—in what meaningful sense may it be asserted that these new doctrines are not 'new revelation'?

# NOTES

PAGE 3

1 Featley, *The Romish Fisher caught and held in his own Net* (London, 1624); *A Remonstrance*, f. L, 3; *Refutation of an Answer*, pp. 72–3, 170 ff.; *An Appendix to the Fisher's Net*, p. 46; Thomas Bedford, *Luther's Predecessors* (London, 1624).

PAGE 5

1 N. Alexander, *Hist. Eccl. Saec. I, Praef.*; Mabillon, *Traité des études monastiques* (1691), Pt. II, pp. 219 and 225; Melchior Cano, *De locis theologicis*, lib. XI, cap. 2. And when Mabillon wrote about theological controversy the opponents he had in mind were dominantly historians—the Magdeburg Centuriators, Aubertin, de Dominis, Hospinien, Daillé, Goldast: cf. *Traité*, p. 450.

PAGE 7

1 *Apologie pour Fénelon* (1910), p. 351. Bremond made partial amends to Bossuet later in his life.

PAGE 8

1 See the very important study by Martimort, *Le Gallicanisme de Bossuet* (Paris, 1953); Hallam, *Introd. Lit. Europe* (1839 ed.), vol. IV, p. 135. For an interesting illustration of Bossuet's subsequent attitude to the defence of the *Variations* cf. Le Dieu, *Journal*, 1 March 1700 (vol. 1, p. 22).

PAGE 10

1 *Discours* (ET, vol. II, (1778) p. 280).

PAGE 11

1 H. de Jongh, *L'ancienne faculté de théologie au premier siècle de son existence* (Louvain, 1911); Polman, *L'élément historique dans la controverse religieuse du XVIᵉ siècle* (Gembloux, 1932), pp. 329 ff.; R. Guelly, 'L'évolution des méthodes théologiques à Louvain', *RHE*, vol. XXXVII (1941), pp. 128–30.

PAGE 12

1 T. Harding, *A detection of sundrie foule Errours, lies, sclaunders, corruptions, and other false dealings* (Louvain, 1568), p. 277b; Jansen, *Augustinus* (1643), vol. III, p. 9.

1 *Traité des études monastiques*, Pt. II (1691), pp. 207 ff. To Mabillon's school Melchior Cano's *De locis theologicis* represented the best type of reformed Catholic theology. Mabillon recommended among his books for monastic libraries such a work as Christophe Cheffontaines, *Varii Tractatus* (Paris, 1586) who was arguing against the scholastics a quasi-Greek theology of consecration. The 'chicanerie' of the scholastics, e.g. G. Cortade, *Octave du Saint-Sacrement* (Toulouse, 1661), p. 208 (Cortade was an Augustinian); cited Bremond, *Hist. litt. du Sentiment religieux en France*, vol. 1 (1916), pp. 180 ff.; Laurent Bénard, *Paraeneses chrétiennes* (Paris, 1616), p. 361; and also F. Bonal in Bremond, vol. 1, pp. 310 ff. (though anti-Jansenist in intention). Even the greatest of the theologians seemed somehow to feel the need for an apology for the scholastics before they began their inquiries. Cf. (e.g.) Maldonat (see Saltet, 'Les leçons d'ouverture de Maldonat' in *Bulletin de litt. ecclés.* (1923), pp. 335 ff.; *DTC*, vol. XII, p. 1322); and Petau, *Dogmata Theologica, Proleg.* I. i. I.

This 'neglect' of scholasticism is not identical with the anti-scholastic tone of some of the 'enlightened' theologians of the eighteenth century, though perhaps it was a necessary background for it: for Catholic attacks upon the scholastics in the eighteenth century see among others Benedict Stattler, *Anacephaleosis ad DD. Protestantes* (undated, about 1780).

For Melchior Cano's reputation among the French, cf. N. Alexander, *Hist. Eccl. Saec. XVI*, v, 2, 18; Marín-Sola, *La Evolución homogénea del dogma católico* (3rd ed. Biblioteca de Autores Cristianos, Madrid, 1952), pp. 696-7.

2 Bossuet has a philosophy perhaps: at least it is possible for writers upon Bossuet to discuss his philosophy, though no one suggests that he was an original philosophical thinker. The scholastic method and tradition appears not to play any significant part in his attack upon philosophical problems. It is true that in his library he had editions of Duns Scotus, Aquinas, Bonaventura, as well as of Suarez, Petau, Thomassin. ('La Bibliothèque de Bossuet', in Brunetière, *Bossuet* (1913), p. 208.) But his interest in Scotus and Aquinas is more theological than philosophical. In the controversy with Fénelon he believed it important that scholastic thought supported him. He admired St Thomas Aquinas as an excellent writer: but this is not so much because he was an eminent philosopher as because he was an eminent Augustinian and momentous evidence for the continuity of the Augustinian tradition. Almost his only serious treatment of the question is to quote extracts from Melchior Cano, *De locis theologicis*, VIII. 5 in order to show that theologians might depart from the opinions of the schoolmen without being

un-Catholic. There is indeed a significant difference of emphasis between Bossuet and Cano. Cano distinguished the opinions of the school from their 'certis constantibusque decretis'. Bossuet understands by this second phrase the rule of faith, dogmas defined and declared by the Church. But Cano did not intend to confine so narrowly the judgments of the school which posterity must in bounden duty follow. Cf. Bossuet, *Defensio declarationis cleri Gallicani*, IV, 18. Here Bossuet gave no sign that he knew that he was departing from Cano's mind. But elsewhere he avowed a difference from Cano which amounts to the same thing, cf. *Defensio*, Appendix II, 14. Cano said in effect 'scholae auctoritate res plurimas ab Ecclesia esse definitas'. Bossuet thought that he ought to have said that these doctrines had been defined by the authority of continuous tradition—of which the teaching of the schools is an important part.

### PAGE 16

1 *Traité des études monastiques* (1691), Pt. II, pp. 219, 225.

### PAGE 17

1 *Première Instruction Pastorale sur les promesses de l'Eglise*, XXVIII (*Works*, (1815 ff.) vol. XXII, pp. 418–19).

2 R. Struman, 'La perpétuité de la foi dans la controverse Bossuet-Jurieu' in *RHE*, vol. XXXVII (1941), pp. 145–89.

### PAGE 19

1 Steeped in Augustine's writings, Bossuet often cited the texts of Augustine for this view: *In. Ps.* 54, n. 22; *De dono perseverantiae*, XX, 53; *Confessions*, VII, 19, 25; *De praedestinatione sanctorum*, 27.

See the strong assertions of *Hist. des variations*, XV, no. 134; Bossuet to Leibniz, 28 August 1692 (*Corr.* vol. V, 228–9); *Lettre pastorale sur la communion pascale*, ii: *La tradition défendue sur la matière de la communion sous une espèce*, *passim*; and the argument and text of Struman, p. 159. Cf. also *Premier Avertissement*, 3 (*Works*, vol. XXI, pp. 5–8); *Réfutation du Catéchisme de Ferry* (*Works*, vol. XXIII, p. 204); Bossuet to Leibniz, 9 January 1700 (*Correspondance de Bossuet*, vol. XII, pp. 123 ff.); Struman, pp. 153–4.

Perhaps M. Struman's statement of this question does not do full justice to the inconsistency *in detail* of which Bossuet is guilty. He states the view that heresies have led to clarification in *Première Instruction Pastorale sur les promesses de l'Eglise*, XXXIV ff., esp. XXXV. 'Les hérésies sont venues pour donner lieu à de plus amples explications; et de la foi simple, on vous a mené à la plus parfaite intelligence qu'on puisse avoir en cette vie. Ainsi

l'Eglise sait toujours toute vérité dans le fond: elle apprend par les hérésies, comme disoit le célèbre Vincent de Lérins, à l'exposer avec plus d'ordre,
avec plus de distinction et de clarté.' The same Vincentian passage is used to
the same effect in *Premier Avertissement*, 35, and in *Défense de la tradition et
des saints pères*, VI, 1 ff. In this latter section he admits that there must be
heresies and that they have helped the theologians to clarify their language.
Cf. *ibid.* VI, 2, 'La face de l'Eglise est une, et sa doctrine est toujours la
même; mais elle n'est pas toujours également claire, également exprimée...',
etc., as St Vincent. The uncomfortable fact was that Simon, in charging
St Augustine with innovation, had appealed to 'antiquity'—Augustine's
predecessors—against him. Cf. *Défense*, VI, 4. 'Il faut suivre, dit-il,
l'antiquité. Cela est vrai; mais il y falloit ajouter que la postérité s'explique
mieux, parce que les questions ont été agitées....Il tombe dans l'absurdité de
nous faire chercher la saine doctrine dans les auteurs où elle est moins claire,
plutôt que dans ceux où elle a reçu son dernier éclaircissement; ce qui est
faire à la vérité un outrage trop manifeste.' Cf. *Défense*, VI, 21, where
he is even prepared to quote Petau's principles on the question, and *Défense*,
IX, 21, 'the profit which God can bring to the Church through heresies'.
But this very passage shows that he does not quite mean what was meant by
the normal adherents of the theory of explication...'Ce qui s'étend du
degré et non pas du fond, par comparaison, et non pas en soi; car on trouve en
tous les temps et en gros, dans les Pères, des passages clairs en témoignage de
la vérité———'. In a passage like *Premier Avertissement*, 35 (*Works*, vol. XXI,
pp. 67–9) he came near to St Vincent's thought in the *Commonitory*, I,
22, but Bossuet was not adequately representing the analogy of growth in
*Commonitory*, I, 23, which cannot easily be fitted altogether into the frame-
work in which Bossuet tried to interpret it.

Leibniz raised (11 December 1699, *Corr.* vol. XII, p. 115) the question of the
canonicity of the Apocrypha as defined by the Council of Trent. Bossuet
replied (9 January 1700, *Corr.* vol. XII, p. 126 and 17 August 1701, *Corr.*
vol. XIII, p. 112) by denying that this militated against his argument. He
could show that the doctrine of the canonicity of the Apocrypha was held by
many thinkers in the fourth century, and since we cannot show any point
when it was a novelty we may presume that it was held continuously from
apostolic times. Cf. also Struman, pp. 167 ff.

1 III, 25. For the development see especially Aquinas, *ST*, II. 2. i. 5 ff.; *In
Sent.* III, dist. 25, q. 2, art. i, sol. 3; cf. *In Sent.* III, dist. 13, q. 2, art. 1, ad 6;
*In Sent.* I, dist. 33, i. 5. Durandus of St-Pourçain in *In Sent.* III, 25, 1.

PAGE 28

1 Arriaga, *Disputationes Theologicae*, I, vii (Antwerp, 1643, vol. I, p. 23).

PAGE 32

1 Vasquez, *Comm. in I. D. Thomae*, I, art. 2, disp. v. cap. 3 (Lyons, 1631), p. 15; Andreas Vega, *De Justificatione Doctrina Universa* (Aschaffenburg, 1621), IX, 39, pp. 320 ff.; Lugo (*Opera Omnia*, vol. III, disp. I, xiii, I, no. 257, Venice, 1718, pp. 40 ff.) quotes Melchior Cano, *De locis theologicis*, VI, 8, 10 in support, but the interpretation of Cano's total view is more complex. Cf. Marín-Sola, *La Evolución homogénea del dogma católico*, pp. 696 ff. On the other side E. Marcotte, O.M.I., *La nature de la théologie d'après Melchior Cano* (Ottawa, 1949).

PAGE 33

1 Molina, *Comm. in I. D. Thomae*, I, art. 2, disp. II (Venice, 1602), vol. I, p. 7; James Granados of Cadiz, S.J., *Commentarii in Summam Theologiae Sancti Thomae* (1624), I, i, disp. III, sect. 2, pp. 10–14: cf. Giles de Coninck of Louvain, *De Moralitate, Natura, et Effectibus Actuum Supernaturalium* (Antwerp, 1623), I, disp. IX, dub. 9, no. 126.

PAGE 34

1 Suarez tried to claim the Fathers for this view of faith, *De fide*, disp. VI, 5, 10, basing himself chiefly on the hyperbolical phrase of St Augustine, *Confessions*, VII, 10, 'Facilius dubitarem vivere me, quam esse vera quae audivi', and on a faulty reading in Chrysostom, *Hom.* 21, *In Heb.* XI (*PG*, vol. LXIII, col. 151). Chrysostom wrote almost the opposite of what Suarez supposed that he meant.

PAGE 37

1 Suarez, *De fide*, disp. III, 13; cf. v, i, 2.

PAGE 38

1 *De fide*, disp. v, i, 1.

2 Suarez, *De fide*, disp. II, 6; cf. III, 12.

PAGE 40

1 The most powerful statement against the view that it is *de fide* was presented by Gabriel Vasquez, S.J., in a statement prepared for the Pope and now to be found in the Biblioteca Nacional at Madrid, MS. 8085, fols. 1–25.

1 Bañez's text in *Comm. in D. Thomae*, II, 2, i, 10, 2 (Venice, 1586), cols. 319 ff. The troubles of Bañez were multiplied because the Jesuit house at Valladolid felt anxious to dissociate itself from the theories of the Jesuits at Alcalá. One of its members, Miguel Vasquez of Padilla, was anxious to prove that the Alcalá thesis was not the traditional Jesuit thesis and on the contrary that it was the traditional Dominican thesis. He pointed to Jesuits like Salmeron and Gregory of Valencia as having taught that it was *de fide* that a particular individual was the Pope (cf. Salmeron, *Commentarii in Epist. B. Pauli*, part III, disp. II, (Cologne, 1604), vol. XIII, p. 182; Gregory of Valencia, *Commentarii* (Venice, 1598), vol. III, disp. I, col. 226; and see also Albertinus, *Corollaria Theologica ex tertio principio philosophico* (Lyons, 1610, dedicated to Bellarmine), q. 3, no. 10, pp. 237 ff.); and Suarez, according to his auto-biographical statement, was teaching the same doctrine at Rome as early as 1585, *De fide*, disp. V, 8, 12, *Opera*, ed. Vivès, vol. XII, pp. 164–5. Suarez moved from Salamanca to the chair at Coimbra in 1597, but followed with keen attention the debate of 1602 (in which several of his colleagues were taking leading parts), and he was able to point to a number of eminent Dominicans who had held the contrary—including Albertinus, bishop of Patti (not to be confused with the Jesuit theologian of the same name) in his *De agnoscendis assertionibus catholicis et haereticis* (Rome, 1572), q. 1–3—a work with a decidedly 'static' outlook: Cajetan, etc.; and the list culminated inevitably in Bañez. Miguel Vasquez of Padilla first complained of Bañez before the Madrid Inquisition and the Papal Nuncio, and then (on 7 May 1902) wrote to Cardinal Baronius at Rome, sending him the offending extract from Bañez's *Commentary*, complaining vehemently that it was not fair dealing when the Dominicans, though guilty of the same error, were triumphing and laughing at the imprisonment of the Alcalá Jesuits. (Cf. Serry, *Historia Congregationum de Auxiliis* (Antwerp, 1719), cols. 285 ff.) Baronius seems to have reported favourably on Bañez's text: and the Pope himself, when he read it, appears to have regarded the conclusion as tolerable. According, however, to one authority hostile to Bañez, a Jesuit Father Sarmiento had tried to maintain the opposite of the Alcalá thesis a few years before at Salamanca itself and had been defeated by the reasoning and reputation of Bañez (Meyer, *Historiae Controversiarum de Auxiliis* (Venice, 1742), IV, cap. 36, vol. I, p. 334). The statement needs confirmation, but it is clear that Sarmiento did believe the proposition *de fide* and refrained from maintaining it in order not to cause scandal, cf. the packets of papers labelled *Scripta de thesi a Patribus SJ Compluti propugnata* in Biblioteca Vittorio Emmanuele, MSS. Gesuitici 679. For Miguel Vasquez of Padilla cf. Biblioteca Vittorio Emmanuele, MSS. Gesuitici 678, containing his letter to

Pope Clement VIII and announcement of the forthcoming disputation at Valladolid on 10 July, to prove that Bañez's modification was inadequate: for Bañez's reply to Padilla, cf. MSS. Gesuitici 677.

For the controversy cf. A. Astrain, *Historia de la Compañía de Jesús en la Asistencia de España* (Madrid, 1913), vol. IV, pp. 315 ff. There is an interesting series of documents in MSS. Gesuitici 678–9 (especially 679, *De carceratione PP Complutensium*, 1602).

Bañez journeyed to the court of Valladolid in the middle of June 1602 to make public satisfaction. He published a thesis which half avoided the crucial question: he asserted that though it is not *per se primo et immediate* that a man believes a particular individual to be the Pope, faith makes secondarily such a firm assent to the statement that a denier or doubter would not only be very temerarious and scandalous, but would deservedly be suspect of heresy. On 2 July, at a great concourse of gentlemen and ladies, in the presence of the Constable of Castile and the Papal Nuncio, he presided from the pulpit over a disputation in this sense maintained by a young Dominican. (MSS. Gesuitici 676 contains the thesis maintained—Bañez dedicated a copy to Pope Clement VIII.) The statement contented Rome: but it dissatisfied the extremists in favour like Zumel and Padilla, on the ground that it was ambiguous and consonant with heresy: and on the other side Gabriel Vasquez dismissed it immediately on the ground that he did not know what it meant, cf. his judgment in Biblioteca Nacional at Madrid, MS. 8085, fols. 3–4.

The most important letters to and from Rome will be found in VA Nunziatura di Spagna, vol. LV, fols. 191 ff.; 218–19; 231 ff. (Nuncio enclosing to Aldobrandini a copy of similar conclusions maintained at Saragossa on 7 May 1601); 254 ff.; 295 ff.; 368–9; 423 ff.; *ibid.* vol. LIX, fols. 40 ff.; 252 ff.; 337. Aldobrandini's letters in Nunziatura di Spagna, vol. CCCXXX, fols. 33–4, 40, 42 (at this stage he is calling the conclusions a 'heresy'); 68 ff., 87 ff.; vol. CCCXXXI, fol. 93. Clement VIII's brief to the inquisitor in VA Armarium XLIV, vol. XLVI, no. 221, fols. 216 ff. (19 July 1602). Aldobrandini's letter to Ginnasio of 12 April 1603 drawing the controversy into silence, VL Barberini Lat. 5852.

Cf. also Bañez to Lemos in VA Lettere di Particolari I, 499: to the Pope *ibid.* 502.

VA Fondo Borghese I, 60, 158 appears to be an attempt by some pupil or friend of Vasquez to distinguish for the benefit of the opponents the proposition 'Clement is the true Pope' from the proposition 'it is not *de fide* that Clement VIII is the true Pope'.

In France a similar problem was raised by the Jansenists. The Church has condemned the doctrines of Jansenius. The Church, it was argued by Nicole and Arnauld, may rightfully declare that certain doctrines are erroneous. But it may not infallibly insist that a particular person, e.g. Jansen, taught those particular doctrines, or exact as of *fides divina* the question of fact. Some of the antagonists of the Jansenists undoubtedly sought to prove that the fact, which could only be known by human inquiry, was nevertheless of *fides divina*. Here the Archbishop of Paris, Hardouin de Péréfixe, stepped in to assert that the fact was to be held not *fide divina* but *fide ecclesiastica*. For the arguments over the Five Propositions see especially P. Nicole, *Lettres sur l'hérésie imaginaire* (1664); Nicole, *Traité de la foi humaine* (1664).

PAGE 42

1 Gaspar Hurtado, whose doctoral thesis had caused the original trouble, continued to maintain it, and to maintain that the release of the Alcalá Jesuits was a proof that the opinion was not forbidden (*Commentarii, De fide* Tract. disp. XI, diffic. 13, Madrid, 1632) and that it was 'sana' doctrine. In Spain theology tended henceforth to follow Suarez, e.g. Lugo (*Opera*, vol. III, p. 48) and partially even the Salmanticenses, who on kindred questions were not altogether inclined to follow Suarez and Lugo; cf. *De fide* Tract. 17, disp. 4, 2, 1. Luis de Torres, who had presided at Oñate's original public act, did not recant in his disputations published thirty years later—he remained all his life a vehement adherent of the opinions of Vasquez and a vehement assailant of the opinions of Suarez all along the line: but he concluded on this particular question that it was not now (1634) possible to maintain the Alcalá thesis without scandal, *Selectis Disputationibus*, part I, disp. 35 (Torres had omitted the question from his *Disputationes in II. 2 D. Thomae* (Lyons, 1617) though it fitted naturally into his scheme).

On 4 January 1606 the Jesuit Raphael Gueran maintained at Barcelona an interesting variant of the Alcalá thesis—(it was now the pontificate of Paul V) —that we ought to believe *de fide* that Clement VIII was rightfully elected and was the true Pope; but we believe with moral certainty that Paul V is the true Pope. The Bishop suppressed the debate at the request, it is alleged, of the Dominicans, Serry, cols. 288 and 840. At Granada on 16 June 1614 Father Hyacinth de Soçes, O.P., of the Convent of Santa Cruz, defended the extreme opinion of Miguel Vasquez of Padilla and the Jesuits of Valladolid that the individual Pope was *de fide immediate*. Again the local inquisition prevented the discussion, and appeals by Soçes to the grand inquisitor and to Rome do not seem to have produced any result (letters in Serry cols. 840 ff., Meyer having incredulously denied that the story could be true).

Outside Spain a rather similar debate took place at the general assembly of the Dominicans in Paris in the convent of the Rue Saint-Jacques, near the Sorbonne, 20–28 May 1611: though the thesis was framed more loosely. For the agreement of Lessius at Douai with Vasquez, see his letters to Vasquez of

24 October 1602 and 8 October 1603, cf. F. Scorraille, *François Suarez* (Paris, 1912), vol. I, p. 231: Vasquez's opinion is held in the universities generally, and he is afraid that the opposite opinion will seem like adulation. These letters are now in the S.J. archives of the province of Toledo, *Cod. Belero*, fols. 101, 102: cf. E. M. Rivière, *Corrections et additions à la Bibliothèque de la Compagnie de Jésus*, fasc. III (Toulouse, 1913), p. 858.

2 See especially the theological comments on the Alcalá thesis in Biblioteca Angelica MS. 883, fols. 3 ff. (cf. MS. 895, fols. 179–81) where two commentators (one of them that hammer of the Jesuits F. Peña) try to resist the force of the thesis by claiming that an inference from a *de fide* premise and a natural premise is itself *de fide*. It is observable that Suarez explicitly eschews this method of defending the proposition that it is *de fide* and rests his case upon the infallibility of the Church in *applying* to a particular instance the general proposition which has been revealed explicitly though *in confuso*. *De fide*, disp. X, 5. Lugo (*De virtute fidei divinae*, disp. I, xiii, 5) followed him, though (characteristically) resting upon the general proposition that the universal Church cannot err and the universal Church has received this man as Pope.

## PAGE 43

1 *De fide*, disp. III, 11, 11. '*Confirmatur* primo, quia non est minor auctoritas Ecclesiae quando veritatem definit, quam sit Scripturae sacrae in his quae continet; sed omnia quae sunt in Scriptura, sunt proprie et immediate de fide; ergo etiam omnia quae Ecclesia definit…Denique non solum definit veritates per discursum elicitas ex principiis fidei, sed etiam definit verum sensum Scripturae, et intentionem Spiritus Sancti in his quae revelavit, vel per Scripturas vel per traditionem; ergo signum est habere infallibilitatem proximam et immediatam, ex assistentia ipsius Spiritus Sancti, quae aequivalet revelationi, vel consummat illam, ut sic dicam. Quapropter, licet Ecclesia dicatur non docere novam fidem, quia semper explicat antiquam, nihilominus sua definitione facit, ut aliquid sit nunc de explicita et formali fide, quod antea non erat….' Cf. disp. II, 6, 18 ('An materia fidei successu temporum creverit'), to the effect that the definition with the assistance of the Spirit has 'vis revelationis', in the application of the general revealed proposition to particular and contingent circumstances.

For the private revelation, *ibid*, III, 10.

2 *De virtute fidei divinae*, disp. I, xiii, 1. F. Marín-Sola's *La Evolución homogénea del dogma católico*, which is probably the most able, and perhaps the most influential thesis upon the theory of development written during the twentieth century, is in one of its aspects an attempt to restate the theory of Lugo in such a way that it is not liable to the obvious objections. Amid a

wealth of doctrinal discussion of the most delicate variety, he also put forward a particular historical theory or account of what happened in the seventeenth century.

He assumed that the only true doctrine of Thomism included the following propositions: (1) all 'virtual' revelation is logically implicit, and its explication is an unfolding from within, not the addition of new God-given truths, (2) to be *de fide* it must be proposed by the Church, and it is not *de fide* until the Church has proposed it. He therefore regarded *all* the chief theologians of the Counter-Reformation as departing from the truth—Vasquez and Vega because they believed that an inference could be *de fide* before it was proposed by the Church, Molina and his disciples because they did not think it *de fide* at all, Suarez and Lugo because they were prepared in some sense to countenance additions that could not be called logically implicit. Melchior Cano may have been nearest to his own view: but Melchior Cano's own theory is still a matter of controversy.

Marín-Sola regarded Molina and Suarez as the villains of the piece. Molina had instanced the doctrine of the two wills in Christ as a doctrine which, though theologically certain, could not be said to be revealed (or among the *principia* of the faith) because the Holy Spirit was not given in order that the Church might make new doctrines. Suarez was surprised, even shocked, at this innovation. He therefore postulated three kinds of revelation instead of two: instead of the old explicitly or virtually revealed, Suarez proposed (1) explicitly revealed, (2) revelation *confusa* (the part in the whole, the particular in the universal), and (3) 'virtual' revelation. Both (1) and (2) were *de fide* before definition, (3) was *de fide* only after definition. Marín-Sola thought that by this distinction between revelation *virtualis* and revelation *confusa*, Suarez was transferring the old idea of the logically implicit from 'virtualis' to 'confusa' and thus leaving 'virtual' revelation to mean nothing but revelation of that which was *not* logically implicit in the original revelation. Consequently Suarez needed his theory of an 'equivalence to revelation': consequently Lugo needed his theory of the transforming assistance of the Holy Spirit: consequently the Carmelites of Salamanca, rightly unable to accept the doctrine that what was not revealed could become revealed, denied any possibility that virtual revelation could become *de fide divina*, and so affected adversely, and away from St Thomas, the whole idea of doctrinal development until the nineteenth century.

This historical thesis is in no sense necessary to Marín-Sola's general doctrinal theory. But if we judge it as a historical theory, there is cause to wonder whether the matter is quite so clear and tidy as he suggested. The following questions may reasonably be asked:

(1) Whether the reason for the innovation of Suarez is rightly stated?

Suarez allows that in virtual revelation a new element has come in, much more because he has raised a chasm between divine faith and theology than because he has framed an idea of revelation *formalis-confusa*. The tendency manifest in Suarez and Lugo is primarily the result of the quest for infallible certitude *plus* argument about, and increasing perception of, the human element in many inferences which the Church had in fact made.

(2) Whether the Thomist tradition before Molina was so stable as Marín-Sola needed to imply? Of course all these theologians were 'innovators' because they were the first to probe this particular problem to its depths. But they were not innovators if by that charge is meant that they were departing from a coherent and framed tradition of thought upon the question. All the medieval treatments of the problem touch it casually and haphazardly: so do the earlier Spanish theologians of the sixteenth century like Michael Medina (*Christiana Paraenesis*, Venice, 1564). It is true that the Thomists, with their clearer distinction between the habit of faith and the habit of theology, were more likely than others to accept the view that a proposition by the Church was necessary for virtual revelation to become *de fide*. (Rather similar language even in Scotus, cf. *IV Sent.* dist. 5, q. 1, 6, 5. *Opera Omnia*, ed. 1639, vol. VIII, pp. 285-6.) But the medieval texts upon the question are vague, unsubtle, undefined. Universally they allow that it is error (at least) to deny theological inferences made by the Church: but whether these inferences are *de fide* after definition, or whether they could be *de fide* before definition, are matters which they do not profoundly discuss: and these are the two most essential problems for the framing of a rational theory of development along these logical lines. The most that can be said is that some of the medieval theologians assert explicitly that a man who denies pertinaciously an inference, would be a heretic (e.g. Aegidius Romanus, cf. Marín-Sola, p. 641). But Vasquez would have accepted this statement, because the inference was *de fide*. And theologians like Occam, Gerson, Aureolus, Biel, Dominic de Soto, form a sturdy tradition on which Vasquez and Vega were reposing.

(3) Whether the Carmelites of Salamanca are not charged with too much responsibility? Influential they were. Though affected by Suarez and Lugo, they were certainly denying their view on this point. But in theologians like Coninck they could find a similar standpoint and good precedent for their view. The relatively more static theory of explication so common in the seventeenth and eighteenth centuries, the prevalence among so many thinkers of a denial that theological inferences could ever become *de fide* and the consequent use of conceptions like *fides ecclesiastica*, stem from a wide area of thought—not only from the simple fact that the Carmelites of Salamanca rightly recognized that what had not been revealed through the apostles

could never become revealed subsequently—and carried the recognition to an allegedly erroneous length because Suarez had muddled their minds about the nature of the implicit.

The criticism of the historical part of Marín-Sola's case was illustrated by R. M. Schultes, in *Introductio in Historiam Dogmatum* (1922) and in *Divus Thomas* (1925), pp. 83 ff., 768 ff., and in *Revue des sc. phil. et théol.* vol. xiv (1925), pp. 286 ff.; by G. Martinez ('La solución del Suárez al problema del progreso dogmatico') in *Estudios Eclesiásticos*, vol. xxii (1948), pp. 151 ff.; and cf. M. Flick, 'Il problema dello sviluppo del dogma nella teologia contemporanea', in *Gregorianum*, vol. xxxiii (1952), p. 5 ff.

PAGE 44

1 E.g. Granados, *In* ii. 2. *S. Thomae, De Fide*, tract 7, disp. ii, 2, 13.

An important method of expressing the theory, among Thomists, that only the Church can convert an inference which (though revealed) was not yet historically 'revealed to be revealed' led the theologians of this school to a deepening, and perhaps slight altering, of the old distinction of St Thomas Aquinas between propositions which are 'immediate *quoad se*' but 'mediate *quoad nos*'. 'Immediate' really means self-evident, and to suppose a proposition which is immediate *quoad se* but not yet immediate *quoad nos* appears at first sight to be a self-contradictory idea, as indeed Duns Scotus had held it to be (followed by Molina and Vasquez). But St Thomas and many Thomists have held that with, e.g., mathematical propositions the words are significant. The ramifications of an equation, it might be held, are in one sense self-evident. Yet they need our rational deductions before we can understand them fully. If applied to doctrinal development, the language must mean that the Church (or a theologian) turns what is said to be immediate *quoad se* into what is immediate *quoad nos* by making us see the necessary consequences of that which is indeed self-evident to us so that these necessary consequences become as self-evident as the truths on which they repose.

The principal difficulty of the language is its application to the problem whether a theologian, or only the Church, can make a theological conclusion *de fide*. The distinction between *fides acquisita* and *fides divina* led some Thomists to argue that a proposition originally immediate *quoad se* but mediate *quoad nos* became immediate *quoad nos* only by the definition of the Church, because it was now known, no longer by rational argument, but by the simple assent of divine faith. But if this is so, it appears to be removing the real point of the original idea that 'mediate' propositions were logically implicated in 'immediate' propositions. Immediate *quoad se* had meant $x + y = a$: mediate *quoad nos* had meant $2x + 2y = 2a$. If the latter (or what is alleged to correspond to it in doctrinal explication) is calculated by an individual theologian, he may either regard the new consequence as *now* an immediate self-evident proposition: or he may continue to say that it is mediate but self-evident when 'worked out'. On a strict logical view the Church cannot do more. If the Church is thus capable of turning mediate into immediate, so is the individual thinker. If on the other hand it is claimed that a definition makes what was not immediate *quoad nos* into that which is immediate *quoad nos*, then the implicated proposition is no longer in any sense *self-evident because it is implicated*, and was therefore in no meaningful sense immediate *quoad se* before the Church made it immediate *quoad nos*: unless this whole language is regarded, not as truly explaining a logical development, but simply as another and particularly complex way of asserting what it is desired to assert, that only the Church can make a deduction *de fide*. Duns Scotus was using the term *nota per se* in a significant sense. Its use by some of the Thomists appeared at times to make more confusing what they were seeking to make clear. However, for a very stout and able defence of the usage, see Marín-Sola, pp. 305 ff. For formally expressed but acute criticism, cf. G. Huarte in *Gregorianum* (1925), vol. VI, pp. 139 ff.

On the other side of Vasquez, the school of Molina, with its strongly static sense of an unchanging revelation, ran into difficulties over the nature of the certitude provided by the definitions of the Church. They were driven, eventually, to postulate a kind of faith called *fides ecclesiastica*. Molina, who did not think the Church could make its deductions into part of the revelation, nevertheless believed that on account of the Church's inerrancy, those deductions were certain. They were thus believed, not by *fides divina* but by *fides ecclesiastica*. For the development of the idea of *fides ecclesiastica* cf. especially Marín-Sola, pp. 440 ff. The idea is integral to the whole school represented by Molina, and begins to appear among his defenders like Granados (*Comm. in S. T. Sancti Thomae*, I, i, disp. III, sect. 2, p. 10 ff.)—faith in the deductions is so near to divine faith that it may be called *fides humana certissima*. In the Jesuit Becan (*Summa Theologiae Scholasticae*, part III, *Tractatus* I, *De virtutibus theologicis* cap. VIII, 8 (Paris, 1634), p. 583; *De fide*, 8, 8) it is of divine faith to believe the articles of the faith because God has revealed them: to believe them because the Church teaches them is to believe with a faith which is *nec pure divina, nec pure humana, sed quasi media*. This view became canonized as *fides humana* in the mandate of 7 June 1664 by the Archbishop of Paris, Hardouin de Péréfixe (cf. Gerberon, *Histoire générale du Jansenisme* (1700), vol. III, pp. 96–8, and the subsequent attack by Pierre Nicole, published 20 August 1664, *Traité de la foi humaine*). For the Scotist sharing in this view of *fides humana*, cf. Mastrius de Meldola, *Disputationes Theologicae in III. Sent.* vol. III (Venice, 1698), pp. 335–6. For a recent treatment of *fides ecclesiastica*, cf. F. G. Garcia, *Estudios teológicos en torno al objeto de la fe y la evolución del dogma* (Publicaciones de la Sociedad Internacional Francisco Suarez, 1953).

If *fides humana* meant 'moral certainty' and had nothing to do with *fides divina*, why had the Church acquired this power of compelling the faithful to adhere to it? It seemed clear that a man who denied what was of *fides humana* could not be accused of heresy. In more recent times one school of theology has sought to elevate it a little nearer *fides divina* by calling it 'supernaturally certain'. It is not clear what precisely is meant. To distinguish between what is 'supernaturally certain' and what is of *fides divina* appears to be near to a distinction without a difference. To say that 'it is as humanly certain as an unrevealed proposition can be' is to imply degrees of certainty, and perhaps come near to making 'certainty' into 'a very high degree of probability'. The difficulty into which the distinction has led some theologians is shown, e.g., by Quilliet's article in *DTC*, s.v. *Censures doctrinales*. He argued that a theological deduction from the revelation presents 'un caractère de surnaturelle certitude', but is not doctrine 'formellement et immédiatement révélée de Dieu'. It is difficult to deny that a doctrine is revealed and simultaneously to attribute to it 'supernatural certainty'. Nor is he resting upon the word *immédiatement* and claiming that it is revealed mediately. For he proceeds to argue (rather in the tradition of Molina and Granados) that even after definition by the Church it 'exigera l'adhésion surnaturelle des intelligences fidèles' in obliging them to hold it as true, but not to believe it to be revealed by God. And if a man denied a deduction which had been thus defined, he would not certainly be a heretic (but only a teacher of erroneous or temerarious doctrine). Such a man would not be denying the infallibility of the Church; since it is not yet defined (though it is 'supernaturally certain'—the phrase again) that the Church is infallible when it makes theological inferences from two premises of which one is not revealed.

All this appears to amount to an attempt to deny that the deduction is virtually revealed and yet to assert that it is certainly true. Of course there are many things which are not virtually revealed and yet are certainly true, e.g. two plus two equals four. But this theory is not asserting that it is certainly true in the sense in which a mathematical proposition is certainly true, for the deduction is 'supernaturally certain'. There appears to be little meaning in the phrase (when distinguished from 'virtually or implicitly revealed') except to assert that the major premise in the syllogism is revealed. The deduction in fact has a far higher degree of probability because one of its premises is absolutely certain, being revealed by God. Thus 'supernaturally certain' appears only to mean 'Since the revelation is known to be true, there is a very high degree of probability that proposition $x$, which natural reason connects with the revelation, is also true.' And it does not seem to help here to introduce the idea of the infallibly assisted Church, in order to turn this high degree of probability into a genuine certainty. For the nature of this infallible assistance in such a matter is not defined, but is only 'supernaturally certain'—which amounts again to a very high degree of probability based on a syllogism of which only one premise is (believed to be) revealed.

This kind of language surely shows that (given these notions of revealed certitude) there was no satisfactory standing-ground other than a theory like that of Vasquez, which makes true deductions *de fide* without definition, or a theory like that of Suarez, which takes definitions so seriously that it must admit their 'equivalence' to revelation.

## PAGE 47

1 *Disp. Theologicae in 2.2 D. Thomae*, vol. v (Antwerp, 1649), disp. 6 and 11, 4: cf. 3, 1 and 4, 7, 8. It is also to be observed that Arriaga's principles about 'private revelations' force him to suppose that he who disbelieves a private revelation made to himself (if true) is guilty of heresy, though not liable to its penalties.

2 For the Carmelites, see *Collegii Salmanticensis Cursus Theologicus* (ed. 1879), vol. xi, disp. i, 4, 3, and 7. The individual's inference is not *de fide* (*contra* Vasquez): the only true implicit revelation is what Suarez had called *formalis-confusa*, especially in the application of the revelation to a particular. The Church never defines, and cannot define as a dogma, what is not revealed in scripture at least *confuse et implicite*. But the writer (here John of the Annunciation) appears to be guilty of illogicality in his application of these positions to dogmatic facts, see esp. disp. iv, 2, 23 ff. (vol. xi, pp. 261 ff.). Contrast pp. 267–9 with p. 273 on the *hostia*. Further the distinction here made between the proposition 'I believe that *x* is *de fide*', and the proposition 'I do not believe it is *de fide* to believe that *x* is *de fide*', and the contention that these positions are in the last resort compatible, leads to remarkable consequences. For the Scotist tradition see especially Mastrius de Meldola (died 1673), *Disputationes Theologicae*. Mastrius was not uninfluenced by Lugo, but is ultimately more static in his outlook, cf. his important discussion on the nature of a theological conclusion, *In III. Sent.* disp. iii. 12, vol. iii (Venice, 1698), pp. 332 ff. For other Scotists, John Ponce, *Theologiae cursus integer ad mentem Scoti* (ed. novissima, Lyons 1671): Cardinal Brancatus de Laurea, *Comm. in III. Sent. Scoti* (Rome, 1673). Ponce helped Wadding and others to edit the works of Duns Scotus (Lyons, 1639). Cf. Caylus, in *Études franciscaines*, vol. xxv (1911), p. 633: *DTC*, s.v. *Mastrius*. The tradition was being continued into the eighteenth century by the Spanish friar Antonio Perez (died 1710), cf. Hurter, *Nomenclator*, vol. iv[3], pp. 675–6.

PAGE 48

1 Cf. e.g. Marín-Sola, p. 279. 'En la definición de la Iglesia el razonamiento precede, pero no influye *formalmente* en la definición; la definición, aunque no se hace sin razonamiento, no se hace *por razonamiento*. A la definición antecede una menor, pero es mera precedencia material, sin influencia *formal* en la definición. La definición sucede y sigue a la menor, pero sin lazo formal con ella: *no es conclusión de esa menor*' (italics original).

In recent times a somewhat different description of the place of logic has won some favour, along these lines. The development is asserted to be strictly logical, strictly an inference. But the Church, or the theologian, cannot perceive, or cannot always perceive, the logical connection until afterwards. Though the definition occurs without conscious inference, we look back subsequently and we see that it was a strictly logical explication. For this view see, e.g., C. Boyer in *Gregorianum*, vol. XXI (1940), p. 265; T. Zapelena, *Gregorianum*, vol. XXV (1944), pp. 262 ff. But can we always perceive it afterwards? Or is the perception itself also a kind of act of faith? For Mgr Charles Journet, the perception is itself an act of faith: the explication must be asserted to be 'rigorously logical', but the inference is discerned itself in 'the night of faith' (*Esquisse du développement du Dogme Marial* (Paris, 1954), pp. 53 ff.). Alternatively, it is suggested by Clément Dillenschneider (*La sens de la foi et le progrés dogmatique du mystère marial*, Rome, 1954) that though the logic of the development is not perceivable by the human mind we ascribe to it 'a higher logic', a kind of logic in God's sight but not man's.

The difficulty of these assertions is that they appear to remove the utility from the logical explanation. The development must be asserted by faith to be logical though we cannot always see how. This is not using the words 'logical explanation' in a meaningful sense; except to assert 'definitions do not (in spite of appearances) change the unchanging revelation: how this is we cannot see, but logical explication makes a good illustrative analogy how such a thing may be without being self-contradictory'. In the case of Dillenschneider the language expresses a recognition of the traditional importance, but nevertheless the inadequacy, of the logical language, while his real case rests upon 'la sens de la foi', in effect Newman's *intimus sensus*.

PAGE 49

1 The list changed. At an earlier period of his life he had regarded all Cicero as genuine.

PAGE 50

1 *Prolegomena* (1766), III, 19: the seven writers were Salmeron, Vasquez, Suarez, Bellarmine, Lapide, Raynaud, Petau. For Virgil, etc., see *Pseudo-*

*Virgilius* (1733), pp. 282, 292; *Pseudo-Horatius* (1733), p. 336. For the general theory cf. *Doutes proposés sur l'âge du Dante*, ed. 1847 (*Mémoires de Trévoux*, 1727); *Chronologiae ex nummis antiquis restitutae prolusio de nummis Herodiadum* (1693); *Chronologia Veteris Testamenti* in *Opera Selecta* (1709), pp. 513 ff.; *Athei Detecti* in *Opera Varia* (Amsterdam, 1733); above all the *Prolegomena*, published at London in 1766 with a preface by William Bowyer. See the criticism in Cellarius, *A Dissertation against Hardouin* in Court's *Josephus* (London, 1733), pp. 873 ff.; *Mémoires de Trévoux* (1734), pp. 77 ff., 306 ff.; *ibid.* (1709), pp. 163 ff. Cf. F. W. Bierling, *De Pyrrhonismo historico* (Leipzig, 1724). All the relevant works of Hardouin found their way, successively, to the Index. In December 1708, after various hostile claims that Hardouin was a spearhead for a conspiracy by the Society of Jesus, his superiors published a disavowal by the Society and a recantation signed by Hardouin: and Hardouin's own colleagues, especially Tournemine, continued to attack the theory consistently. But it is evident from Hardouin's sense of prophetic inspiration that no recantation could mark more than a temporary change in his opinions.

PAGE 51

1 For d'Olivet's views, cf. the hostile remarks of the Marquis d'Argens, *La philosophie du Bon Sens*, vol. III, pp. 168 f. He held that Cicero, whom he edited, and the *Timaeus* were genuine, but does not otherwise appear to have been confident about the works of the Greek fathers. Through the modified version of Berruyer (for whom see below) the sceptical views affected a certain number of the clergy—so at least the assailants believed, cf. *Requeste des curés du diocèse de Rouen à M. leur archevêque* (1764), p. 36. Among the Stonyhurst College MSS. is a list of Hardouin's supporters, or partial supporters, among the French Jesuits, in a report sent to Rome, A, III. 27, fol. 4. Among them is the eminent astronomer Mahoudeau. The most spectacular is François de la Pillonnière, who subsequently took refuge in Holland and England and became tutor in the household of Bishop Hoadly. The report in Stonyhurst College MS. A, III, 27 attributes his secession to the influence of Hardouin. His own apologia or quasi-autobiography shows that, after being unsettled by Hardouin, he went to the opposite extreme and became a vehement disciple of Malebranche: and that the immediate intellectual cause of his departure was the principle of Cartesian doubt which led him to study Boyle and Grotius, cf. F. de la Pillonnière, *An Answer to the Reverend Dr Snape's Accusation* (London, 1717), with preface by Bishop Hoadly. Pillonnière possessed the kind of mind which, though courageous, is unstable in the sense of easily shifting its ground, and yet is a warm and vehement defender of each successive position which it holds. His apologia, though not published

until some nine or ten years after his conversion to Protestantism, is drawn from a manuscript which he composed for his own defence soon after he left the Roman Catholic Church, and of which another large section was published (without his permission) by his friend Hyacinthe Cordonnier in *Mémoires littéraires* (La Haye, 1716), vol. I, pp. 403 ff., under the title *L'Athéisme découvert par le R. Pére Hardouin, jésuite, dans les Écrits de tous les Pères de l'Église et des Philosophes modernes*. It is a most interesting, and without doubt in substance an authentic portrait of the way in which a fairly reasonable though easily led young student could little by little come to accept the bizarre theories of Hardouin. Cardinal de Bissy, *Instruction pastorale*, has been claimed as a backer of Hardouin, but without any sufficient reason.

PAGE 53

1  F. de la Pillonnière, *An Answer to the Reverend Dr Snape's Accusation*, pp. 12–13. It is also certain that Richard Simon's dislike of Jansenism, and his convinced Molinist ideas, were the reasons why he wrote so irreverently about Augustine in his *Histoire des commentateurs*: and cf. *Lettres choisies*, vol. II, p. 233: and Molien in *DTC*, vol. XIV, col. 2112. He likewise admired Petau.

The seed of this line of defence can be seen even in very early anti-Jansenist works like Petau's *De la pénitence publique* of 1644, in which he was challenging Arnauld's appeal to the practices of the primitive Church. But only after *Unigenitus* was the argument beginning to be 'theological' rather than 'practical' in its implications, cf. for example the *Instructions Pastorales* by Languet (Bishop of Soissons and then Archbishop of Sens), e.g. *Première Instruction Pastorale* (1718), XLV and LXVII–LXVIII. (Cf. also *Lettres écrites à un ami sur les disputes du Jansénisme*, p. 7: 'Strictly speaking the Church does not need the witness of antiquity to establish truth, and in consequence the perpetuity of its faith. Its own witness is sufficient...'; quoted by Hardouin, *Prolegomena*, ix.) The Abbé Longuerue half-excepted Languet alone from a very sweeping judgment upon the low standard of scholarship among the bishops of his time, *Longueruana* (1754), p. 275.

PAGE 54

1  Rancé, *Réponse à Mabillon* (1692), pp. 46 ff. Mabillon conscientiously went through the long catalogue in replying to this odd charge, *Réflexions*, pp. 355 ff. Rancé was not without support even among learned Benedictines, cf. Claude de Vert, *Explication du chap. 48 de la règle de S. Benoît* (1693); and *Mémoires de Trévoux* (1708), pp. 1352 ff. The English parallels to this anti-rational trend are to be found in such writers as Thomas Baker, *Reflexions on Learning* (1700), and Edwards, *Some new Discoveries of the Uncertainty, Deficiency and Corruptions of Human Knowledge* (1714); Dryden's *Religio Laici* has

something of the same purpose. In another English work, Henry Dodwell's *Christianity not founded upon argument* (1742), the fideist trend of thought reached its theological and paradoxical apogee. We find an equally extreme variety of fideism in Germany as early as 1676, in Jerome Hirnhaim, who was general of the Praemonstratensians, *De Typho Generis Humani*, published at Prague: (C. S. Barach, *Hieronymus Hirnhaim, Ein Beitrag zur Geschichte der Philosophisch-Theologischen Cultur*, Vienna, 1864). Cf. La Pillonnière, *An Answer to the Reverend Dr Snape's Accusation*, p. 10: Hardouin 'cautioned me vehemently and passionately against Reason, begging me to fly from it as from the Plague, and making Rapturous Exclamations upon the unspeakable blessings of Orthodoxy, and Blind Faith': and C. J. Develles, *Traité de la simplicité de la foi* (Paris, 1733), and *Mémoires de Trévoux*, vol. CXXXII, pp. 2094 ff.

## PAGE 57

1 Thomassin, *La Méthode d'étudier et d'enseigner chrétiennement et solidement les lettres humaines* (1681–93): Huet, *Quaestiones Alnetanae* (1690), of which the argument, crudely, is that whatsoever in Christianity is unusual, is confirmed by the consensus of antiquity and of the sages. The thesis was at its oddest in G. de Lavaur, *Conférence de la fable avec l'histoire Sainte* (1730), where Niobe is Job, Jason Joshua, and the Argo is the ark of the covenant. Faydit (a vehement and eccentric Cartesian, 'qui avoit', said Longuerue, 'de l'esprit et du savoir, mais un peu fou'), *Remarques sur Virgile et sur Homère* (1705 and 1710), sought to prove that the theology of Homer and Virgil was more orthodox than that of the Socinians and even on some points than that of Malebranche: cf. Monod, *De Pascal à Chateaubriand*, (1916) pp. 258 ff. Richard Simon took the trouble to refute much of this, *Bibl. crit.* II (1710), cap. 32.

For the relation of China to this, see Pinot, *La Chine et la formation de l'Esprit philosophique en France* (Paris, 1932), and for the kind of argument thus produced, see de Prémare, *Vestiges des principaux, dogmes chrétiens tirés des anciens livres Chinois* (which, however, remained in manuscript until 1878); for Persia, Hyde's *Historia religionis veterum Persarum* (1700); for the Indians, L. Hontan, *Nouveaux Voyages dans l'Amérique septentrionale* (1703); for Mahomet, especially Reland, *De religione mohammedica* (1705).

Even as early as 1666 you find the argument of consensus which Thomassin was to carry through so remarkably. P. Beurrier, in *Speculum Christianae religionis in triplici lege*, argued that the different religions of the world are the mirror of the Christian religion, and that primitive Chinese religion contains all the fundamental Christian dogmas. In his memoirs (cf. Pinot, pp. 202 ff.) he tells us that having to convert an anti-Christian philosopher at the hour of death, he succeeded in proving to him that all the philosophers and sages of the heathen—Zoroaster, Trismegistus, Orpheus, Pythagoras, Plato—have recognized the doctrine of the Trinity and that Trismegistus prophesied the Incarnation.

The English parallels to Thomassin are to be found chiefly among the Cambridge Platonists like Cudworth.

2 Huet to Martin, 19 January 1705; cf. Bartholmèss, *Huet ou le scepticisme théologique* (1850), p. 30.

PAGE 60

1 Jean Leclerc published the second edition of Petau's *Theologica Dogmata* at Antwerp in 1700, under the pseudonym *Theophilus Alethinus*. In *Bibliothèque universelle*, x, and *Epistolae criticae et ecclesiasticae*, vii, Leclerc launched an attack upon the Platonic influence in the Fathers. He was answered by the Jesuit Father Baltus, *Défense des Saints pères accusez de Platonisme* (Paris, 1711): and cf. *Mémoires de Trévoux* (April 1711), pp. 582 ff.—the controversy centring upon Clement of Alexandria, Justin Martyr, and Augustine. Baltus put as the motto for his book Tertullian's *Quid Athenis et Hierosolymis? Quid Academiae et Ecclesiae?* It is significant that Baltus was almost the only Jesuit to approve of Huet's treatise *Of the Weakness of Human Understanding*: and Huet likewise approved of Baltus' defence of the Fathers, cf. Bartholmèss, *Huet ou le scepticisme théologique*, pp. 47–8. Baltus continued in 1719 with *Jugement des saints pères sur la morale de la philosophie paienne*.

For the Socinian use of Petau, see e.g. Sandius, *Enucleatae Historiae Ecclesiasticae* (1669), lib. i, pp. 217–18; Hermann Cingall (which was a pseudonym of Johann Crell) *Scriptura S. Trinitatis Revelatrix* (Gouda, 1678), pp. 30–2; Daniel Whitby, *Disquisitiones Modestae in Clarissimi Bulli defensionem Fidei Nicenae* (1718), p. iv; and for a particular Socinian attack upon the Platonism of the Fathers and their Trinitarianism, see M. Souverain, *Le Platonisme dévoilé* (Cologne, 1700): and, in defence, the Jesuit M. Mourgues, *Plan théologique du Pythagorisme* (Paris, 1712).

Hardouin, who spent all his adult life at the college in Paris where Petau had worked, certainly had Petau's MSS. under his eye, cf. Sommervogel's examples in *Bibliothèque de la Compagnie de Jésus*, vol. iv, col. 91, no. 33. His edition of Themistius also (1684) is based upon Petau's edition.

Huet knew, admired and was a pupil of Petau, cf. Huet's *Mémoires*, ET (1810) by John Aikin, vol. i, p. 54. For Huet, Petau 'recalled theology from the frivolities and fetters of the schools to the open fields of the ancient Church, trodden by the feet of the ancient Fathers'. There are charming pictures of him in these memoirs and in *Longueruana* (1754), pp. 66–7.

The legend that Petau was forced to retract, and (in the more colourful version) did so because, as he said, he was now too old to change his lodgings, appears to be baseless. (See especially P. Galtier, 'Petau et la Préface de son De Trinitate', in *Recherches de science religieuse* (1931), pp. 462 ff.; and J. Vital-Chatellain, *Le Père Denis Petau* (Paris, 1884), p. 407.) It has sometimes been alleged that du Perron in his *Reply to King James I* anticipated Petau in thus weakening the authority of the Fathers, e.g. Lord Acton, *History of Freedom and other Essays*, p. 592. It is true that du Perron freely admits of individual ante-Nicenes that their language has strayed, e.g. that the historian Eusebius was an Arian. But nowhere are the same admissions heaped together as by Petau, for du Perron has not the particular motive which led Petau to heap them together. William Chillingworth had charged du Perron with damaging admissions about these early Fathers (cf. *Preface to the Author of Charity Maintained*, sections 16–18, *Works*, vol. I, pp. 18–20): and later in the century, when the Socinians had taken to using Petau, Anglican writers who were familiar with Chillingworth assumed that du Perron was a sort of early version of Petau, e.g. Tenison, *The Difference between the Protestant and Socinian Methods* (1687), pp. 21 ff. No doubt there is a relation between the readiness of both to make their admissions. No doubt also both writers are fundamentally conservative in their theories of doctrinal tradition. The nearest du Perron approaches to a theory of development may be found in *Replique au Roy* (ed. 1622), pp. 632–3, especially, in arguing that we should appeal to the Church of the fourth and fifth centuries rather than the Church of the third and fourth centuries:

> Though the doctrine was no purer, it was much more formulated, investigated, elaborated: and consequently it was much more suitable as a model for modern societies which claim to be its successors. The earlier centuries, though they believed confusedly and implicitly the same doctrine, had not expressed it with the same distinction and clarity....If anyone had asked Arius or Eutyches to submit himself to the judgment of the Church in the centuries before Constantine or Marcion respectively, he would have had no difficulty.

For du Perron in general, see a useful study by R. Snoeks, *L'argument de tradition dans la controverse eucharistique entre catholiques et réformés français au XVIIᵉ siècle* (Louvain, 1951). Longuerue's very unfavourable judgment of du Perron's scholarship ('avoit plus de fanfaronnade que de savoir') is quite unjustified, cf. *Longueruana* (1754), pp. 11, 276.

You find 'Ultramontane' opponents of Bossuet's Gallicanism using kindred language to that of du Perron to defend the Papacy against the Articles of 1682: e.g. Charlas, *Tractatus de libertatibus ecclesiae Gallicanae* (1684), VI, 3, 13. 'Truth, like the sun, before showing itself to our eyes, begins to send a half-light which...grows bit by bit to high noon. Although the monuments of antiquity do not show with extreme clarity certain truths which afterwards, when studied and examined with greater care, find at last their full light, or at least a greater light, nevertheless we should not despise these first *vestigia*, particularly when they are obvious.' Cf. A. G. Martimort, *Le Gallicanisme de Bossuet* (Paris, 1953), pp. 609 ff.

PAGE 64

1 *Réflexions*, Pt. II, pp. 76–8. There is an important series of reviews of Honoré in *Mémoires de Trévoux* (1713), pp. 1305 ff. (1722), 1991 ff., 2033 ff.

PAGE 65

1 Tillemont was still clinging to tradition surprisingly often. He made a life of Timothy on the acts which Bollandus had given in *Acta Sanctorum*, though he thinks that the author is an Ephesian ecclesiastic who lived in the fifth or sixth century: cf. Honoré's criticisms, vol. I, pp. 170–1; and cf. vol. II, p. 264: 'His first volume would not be long if you removed from it all the evidence about the Virgin, St John Baptist and the other apostles which is given you by the Fathers and not by scripture.'

PAGE 68

1 *De veteribus haereticis ecclesiasticorum codicum corruptoribus*, pp. 571 ff., 591–2, 624–5. Hardouin thought it worth while defending Germon from the attack that the acknowledgment of corruption in the Fathers logically led to the possibility of corruption in the scriptures: cf. *Prolegomena*, v. The argument of Germon was not in detail new. The case of Hermas had already been a matter for controversy between Labbe (*De scriptoribus ecclesiasticis* (Paris, 1660), vol. I, p. 431) and Cotelier and Natalis Alexander. Possevinus, *Appar. sacer* (1603), vol. I, p. 327, s.v. *Clemens*. But Germon was the first to make a systematic apology out of it.

Germon's attack upon Mabillon's *De Re Diplomatica* was in three parts, 1703–7, and largely influenced Honoré's attack upon Mabillon's alleged 'Subjectivism'. There were other assailants of the *De Re Diplomatica*, notably G. Hickes, *Thesaurus Linguarum Septentrionalium* (Oxford, 1705), but these were standing on grounds less doctrinaire than those of Germon. For the bibliography of the whole controversy see especially Sommervogel, *Bibliothèque*, etc. s.v. *Germon*. The principal supporter of Germon was the historian of the controversy, Lallemant, *Histoire des Contestations sur la*

*Diplomatique* (1708). We know from the memoirs of Bossuet's secretary Le Dieu that Mabillon privately thought Germon's attack 'very feeble' (Le Dieu, *Journal*, 16 January 1704, 1928–9, vol. II, p. 189).

PAGE 69

1 E.g. Hurter, Funk. For Schelstrate cf. Batiffol in *DTC*, s.v. *Arcane*: Vacandard in *DHGE*, s.v. *Arcane*. The theory in its crudest form may be found in Merlin, *Traité historique et dogmatique sur les paroles ou les formes des sept sacrements de l'Eglise* (1745). See J. P. Migne, *Theologiae cursus completus*, vol. XXI (1841), pp. 119 ff. Cf. also P. de Vallemont, *Du secret des mystères ou l'apologie de la rubrique des missels* (Paris, 1710). Schelstrate had first uttered the doctrine in *Antiquitas illustrata* (1678) and *Sacrum Antiochenum concilium* (1681). Tentzel replied with *Dissertatio de disc. arc.* (Wittenberg, 1683). Schelstrate's *De Disc. arc.* was the answer to Tentzel. Tentzel replied, and a general controversy ensued in which the English Bingham participated, *Antiquities*, VIII, viii, 6.

Schelstrate was a friend and correspondent of Mabillon, see E. de Broglie, *Jean Mabillon et la Société de l'abbaye de S. Germain-des-Prés* (1888), vol. I, pp. 411 ff.; vol. II, pp. 32, 44. For the way in which the public wrongly regarded him as the 'inventor' of the notion of *Doctrina Arcani*, cf. *Longueruana* (1754), p. 77.

2 *Réflexions*, vol. I, pp. 288–9. The reform of the liturgy, which many French bishops were at this period undertaking in their dioceses, was a particularly thorny battlefield between conservative and scholar, since some of the critical revisers, influenced by St Maur, etc., wanted to remove elements in the liturgy which seemed to them the product of excessive credulity. How severe a strain the unreformed Breviary could impose upon the scholarly may be seen by remarks like that of the Abbé Longuerue, 'Quand je lis les Légendes du Bréviaire, il me semble lire un roman', *Longueruana* (1754), p. 239.

PAGE 70

1 Just as, a century later, the anti-intellectualism in the philosophy of Lamennais and the Ultramontanes is paralleled by the attempt to replace the work of Ruinart and others with the less critical productions of men like Guéranger.

The anti-intellectualism of Rancé in regard to monastic studies can be paralleled many times over from writers dealing with general studies. Cf. Laubrussel, 'La Critique et l'Hérésie, fidèles compagnes', *Traité des abus de la Critique* (1710), vol. I, p. 88; and cf. Honoré, *Réflexions*, vol. II, p. 154, note. Cf. Laubrussel, p. 239: 'If independently of any recourse to Providence or to the authority of the Church, the truth of the monuments of the faith is regulated by the oracles of criticism, to what uncertainties shall we not deliver ourselves? There will be doubt about the text of the Bible, and the inviolable deposit of tradition, and the decrees of the Councils, and consequently about the rule of faith.' For Laubrussel cf. *Mémoires de Trévoux* (1711), pp. 1311 ff.; *Journal des Sçavans* (1711), pp. 89 ff.

See also Dom Liron's *Les Aménités de la Critique* (1717–18); and *Mémoires de Trévoux* (1719), pp. 389 ff., 1113 ff.

### PAGE 71

1 Stonyhurst College MS. A, III, 27. A MS. copy of *Réflexions sur la foi*, with notes by Le Forestier, is there, B, II. 9, III. fols. 99–135.

There is an English parallel to Berruyer, in Francis Hare's satire of 1714, *The difficulties and discouragements which attend the study of the Scriptures*. The chief difference is the opposite intention of the authors. Berruyer intended his case seriously: Hare believed that merely to state the case was to convince the reader of its absurdity.

### PAGE 75

1 It was preceded by the publication of an *Introductory Discourse* in April 1747. Many critics, beginning with the contemporary opponents or friends (for example John Brette in a letter to Middleton, 26 October 1748, B.M. Add. MSS. 32457, fol. 172) have asserted that Middleton's intention was to deny that miracles have occurred. Middleton denied that this was his intention, and forcibly asserted that what he was denying was not the occurrence of individual miracles but a general miracle-making power in the Church, alleged to have existed in the first three or four centuries but to have been later withdrawn. See especially his *Vindication of the Free Inquiry* (*Works*, vol. II, pp. 166 ff.).

For the kind of influence exerted by these attacks upon the primitive Church, see Francis Blackburne's attack upon Warburton's *Julian*, in *The Confessional* (2nd ed., 1767), p. 327, which he regards as 'a late attempt to restore the Fathers so-called to some part of the credit they had lost under the examination of Daillé, Whitby, Barbeyrac, Middleton and others. . .'.

### PAGE 76

1 Archdeacon Chapman published his Charge to the Clergy of Sudbury in 1746. Middleton animadverted on it in his postscript to the *Introductory Discourse*, pp. 58 ff. Chapman replied with a defence of his Charge. *The Jesuit Cabal further opened*. Middleton replied with 'Remarks on the Jesuit Cabal', printed *Works*, vol. II, pp. 71 ff. Middleton was sensitive about depredators of antiquity; because since 1741 he had been engaged in contro-

versy with James Tunstall and Jeremiah Markland in the effort to defend the genuineness of Cicero's letters to Brutus.

The postscript to an anonymous letter to Middleton in B.M. Add. MSS. 32457, fols. 182 ff.: 'I have long wished to see some able writer undertake the Cause which you are now engaged in, as it cannot fail to show, that the Religion of the Primitive Fathers and of the Church of Rome, is the same....'

Middleton is the most lucid and outspoken of the school; but the same sentiments may be found, less worked out, in Hoadly, who is so anxious to show that no authority from the past is sufficient to warrant our belief (e.g. Sermon on Matthew x. 34, *Works* (1773), vol. I, p. 35). In the field of ecclesiastical history—because the writer was after all an eminent historian —John Jortin's *Remarks on Ecclesiastical History* (1751–4), which became the standard history of the primitive Church for the second half of the century, set a far more moderate and balanced tone, even if the book did furnish much material for Gibbon's celebrated chapters on the primitive Church.

PAGE 78

1 John Edwards, Πολυποίκιλος Σοφία: *a Compleat History or survey of all the dispensations and methods of religion, from the beginning of the world to the consummation of all things; as represented in the Old and New Testament* (London, 1699), vol. I, p. 396; vol. II, pp. 578, 612 ff.

Edwards appealed to St Vincent of Lérins (vol. II, p. 611), the only one of this school to lay any stress upon the wording of the *Commonitory*. He is clear that doctrines cannot change; they can only be better understood—God 'hath done adding'. He is careful to maintain this position firmly against the Socinians: 'They are vain men, and intend nothing but Imposture, who hoist up sail for the Discovery of an unknown Continent, some new Plantation in Religion. We must expect no Columbus to discover new Worlds and Treasures to us of that kind. Our religion hath been professed in the world very near seventeen centuries of years and it is still the same, and will never be superannuated, and out of date, but will continue to the end of all things: for it is the Top and Flower, the Crown and Perfection of all Divine Institutions...'. But in vol. II, pp. 597 ff., he is also anxious to show that the primitive Church was then in her infancy and no due model for uncritical imitation: and he takes the trouble to controvert Daillé on the point.

The early date of John Edwards, who is not countering Deists but Socinians, Quakers and what he calls 'the sects', is a reminder that traces of the same general kind of approach, though never so articulate, are really contemporaneous with the Latitudinarian trend.

The same general analogy between the progress in knowledge and progress in religious knowledge appears in Law's *Theory of Religion*; in William

Worthington (Vicar of Blodwell in Shropshire), *Essay on the Scheme, and conduct, procedure and extent of man's Redemption, wherein is shown from the Holy Scriptures that this great work is to be accomplished gradually* (1743); in a number of sermons such as that of Law, *Sermon at the Anniversary meeting of the S.P.G.*, 18 February 1774; or of J. Napleton, *A sermon preached in Hereford Cathedral at the meeting of the Three Choirs*, 9 September 1789, pp. 10–12.

PAGE 79

1 Thomas Balguy, Charge II (1763) in *Discourses on Various Subjects* (Cambridge, 1822), vol. I, p. 169. Balguy was a fellow of St John's College, Cambridge, then Canon of Winchester and Archdeacon of Hampshire: he refused the see of Gloucester in 1781 and died in 1795. That he was nominated by Hoadly to this canonry is not surprising, for he is one of the rare representatives of that kind of divinity which so many theologians in the nineteenth century thought to be characteristic of the eighteenth century—prudential ethics, simplicity, prosaic earthiness, good sense, strongly Erastian, antidogmatic. His lectures on moral philosophy and his *System of Morality* are among the MSS. in the library of St John's College (O. 62).

2 Hey, *Lectures in Divinity* (published 1796), ed. 1822, vol. I, p. 110.

PAGE 80

1 The most illuminating and level-headed student of the relation of doctrinal truth to a changing and developing language is the aforesaid John Hey.

But the subject recurs in every thinking opponent of literal subscription to the Thirty-nine Articles, as most strikingly in Dr Powell's *Discourses* (1776, the year after his death: but the sermon in defence of subscriptions, preached to the University on Commencement Sunday, 1757, had been immediately published). Powell argued (*Discourses*, pp. 37–9) that the value of money imperceptibly changes. A man who pays another after a lapse of time must pay the equivalent in the new value of money; but it may not be the same sum of money. Exactly this happens to language. Hence the force of the assent cannot have been intended to 'exclude all improvements from theology. For as new discoveries have sprung up, new explanations have been gradually framed and adapted to them, and almost every commentator has added something to the common stock. And if among this great variety, a free inquirer should not find all his own opinions, the same liberty of adding to it still remains....' (For indignant criticism of this method of escape from the force of subscription, cf. Francis Blackburne, 'Remarks on Dr Powell's sermon' (1758), in *Works*, vol. VI, esp. pp. 90 ff.: with the retort that if dogmatic language may in course of time become ambiguous, why not scriptural language?) Blackburne has some able and lively comments upon the same theme in *The Confessional*, 2nd ed. 1767 (first published 1766), pp. lxxii ff., 397 ff.; for others, see Edmund Law, *Considerations on the propriety of requiring a subscription* (Cambridge, 1774), pp. 32–4; J. Firebrace, *A Letter to the Reverend James Ibbetson* (London, 1771), pp. 6–7; G. Tytler, *The Plea of the Petitioners Stated and Vindicated* (London, 1773), pp. 63–5: and some brief but interesting MS. notes by Edmund Law upon the same general subject among the Ellenborough MSS.

## PAGE 83

1 *Considerations on the state of the World with regard to the Theory of Religion* (Cambridge, 1745), pp. 165, 183–4, cf. pp. 187–9, 249: Christianity 'was in its infancy in Christ's time, who communicated the things of it to his disciples by little and little, as they were able to bear them; beginning with the plainest and most obvious: laying the foundation and first Principles of the Doctrine during his Ministry and Conversation with them after his Resurrection, and leaving the more full opening of it till the Descent of the Holy Ghost; which likewise led them gradually into its several Truths'. And perhaps something of the same progressive assimilation may be seen in the history of the Church, as at the Reformation 'a brighter Light perhaps than ever' was given: 'As every branch of knowledge has been all along enlarging and improving itself, and every successive age not only enjoys the Discoveries of the foregoing, but adds still greater and more valuable ones of its own; so it is probable that the Knowledge of Religion alone is not at a stand; but on the contrary, that as we continually advance in the study of God's Works, so we shall come to a proportionably better understanding of his Word: as by all these means Human Reason is still growing more perfect, so by the same means Divine Revelation will gradually clear up, and Christianity itself draw nearer to its fulness.' This is not the delivery of a new Revelation: it is the ever more perfect assimilation by humanity of the revelation given. For other writers, see Edwards, *Patrologia*, p. 57, cited by Law, *ibid.* p. 173: 'It is with Religion as it is with Arts and Sciences, the first Essays are seldom perfect; they arrive not to their height at first, they require a gradual Improvement. And so it is here: the primitive Christians were not grown up to that perfection of Knowledge and Understanding which was designed by the Author of our Religion. Christianity was in its infancy, at most in its Childhood, when these men wrote, and therefore it is no wonder that they spake as Children, that they understood as Children, that they thought as Children. This was according to the Oeconomy they were then under. And besides they had not sufficient time and leisure to search into the Christian Doctrines, nor

had they laid in a sufficient stock and fund for that purpose, they being but newly adopted into the Christian Church; yet they were willing to appear in its behalf, to defend it as well as they could, which was accepted by Heaven.'

For Law's interesting liberalism on Biblical inspiration ('Examine the sacred books with the same freedom that we do and find we must do every other book which we desire to understand'), cf. *Theory of Religion*, pp. 250 ff.

These passages of Edwards and Law were both known to, and used by, Conyers Middleton: cf. *A Free Inquiry* (1755), pp. 180–1. The same notions appeared in other members of the Latitudinarian left wing, e.g. Bishop Richard Watson (pupil and admirer of Edmund Law), *Anecdotes* (1818), vol. I, pp. 378–80. On the question whether the ordinary operation of the Holy Spirit is revealed in scripture: 'I am not prepared to say that the latter is an unscriptural doctrine: *future investigation may clear up the point*, and God, I trust, will pardon me an indecision of judgment proceeding from an inability of comprehension' (my italics). Cf. John Jones, *Free and Candid Disquisitions* (1749), p. 10, and Francis Blackburne, *Works*, vol. I, pp. 230 ff., the parable of the catacombs. For the relation to a Latitudinarian view of doctrine in a thinker like Blackburne, cf. *Works*, vol. III, p. 38. 'It has been the opinion of some eminent men who studied the scriptures with great judgment, application and success, that if our forefathers, who had the management of the Protestant reformation, had enjoyed the lights and aids with which succeeding times have been favoured, and could have divested themselves of their scholastic manner of reasoning, the differences (of the several churches)...might have been, in a great measure, prevented. If this is true, or even probable, much edification may still arise from clearing up the genuine sense of scripture, and freeing it from those mistaken interpretations which unskilful men first adopted....': cf. *ibid.* vol. IV, pp. 345–6, 360 ff.

Law's disciple John Gordon, archdeacon of Lincoln, has a stern attack upon the doctrines of original sin and eternal punishment in *A New Estimate of Manners and Principles* (Cambridge, 1760), and his theological expressions are most revealing in this connection: especially pp. 108 ff., on religion considered as a science.

The expression of a similar theological quest is ironically set forth in Hoadly's 'Dedication to Pope Clement XI', *Works* (1773), vol. I, p. 545.

One of the earliest to make the parallel between the growth of the sciences and the expected growth of divinity, and to plead that the advantage in secular learning creates a presupposition in favouring the view that Christian doctrine has advanced, was Pierre Bayle, *Nouvelles lettres critiques sur l'histoire du Calvinisme* XIII, capp. 10–12. But Bayle was then in the stage of resisting Bossuet's *History of the Variations*, as was Pierre Jurieu when he used the same argument, *Lettre Pastorale*, VII (1 December 1688), pp. 51–2.

So finally the view that articles of religion restrict inevitable changes and eventually contradict the consensus of the Church received the weight of William Paley's authority in his *Moral and Political Philosophy* (*Works*, vol. IV, pp. 461–2). For modern treatment, especially of the relation of all this to the idea of progress, see a valuable article by R. S. Crane in *Modern Philology*, vol. XXXI (1934), pp. 273 ff., 349 ff.; and R. N. Stromberg, *Religious Liberalism in Eighteenth-Century England* (Oxford, 1954).

2 John Hey, *Lectures in Divinity* (1822 ed.), vol. II, pp. 465–6.

PAGE 84

1 *The Analogy of Religion*, II, iii, 21.

PAGE 86

1 Cf. Thomas Sherlock, *The Use and Intent of prophecy in the several ages of the world* (1725); William Berriman, *The gradual revelation of the Gospel from the time of man's apostasy* (1733): cited Crane, 294.

PAGE 91

1 For the use of Butler, see *Essay* (1845), pp. 50, 101–2, 110–13, 123–4.

PAGE 92

1 *Analogy*, II, 4; *Essay*, pp. 113–14.

2 Mozley, *The Theory of Development* (1878), pp. 115–16.

PAGE 93

1 *Analogy*, II, ii, 7–9.

PAGE 97

1 Mozley, *The Theory of Development*, p. 226; *Frazer's Magazine* (1846), pp. 256, 265. Many others took the same view, e.g. Bishop Blomfield in his charge of 1846; William Palmer, *The Doctrine of Development and Conscience* (1846); the level-headed Isaac Williams, *Autobiography* (1892), p. 48. John Oman, *The Problem of Faith and Freedom* (1906), p. 290: 'Of his indebtedness to Hegel, Newman, with his usual disregard to his contemporaries, is not aware, yet, who that has once heard it, can fail to recognise the accent of that great thinker when Newman goes on to describe the development he believes in?....'

2 'Newman and the Doctrine of Development', *Church Quarterly Review*, January 1933, pp. 245 ff.

3 E.g. J. Guitton, *La philosophie de Newman* (Paris, 1933); J. J. Byrne, *Ephemerides Lovanienses* (1937), pp. 230 ff.; L. Bouyer, *La Vie intellectuelle* (November 1945); M. Nédoncelle, *La Philosophie religieuse de J. H. Newman* (Strasbourg, 1946), pp. 201 ff.

PAGE 99

1 *Essay* (1845), p. 184. For the now well-known story of German influences upon English historical writing, see especially Klaus Dockhorn, *Der Deutsche Historismus in England* (Göttingen, 1950); Duncan Forbes, *The Liberal Anglican Idea of History* (1952); and H. Butterfield, *Man on his Past* (1955).

PAGE 101

1 *The Ideal of a Christian Church*, pp. 38–9.

PAGE 102

1 *Memorials of G. E. Corrie* (1890), p. 36. There is one possibility that Newman knew of a Catholic historian who had been affected by these historical methods and principles. Under Wiseman's impetus, and in the effort to widen the horizon of English Roman Catholics, the *Dublin Review* began from 1838 to interest its readers in German Catholic theology. In January 1839, in its survey of Catholic literature, it reviewed Klee's *Dogmengeschichte*, and asserted its object to be the tracing of 'the gradual development of the truth once committed to the saints'. The review contrasted the dogmatic history of the Protestant communities with that of the Catholic Church wherein the one immutable truth receives 'its increasing development, always implicitly believed, yet not always explicitly declared by the Church'. There is, however, no evidence that the passage struck Newman. He was fully aware by 1838–9 that some apologists appealed to a notion called vaguely 'development'.

Acton remarked (CUL Add. MSS. 5382,94) how so many of the big histories of dogma were published in Germany in a narrow compass, between 1838 and 1841: Kliefoth (1839), B. Crusius (1840), Engelhardt (1839), Hagenbach (1840), Meier (1840), Dorner (1839), Baur (1841), Klee (1838).

The kind of damage which the new Germanic quest for principles and laws and causes in history could do even to able historical minds, especially when writing off their own special field, is pointedly illustrated by Newman's superficial and misleading account of German religious development since the Reformation (*Essay*, pp. 84–5). The account however could only have been written by one who had imbibed the new historical spirit.

PAGE 103

1 For the concern of the Tübingen school with liberty see especially Gratz, *Über die Grenzen der Freiheit* (Ellwangen, 1817): Möhler, *Die Einheit, passim*.

PAGE 104

1 Bautain was censured in 1834: Hermes in 1835 (and 1847): Günther not until 1857.

2 For Hirscher's early views the work of 1823 is important, *Über das Verhältniss des Evangeliums zu der theologischen Scholastik*. See also E. Mangenot in *DTC*, vol. VI, p. 2512: and the introduction to A. C. Coxe, *Sympathies of the Continent* (Oxford, 1852) which translates one of his later appeals.

PAGE 105

1 Vermeil, *Möhler et l'Ecole catholique de Tubingue* (Paris, 1913), pp. 27–30. I must pay tribute to this discursive but excellent book. It has encountered criticism and the conclusions need modifying, but it is still indispensable. Cf. Drey, *Dissertatio historico-theologica in originem et vicissitudinem exomologeseos in ecclesia catholica* (Ellwangen, 1815). The book was regarded unfavourably by some but was not censured.

2 *Kurze Einleitung in das Studium der Theologie mit Rücksicht auf den wissenschaftlichen Standpunkt und das katholische System* (Tübingen, 1819).

PAGE 106

1 For influence of Schleiermacher on Drey, see K. Eschweiler, *Johann Adam Möhlers Kirchenbegriff* (1930), pp. 11 ff.

2 *Einleitung*, p. 230.

PAGE 108

1 *TQ* (1819), pp. 8–23, 193–210, 369–91, 559–74, 'Vom Geist und Wesen des Katholizismus'. The article is anonymous, and Vermeil will only allow that it is 'very probably' by Drey: but style and matter seem decisive, cf. S. Lösch, *Die Anfänge der Tübinger Theologischen Quartalschrift* (1938), p. 52.

PAGE 109

1 For Möhler's ideas see especially Vermeil; and K. Eschweiler, *J. A. Möhlers Kirchenbegriff* (1930); P. Chaillet (ed.), *L'Eglise est une. Hommage à Moehler* (Paris, 1939); J. R. Geiselmann, *Lebendiger Glaube aus geheiligter Überlieferung. Der Grundgedanke der Theologie J. A. Möhlers und der katholischen Tübinger Schule* (Mainz, 1942); S. Bolshakoff, *The Doctrine of the Unity of the Church in the Works of Khomyakov and Möhler* (London, 1946); F. Vigener, 'Drei Gestalten

aus dem modernen Katholizismus', *Historische Zeitschrift*, Beiheft 7 (Munich and Berlin, 1926); H. Fels, *J. A. Möhler, Der Weg seines geistigen Werdens* (Limburg, 1939): J. R. Geiselmann, *Die theologische Anthropologie Johann Adam Möhlers* (Freiburg-im-Breisgau, 1955). Möhler was a lecturer at Tübingen 1823–6, Professor 1826–35, professor at Munich from 1835 until his early death in April 1838.

2 *Die Einheit in der Kirche, oder das Princip des Katholizismus dargestellt im Geiste der Kirchenväter der drei ersten Jahrhunderte*. The title of the French translation of 1839, *De l'unité de l'Eglise*, does not capture the nuance of the original title.

PAGE 110

1 He refused however to make a retractation demanded of him as a kind of condition which accompanied the offer of a professorship at Bonn: and he explicitly recognized that the fundamental ideas of *Symbolik*'s theory of the Church are to be found in *Unity*.

The controversy with Baur, though of interest, was concerned more with the interpretation of dogmatic formulas. Baur first answered the *Symbolik* in a long article in *Tübinger Zeitschrift für Theologie* (1833), III, pp. 1 ff.: and this was printed separately and revised as *Der Gegensatz des Katholicismus und Protestantismus* (1834 and 1836). Möhler replied with *Neue Untersuchungen der Lehrgegensätze zwischen den Katholiken und Protestanten* (1834 and 1835: part used in later editions of *Symbolik*). Baur replied with 'Erwiederung auf Herrn Dr Möhlers neueste Polemik gegen die protestantische Lehre und Kirche', in *Tüb. Zeitschrift* (1834), III, pp. 127 ff., and published separately the same year. Baur was not left a solitary champion: cf. P. Marheineke, *Über J. A. Möhlers Symbolik* (Berlin, 1833); J. F. I. Tafel, *Vergleichende Darstellung und Beurtheilung der Lehrgegensätze* (Tübingen, 1835): A. T. Lehmus, *Die Rechtfertigungslehre der Evangelischen Kirche* (Nuremberg, 1836); C. I. Nitsch, *Eine protestantische Beantwortung der Symbolik* (Hamburg, 1835)— Döllinger thought this the soundest of the replies.

For Baur's comments on the new theory of tradition see especially *Gegensatz*, etc. (1836), pp. 576 ff., 593 ff. For the comments on Hegelian influence among the Catholics cf. *Gegensatz* etc. Appendix V, pp. 669 ff. and *Erwiederung in Tüb. Zeitschrift* (1834), iii, pp. 209 ff.

For moderate statements of Möhler's theory of tradition, which became characteristic of the school, see Gengler, 'Über die Regel des Vincentius von Lirinum', *TQ* (1833), pp. 579–600: Hefele's review of Klee's *Dogmengeschichte*, *TQ* (1838), pp. 514 ff.; Kuhn in *TQ* (1832), pp. 419 ff., and *Einleitung in die katholische Dogmatik* (Tübingen, 1846), pp. 99 ff.; Staudenmaier, *Das Wesen der katholischen Kirche* (Freiburg-im-Breisgau, 1845), pp. 68 ff.

PAGE III

I *Essay* (1845), p. 27.

PAGE II2

I *Quarterly Review* (March, 1846), reprinted in *Savonarola, Erasmus, and other Essays* (1870), pp. 296 ff. The juxtaposition would certainly not have been made by anyone who had read the Tübingen review (by Herbst) of the German translation of de Maistre's *Du Pape*, *TQ* (1822), p.'677. One Anglican critic, W. Archer Butler, taking Newman to task for ignorance upon the point, said he would have found better precedent from the Continent in the language of Lamennais' 'Essay on Indifference' (*Letters on the Development of Christian Doctrine* (Dublin, 1850), pp. 3 ff.). There are occasional passages in Lamennais, e.g. *Essai*, vol. III, pp. 185, 193. But the total effect does not amount to much. It must however be noticed that W. G. Ward believed that Newman had first perceived the idea in de Maistre's *Du Pape* i. 14—Ward being at the time (1847) concerned to show that Newman had first received the idea from a Catholic writer, cf. BP, Ward to Brownson, 7 April 1847.

PAGE II4

I CUL Add. MSS. 5463: Perrone, *Praelectiones: Tractatus de Locis Theologicis* (ed. Migne), vol. II, cols. 855–6, referring to the *profundam theoriam* of Möhler and quoting *Symbolik*, ch. v, *Von der Kirche*. In 1837 Perrone had published an *Analisi della Simbolica...del Prof. Moehler*. An Italian translation of *Symbolik* was published at Milan in 1842 (and again at Naples in 1850). Newman, though probably he had read no word of Perrone before 1846 *did* know that Perrone approved of Möhler: for W. G. Ward, unlike Newman an ardent reader of modern theologians (provided they wrote in English, Latin, or French), stated the fact in an article of 1843 which Newman read, *British Critic*, vol. XXXIV (July 1843), p. 55 n. Ward moreover ascribed a general approval to Perrone, and then quoted Möhler's *Unity*, of which Perrone would not have approved.

2 CUL Add. MSS. 5666, fols. 22, 42; 4990, fol. 226. For Renouf's later, somewhat extreme, views on development, see *Home and Foreign Review*, vol. II (1863), pp. 596–7. Renouf was a scholar of Pembroke College from 1840–2. I owe thanks to Mr J. S. Nurser of Peterhouse, who called my attention to Acton's interest in Möhler and Baur in relation to the theory of development.

3 *Letters and Diaries of J. H. Newman*, ed. C. S. Dessain and others (hereafter LD) vol. IV, p. 320. When Bowden offered to procure the book for him, he replied: 'Pray give yourself no great trouble.... When I shall have an

opportunity of correcting my "Arians" is, of course, very uncertain, and of distant date. I fancy I shall continue fidgety till I have learned a smattering of German, but that, of course, is a date still further removed. You see, we stand a chance of being inundated with German divinity, and they have (I believe) written some useful books, too, in my line; both which reasons make me anxious to understand them.'

Wiseman also expressed a high opinion of the *Symbolik* in the preface to *Lectures on the Principal Doctrines and Practices of the Catholic Church* (1836), a work which Newman reviewed in the *British Critic* of December 1836; see also H. Tristram, *Revue des sciences philosophiques et théologiques*, vol. XXVII (April 1938), p. 188.

On 10 October 1839 Wiseman preached at the consecration of the new Church of St Mary's at Derby, and published the sermon. He had argued from the text on the grain of mustard seed, and from the development in the Old Testament, to the possibility of development under the new covenant. The sermon was vague and generalized. But it may possibly be one of the pleas to which Newman referred in his 1840 article 'On the Catholicity of the Anglican Church', rebuking Roman apologists for appealing to the theory of development to justify their departure from antiquity (*Essays Critical and Historical*, vol. II, p. 43). For this was the article designed to meet Wiseman's criticisms about the Donatists and to quiet the qualms aroused by the celebrated article in the *Dublin Review* which had given him, as he confessed, a stomach-ache.

Thirlwall's preface to *Schleiermacher on St Luke*; Cox, *Recollections of Oxford*, p. 220; Tristram, *Revue des sciences philosophiques et théologiques*, vol. XXVII, pp. 185–6.

PAGE 115

1 *German Protestantism* (Oxford, 1844).

PAGE 116

1 Friedrich, *Döllinger*, vol. II, p. 224.

2 *Christ. Rememb.* (1842), I, p. 484; II, p. 362; 1843, I, pp. 1–25; cf. also *British Magazine* (1840), II (August), p. 167.

PAGE 117

1 *British Critic*, vol XXX (1841), pp. 328 ff.: cf. 'Goode's Divine Rule of Faith and Practice', *ibid.* XXXII (1842), pp. 34 ff., 91 ff.; 'St Athanasius on the Arians' *ibid.* vol. XXXII (1842), pp. 401 ff.; 'The Synagogue and the Church', *ibid.* vol. XXXIV (July 1843), pp. 54–5; 'Mill's Logic', *ibid.* vol. XXXIV (October

1843), pp. 403 *bis* to 407 *bis* (beware of faulty pagination). Cf. also the article, not by Ward but by J. B. Mozley (!) on 'Development of the Church in the seventeenth century', *ibid.* vol. XXXI (1842), pp. 300 ff.

Ward himself later asserted that the book by Goode, 'silly and weak' though it was, drew his attention to patristic texts unpalatable to Tractarians and so drove him to explain them by the principle of development: BP, Ward to Brownson, 7 April 1847.

2 *The Ideal of a Christian Church*, pp. 547 ff. For the public association of the book with the principle of development cf. an interesting letter from W. B. Barter in *The Times*, 12 October 1844.

Thirlwall, *A Charge* etc. (September 1845), pp. 13 ff. Newman did not know of this charge till much later.

## PAGE 118

1 W. Palmer, *A Narrative of Events connected with the publication of the Tracts for the Times* (1843), pp. 45, 57, 63; *On the Church* (3rd ed. 1842), vol. II, pp. 443–5. It therefore seems possible that, if Renouf's memory is to be trusted, Renouf drew Newman's attention in 1842 to the passage inserted into the new edition of Palmer, *On the Church*. For Palmer's distress at Newman's participation in the controversy, see his letter to Hook of August 1843, printed in *Life and Letters of Walter Farquhar Hook*, vol. II, pp. 105–6.

2 Ambrose St John, who arrived at Littlemore on 7 August 1843, brought with him a number of books for the library, among which a French translation of the *Symbolik* was certainly included. For the books in the Littlemore library, cf. Tristram, *Revue des sciences philosophiques et théologiques*, vol. XXVII, p. 184.

For Pattison, see especially BL MSS. Pattison 6, fol. 157; 128, fols. 10–14, 20, 23, 26, 29, 53, 56, 64, 69, 88–9; 7*, s.v. 14 January 1846.

English printers had some difficulty with Möhler. The editor of Pattison's memoirs spelt him Moehrer: the reporters of *The Times* for 20 October 1846, Müller: the printers of Bishop Blomfield's *Charge* of 1846 tried Moëhler.

Acton has a piece of gossip that when Bath came to R. I. Wilberforce with 'difficulties', he was advised to read Möhler. Having done so, the curate announced that he was joining the Roman Church. 'I expected it', said Wilberforce (CUL Add. MSS. 5463).

## PAGE 119

1 OM B. 2. 8. 1, a packet labelled *Papers on the Development of Christian Doctrine* and dated 11 November 1845. It shows that he began serious work on the

*Essay* on 7 March 1844, and that from the first he was consciously resolved to treat the subject 'historically, not argumentatively'. The notes show that the main lines of the published essay were clear to him in 1844, though he had not come yet to any suggestion about 'tests' for distinguishing true developments from false. See also appendix note in Diary for June 1843–June 1844, pp. 118–19: and the appendix for the diary for June 1844–June 1845. For his occasional descriptions of the progress of the work see his letters to Mrs William Froude, OM, 19 May and 9 June and 14 July 1844 ('I find the subject I have now got into is endless'), 1 June and 10 June 1845, the last printed in Ward, *Life of Newman*, vol. I, p. 86. The reference which he noted from Gieseler was vol. I, p. 81, where Gieseler is arguing that the Judaic Christians of the first and second centuries declined because in their isolation they 'did not keep pace with the progress of doctrines'.

PAGE 120

1 Sermon XIV of the *University Sermons*. The collection was sent to the press two days afterwards. 'People went about saying there was a good deal of mischief in it (namely, the sermon of 2 February) and that it must be answered; but I am under no apprehensions', Newman to his sister 21 February 1843 (*Letters*, vol. II, p. 408). For further illustration of Newman's mind at the time see the passages in *Select Treatises of S. Athanasius*, vol. II, pp. 226 ff., discussed by Guitton, *La philosophie de Newman*, pp. 154–5.

What can be said about the 'preparation' of Newman's mind for the idea has been well said by J. J. Byrne in *Ephemerides Lovanienses*, vol. XIV (1937), pp. 230–86. Notice especially the deep sense, from an early period (a sense connected with his 'sceptical' view of reasoning) of the inadequacy, yet necessity, of words to represent mysteries—words 'are but shadows cast, or at best, lines or portions caught from what is unseen, and they attend upon it after the manner of the Seraphim, with wings covering their face, and wings covering their feet, in adoration and majesty'... 'I see herein a great mystery, a hidden truth, which I cannot handle or define, shining "as jewels at the bottom of the great deep", darkly, tremulously, yet really there', *Parochial Sermons*, vol. III, pp. 367–8.

All the early passages are of course 'static': religious knowledge does 'not admit of improvement by the lapse of time'... 'the new ways are the crooked ones'...in the Christian Church 'we cannot add or take away' (*Parochial Sermons*, vol. VII, p. 247); and if he also preaches that the individual Christian may by meditation and conscientious living grow into fuller and fuller understanding of the meaning of scripture, this is a growth into the possession of a treasure which the Church already possesses and transmits.

PAGE 122

1 For what can be said, see R. H. Broker, *The Influence of Bull and Petavius on Cardinal Newman's theory of the development of Christian doctrine*, Rome, 1938 (Pontificia Universitas Gregoriana). And cf. CUL Add. MSS. 5463, 15. 'When Morris came to him, dissatisfied with Bull, he said "I am afraid, Jack, you must go to the Jesuit Petavius."'

PAGE 123

1 *Apologia* (Everyman ed.), pp. 163–4.

PAGE 126

1 The three were Tract 85, the *Essay on Ecclesiastical Miracles* of 1843 and the *Essay on Development* (Huxley, *Essays on Controverted Questions* (1892), p. 471).

2 Acton thought that this was why history 'depressed' Newman and why (unlike Pusey) he took 'no pleasure in erudition', CUL Add. MSS. 4987, fols. 1, 20, 46.

PAGE 128

1 These scriptural instances are used for one of the most astounding arguments to be found anywhere in Newman's works—some scriptural texts are contradictory, yet both must be true; therefore the Church may teach something not obviously in scripture yet both the scripture and the teaching may not be contradictory.

PAGE 129

1 OM B. 2. 8. 1. 'This work must be looked at in connection with Tract 85— that delivered from Liberalism, this persuades to Rome.'

2 CUL Add. MSS. 4990, 298; cf. 4988, 100, and 5463: 'What he meant by Development was *securus judicat*. It was the voice of the present Church superseding the study of the Past.'

PAGE 131

1 Newman, *Sermons on subjects of the Day*, pp. 73, 391.

2 *University Sermons* (1843), pp. 45–6, 176, 194, 217, 227–8, 233, 292; cf. p. 40: the basis of scriptural doctrine is the truth that 'there is no necessary connexion between the intellectual and moral principles of our nature'.

PAGE 132

1 *Quarterly Review*, vol. LXXV (December 1844), p. 183.

PAGE 135

1 *The Ideal of a Christian Church* (1844), pp. 512, 517, 521, 532, 582.

PAGE 136

1 'The Synagogue and the Church', *British Critic*, vol. XXXIV (July 1843), p. 4.

PAGE 137

1 Wilfrid Ward, *W. G. Ward and the Oxford Movement*, p. 295.

PAGE 140

1 *Essay*, pp. 26–7.

PAGE 142

1 *Essay*, p. 138.

PAGE 146

1 *Essay*, p. 170: and the whole argument, pp. 139 ff.

2 *Essay*, pp. 186–8, quoting *Prophetical Office*, pp. 84–7: 'though I condemn its tone and its drift, and think its statements exaggerated,... *mutatis mutandis* I acquiesce in it'.

PAGE 147

1 *Essay*, esp. pp. 28, 147–8, 181.

2 *Essay*, p. 389.

PAGE 151

1 *Essay*, pp. 49, 39, 38.

2 See especially, among the *University Sermons* (nearly all of which are relevant to this theme) the sermon on 'Explicit and Implicit Reason' (preached 1840). There is a valuable and fresh introduction by M. Nédoncelle to the newest French translation of these sermons (1955).

PAGE 152

1 *Essay*, pp. 55–6, quoting *University Sermons*, pp. 330–3. 'What was an impression on the Imagination has become a system of creed in the reason'... 'Religious men, according to their measure, have an idea or vision of the Blessed Trinity in Unity, of the Son Incarnate, and of His Presence—not as a number of qualities, attributes, and actions, not as the subject of a number

of propositions, but as one and individual, and independent of words, like an impression conveyed through the senses.'

Cf. p. 417, on the growth of the doctrine of purgatory—'an instance of the mind of the Church working out dogmatic truths from implicit feelings under secret supernatural guidance'.

For a forcible, though one-sided expression of the view that texts like these are the clue to Newman's whole theory, cf. George Tyrrell, *Through Scylla and Charybdis* (1907), pp. 139 ff.

It should always be remembered that Newman, without defining 'religious experience', does not associate this directly with 'religious sensations'. For him religious experience is not so much the kind of intuitive experience postulated by a Schleiermacher, a von Hügel, or an Otto, as the reception of a testimony and the moral consequences of receiving that testimony.

PAGE 154

1 *Essay*, p. 83 : cf. pp. 27, 344; cf. his letter to Mrs W. Froude, 9 June 1844, OM.

2 *Essay*, pp. 87–8; cf. pp. 452 on the 'incorrigibility' of the Church.

PAGE 155

1 That he realized how integral was this old Tractarian expression to the formulation of his theory of development is proved by his letter to Mrs W. Froude of 9 June 1844, OM.

2 *Essay*, pp. 97, 417, 337. (Contrast the weakening of all these phrases in the 1878 revision, pp. 59, 390, 336.) Cf. also p. 344, '...truth...unknown to them hitherto'.

PAGE 156

1 *Essay*, pp. 80–1.

2 Especially in the quotation from Lapide, *Essay*, pp. 322–3.

PAGE 157

1 *Essay*, p. 83; cf. p. 113: development 'is not an effect of wishing or resolving, or of forced enthusiasm, or of any mechanism or reasoning, or of any mere subtlety of intellect; but comes of its own innate power of expansion within the mind at its season, though *with the use of reflection and argument and original thought*, more or less as it may happen, with a dependence on the ethical growth of the mind itself, and with a reflex influence upon it' (I have italicized one phrase lest any reader of the *Essay* be inclined to exaggerate the a-logical character of Newman's idea of logic).

P. 397. Logical sequence 'will include any progress of the mind from one judgment to another, as, for instance, by way of moral fitness, which may not admit of analysis into premiss and conclusion'.

PAGE 159

1 *Essay*, pp. 353–4. The language is sometimes applicable to the theological debate rather than doctrinal definitions. But it is clear from the context that Newman thinks of preparation for definition as a discovery of truth which might be described as 'an unwearied anxious process of thought'. For anticipations of the thought, cf. Tract 85, p. 83.

PAGE 160

1 The sermon of 1843 contains one of those frustrating passages which from time to time baffle and trouble every reader of Newman. 'The doctrine of the Double Procession was no Catholic dogma in the first ages, though it was more or less clearly stated by individual Fathers; yet if it is now to be received, as surely it must be, as part of the Creed, it was really held everywhere from the beginning, and therefore, in a measure, held as a mere religious impression, and perhaps an unconscious one' (p. 224).

The historian in Newman concedes that the 'doctrine' was not a 'Catholic dogma' in the first ages. The theologian, perceiving (1) that the west now has the double procession in the creed, and (2) that the (western) church is inerrant, and (3) that doctrine is immutable, must contend that the Church has always 'held' the doctrine—not as doctrine (so the historian has conceded) therefore 'in a measure' as an idea or impression, of which the Church was not conscious. The theologian must also (in spite of the historian) contend that the doctrine was 'really held everywhere'—and if so the unconsciousness becomes necessary presupposition and not a mere perhaps.

PAGE 161

1 Baggs to Newman, 11 October 1845, OM, XV: Newman's notes dated September 15 (no year) in OM B. 2. 8. 1. It was one of the last acts of Bishop Baggs. He died at Prior Park on 16 October 1845.

2 Wiseman to Newman 14 October 1845, OM, CXL.

PAGE 162

1 Newman to Hope (Scott), Oscott, 2 November 1845, OM: cf. Newman to Dalgairns, Littlemore 9 November 1845, *LD*, vol. XI, pp. 23, 29.

As long ago as 1 June 1845 he had described the *Essay* to Mrs Froude as 'a sort of obscure philosophical work'.

2 Wiseman to Newman, 7 November 1845, OM, CXL.

PAGE 163

1 On 27 November. Cf. T. W. Allies' *Diary* for that date: 'Went into Oxford to get J. H. N.'s book, so anxiously awaited for, and with a combination of opposite feelings—love, curiosity, and fear.... Returned in evening with my treasure.' *A Life's Decision* (1880), p. 81.

PAGE 164

1 See especially W. J. Irons, *The Theory of Development Examined*; W. B. Barter, *A Postscript to the English Church not in Schism*; *A Review of Mr. Newman's Essay* by an English Churchman; *A Few Words addressed to the Author of an Essay on the Development of Christian Doctrine*, by an Anglican Divine; George Alston, *The Development of Divine Instruction*; *Mithridates, or Mr. Newman's Essay on Development its own confutation*, by a Quondam Disciple; F. D. Maurice, *The Epistle to the Hebrews*, Preface; G. Moberly, *The Sayings of the Great Forty Days*, Preface to the 3rd ed.; W. Palmer, *The Doctrine of Development and Conscience*; G. S. Faber, *Letters on Tractarian secession to Popery* (unfair and only important because it treats Möhler as well as Newman); all these published in 1846. H. H. Milman, 'Newman on the Development of Christian Doctrine', *Quarterly Review*, March 1846, reprinted in *Savonarola, Erasmus, and other Essays* (London, 1870), pp. 296 ff.; W. Archer Butler, *Letters on the Development of Christian Doctrine* (Dublin, 1850), reprinted from a series of articles in the *Irish Ecclesiastical Record*, 1845–7; J. B. Mozley, *The Theory of Development*, 1878 (reprinted from the *Christian Remembrancer* of January 1847 in response to the demand when Newman's third and revised edition appeared); Christopher Wordsworth, *Letters to M. Gondon* (1847). Mozley's reply is the most convincing, Palmer's the most learned and Milman's the most amusing. Butler is also worth reading: and it appears from a letter from Newman to Father Coleridge of 5 February 1871 (*LD* vol. xxv, p. 279) that Newman also regarded it seriously. A letter to J. M. Capes of 15 March 1849 (*LD* vol. xiii p. 86) shows that he did not underestimate the force of Mozley's work.

PAGE 165

1 F. C. Husenbeth to Newman, 5 December 1845 (OM)—Newman had sent him a present of the *Essay* on publication. Cf. Newman's accounts of the correspondence with Husenbeth in his letter to Hope (Scott) of 23 December 1845 from Littlemore, *LD*, vol. xi, p. 76.

2 Wiseman to Newman, 27 December 1845 (OM); *Dublin Review* (March 1844), p. 98, but the estimate was only second-hand.

**PAGE 166**

1 OM, xv, no. 7: 'I do not at all deny that the theory of development requires far closer analysis, or more full elucidation than I have hitherto given it, but I have no doubt whatever it will triumph, the more it is examined'. OM, cxxxii; cf. his letter to Henry Wilberforce, 25 June 1846.

**PAGE 167**

1 *Diary*, 12 May 1846 (*LD*, vol. xi, p. 162); Newman to George Ryder, 22 May 1846, *LD*, vol. xi, p. 165; Newman to Lord Adare, 31 August 1846 (*ibid.* p. 238); Ambrose St John to Dalgairns 29 June 1846 (OML), 'At present we are deep in Melchior Canus and find it somewhat dry'. A little scrap in OM shows that Newman was also reading, during this period, Bellarmine on 'deductions' and 'mediate and immediate faith'. For Dalgairns on his theological instructors see Dalgairns to Newman, 1 August 1846, from Langres (OML).

**PAGE 168**

1 For Perrone and Passaglia, *DTC* and bibliography therewith. For Mazio, Antonio Angelini, *Della vita e degli scritti del P. Giacomo Mazio* (Rome, 1859); *L'Università Gregoriana del collegio romano nel primo secolo dalla restituzione* (Rome, 1924). Mazio was the first whom Newman met. He called at the Collegio Romano on 6 November 1846 and had an 'interesting talk' about the *Essay* and was disappointed when a visitor came in to interrupt the discussion and 'spoilt the whole', cf. Newman's *Diary*, 6 November 1846 and Newman to Stanton, 6 November 1846 (*LD*, vol. xi, p. 267). For Mazio's difficulty in understanding the *Essay*, cf. the oblique reference, probably to him, in *The Rambler*, vol. i (n.s. 1859), p. 201.

**PAGE 169**

1 Ward, *Life of Newman*, vol. i, pp. 166–9; and part of Newman's letter to Dalgairns, 31 December 1846, section not printed by Ward; *LD*, vol. xi, p. 303.

**PAGE 170**

1 This Dr Grant is not to be confused with the English Dr Thomas Grant who was also in Rome at this time and later became bishop of Southwark. For Alexander Grant see his obituary in *The Catholic Directory for the Clergy and Laity of Scotland* for 1875 et seq. His article of spring 1846 was entitled 'Sullo stato passato ed attuale del Puseismo in Inghilterra', *Annali delle scienze religiose, series II*, vol. ii, pp. 153 ff. His cool attitude to Newman in Newman to Wiseman, 14 February 1847; Newman to Dalgairns, 14 February 1847 (*LD*, vol. xii, pp. 33 and 40). For Ryder see H. Tristram, *Newman and his friends* (1933), p. 92.

**PAGE 171**

**1** A. M. Schlesinger, *Orestes A. Brownson* (Boston, 1939): cf. the letter of a priest in St Louis to Brownson, 7 January 1853 (BP). And see a letter to Brownson of 16 December 1846 (BP): 'It [the *Essay*] contains numberless propositions and assertions, which could not come from the pen of any thorough Catholic divine, nor would they now come, at least in the same phraseology, from the pen of Mr Newman himself....As to the danger to be apprehended from the book itself, I cannot say that in this I fully agree with you. It is not a Catholic book, and we are in no manner called upon to defend it....'

Brownson's articles in *Brownson's Quarterly Review*, vol. III (July 1846), pp. 342 ff.: vol. I (n.s. January 1847), pp. 39 ff., and *ibid.* October 1847, pp. 485 ff.; vol. II (October 1848), pp. 525 ff.

**PAGE 172**

**1** *Brownson's Quarterly Review*, III (1846), pp. 345, 367; Brownson to W. G. Ward, 29 September 1847 (BP). Cf. T. R. Ryan, *Orestes Brownson*, Huntington, 1976.

**2** Ambrose St John to Dalgairns, Maryvale, 20 August 1846 (OML). 'I suspect no more than a piece of Yankeeism but it will do mischief.'

**PAGE 173**

**1** Newman to Dalgairns, 15 November 1846 (*LD*, vol. XI, p. 274), partly printed in Ward's *Life of Newman*, vol. I, p. 161. Ward's statement on p. 160 that Newman 'at once took steps to let the Americans know that at least in principle his theory was accepted in Rome' is not true. It is founded on a faulty transcription of the letter of Dalgairns:

Ward's version: 'I am quite right in writing to Knox what people think here.'

Original: 'I am quite right in wishing to know what people think here.'

**PAGE 174**

**1** Newman to Dalgairns, 22 November 1836 (*LD*, vol. XI, p. 279), partly printed Ward, *Life of Newman*, vol. I, pp. 166 ff.; Newman to Dalgairns, 14 February 1847 (*LD*, vol. xii, p. 33).

**2** Newman to Dalgairns, 8 December 1846 (*LD*, vol. XI, p. 288). The passages which at this stage worried him most were *Essay*, p. 120, probable infallibility; p. 9, probability for the existence of God; p. 412, growth of the penitential system; p. 415, 'the doctrine afterwards received' better as 'the doctrine afterwards defined' (interestingly enough, the 1878 revision preserved 'the doctrine afterwards received'), p. 388.

In a passage in the *Apologia* (Everyman, pp. 91–2) he expresses his belief that he has not read the *Essay* 'since its publication'. But he was dipping into it in 1846–7.

PAGE 175

1 Dalgairns to Newman, 7 December and 27 December 1846 (OML): Newman to Dalgairns, 10 January 1847 (*LD*, vol. XII, p. 4). Newman considered rushing through a translation at Rome but was deterred by the prospect of difficulties with the local censors.

2 Dalgairns to Newman, 31 December 1846 and 25 January 1847 (OM). The disavowal was published by the *Univers* of 10 January 1847.

PAGE 176

1 Dalgairns to Newman, 20 March 1847 (OM).

2 H. Tristram, *Gregorianum*, vol. XVIII (1937), pp. 241–60.

PAGE 178

1 Ambrose St John to Wiseman, 17 January 1847; Wiseman to Newman, 27 January 1847 (OM). For the use by other ex-Anglicans see, for example, E. H. Thompson, *The Unity of the episcopate considered*; David Lewis, *Notes on the nature and extent of the papal supremacy*; J. S. Northcote, *The Fourfold Difficulty of Anglicans*; T. W. Allies, *A Life's Decision* (1880, but based on his diary for the period), the *Essay* 'directed my studies, I may say, for the next five years. I read it with avidity' (p. 82).

PAGE 179

1 *Brownson's Quarterly Review*, vol. I (n.s. 1847), pp. 45, 83–5. 'One of the most insidious attacks, though not so intended by its author, on religion, which we remember ever to have read, and that is saying much.' The book which sparked this article was the American edition of J. S. Northcote's *Fourfold Difficulty of Anglicans* (Philadelphia, 1846).

PAGE 180

1 Newman to Dalgairns, 7 February 1847 (*LD*, vol. XII, p. 29) (cf. Ward, vol. I, p. 174 not quite accurate). The letter is important for Newman's efforts to distinguish his views from Bautain's theory of faith, as a little earlier he

had sought to distinguish his views from those of Hermes. Perrone was expert upon the point, having published a refutation of Hermes, entitled *L'ermesianismo*, in 1838–9.

PAGE 181

**1** Newman's postscript in Ambrose St John to Dalgairns, 24 February 1847 (OML); St John to Dalgairns, 16 November 1846; Newman to Wiseman, 17 January 1847 (*LD*, vol. XII, p. 19).

**2** Ward, *Life of Newman*, vol. II, p. 270, *LD*, vol. XXV, p. 280.

**3** Notes dated 15 September, no year, in OM, B. 2. 8. 1. From the similarity to the letter to T. F. Knox dated 10 May 1847 (*LD*, vol. XII, p. 77) it is likely that he said 'Give me time'...etc. to the Bishop of Toronto. Perhaps this is also the bishop referred to in Brownson to Ward, 29 September 1847 (BP).

PAGE 182

**1** *Theses de fide*, published by H. Tristram in *Gregorianum*, vol. XVIII (1937), pp. 219 ff. It should however be observed, not only that it is difficult to reconcile all the theses without contradictions (for example, contrast the consequences of thesis 5 with the consequences of thesis 6—the problem is admittedly thorny) but also that the texts have been lifted out of the respective systems of thought or contexts in which they originally stood. Suarez, with his wide gap between *fides acquisita* and *fides divina*, could provide texts to suit Newman's contention that faith was not *based* on evidence or reasoning upon evidence. But though there are points of contact between the two, the open-eyed reader of the *University Sermons* will not be deceived into supposing that Suarez would have approved of them without grave reservations.

The paper on development was published by T. Lynch in *Gregorianum*, vol. XVI (1935), pp. 402–47. Commentaries by T. Lynch, *The Newman-Perrone Paper on Development* (Southsea, 1935), and by F. Cavallera, 'Le document Newman-Perrone et le développement du dogme' in *Bulletin de littér. ecclés.* (Toulouse, 1946), pp. 132–4 and 208–25.

The importance of the paper has been underestimated because Wilfrid Ward, in his *Life of Newman* (1912), vol. I, pp. 184–5 did not print it, though he commented on it, and himself seemed to minimize its significance. 'Perrone's main objection was confined to Newman's expression "new dogmas" in place of "new definitions". Newman was using the phrase *dogma* to denote the intellectual concept expressed in a new definition. Perrone seems to have taken it as tantamount to new truth added to what was at first revealed to the Church. This was a difference almost entirely of expression.

In principle they agreed. Both held that the "deposit of faith" once for all committed to the Church was so given that Christians were not explicitly conscious of all its intellectual implications which were subsequently defined.' This view of Ward is so far as it goes perfectly true, and if this were the main point at issue we might indeed agree that the difference was 'almost entirely of expression'. All parties of course agreed that *Christians* were not explicitly conscious of all the implications. There are two vital questions in the arguments which Ward glosses over. First, there is the question whether the *teaching* church can in this matter be assimilated to the *Christians*, so that the Church can be said to be not 'conscious' of truths which it later declares. And in this matter Newman is on one side, Perrone on the other. Newman wanted to assert (though not precisely in this language) that the *magisterium* had 'grown' in knowledge because he could not separate in his mind the *magisterium* from the consensus of the faithful, as was later to become evident in his famous *Rambler* article *On Consulting the Faithful*, and which is also evident from occasional letters from Rome in 1846–7. Cf. Newman to Dalgairns, 22 November 1846 (OML) '...Perrone (in what we are reading in lecture) maintains that the canon fixed at Trent depends *solely* on the tradition of the Roman Church. He simply *gives up* Catholic tradition. I asked the lecturer if it was not so: he did not like to admit it, and said the *traditio principalium ecclesiarum* was necessary but not of the particular churches....I asked whether in the case of the canon there was *any* tradition but that of Rome, but I could not get him to say yes or no....All this shows how little they have of a view....'

Cf. Newman to Acton, 8 July 1862 (CUL Add. MSS. 5463; *LD*, vol. xx, p. 224), '*I* should like to say that *the Church* apprehends it more clearly; and I almost think that Bossuet countenances such a notion. When I suggested it to Father Perrone, he disliked the idea. But what *is* the Church as separate from pope, councils, bishops and faithful?' In his Latin paper on development, Newman, knowing that Perrone took a particular view of this particular point, left the question doubtful—'Id solum hic dubito' (*Gregorianum*, vol. xvi, p. 406).

The second great point at issue is of course the question how these implications are explicated and what is meant by an implication being explicated. Nothing can reconcile the views of Perrone and Newman on this point.

PAGE 184

1 Newman to Lord Adare, 31 August 1846 (*LD*, vol. xi, p. 238). Perrone's theology should of course be judged solely on his laconic negotiations of Newman. Though no historian in the modern sense, he was fully aware of the theological problem, and gave a balanced statement of his answer to it in *De immaculato B. V. Mariae conceptu* (Milan, 1852).

1 Father Henry Tristram, who knew Newman's handwriting better than any-one else, told me that he thought this note was probably written in Newman's later years, probably when he was revising the book for the 1877–8 edition. Such a verdict must carry great weight. I attribute the note to 1847–53 partly because this date better fits other evidence about Newman's mood at the time: partly because the evidence of the handwriting is not so clear—the only certain thing about the note being that it was not written at the same time as he wrote his own name in the book (which he dated 1846): and especially because in 1846–8—but not in 1877–8, so far as I am aware—Newman was still describing the book as he had first described it to Wiseman, as not dogmatic but philosophical. See for another example a letter to his friend Dr Russell of Maynooth dated 20 February 1848, (*LD*, vol. XII, p. 170) '...It does not pretend to be a *dogmatic* work, it is an external philosophical view....I think it very possible that my theory may require some modification, though I don't mean that I am aware of it. It is an attempt to give the *laws* under which implicit faith becomes explicit—this is the very subject of the book—now is it wonderful that, in so arduous an undertaking, it should not be anything more than it professes to be, "an Essay"?' James Walker's criticisms may show the kind of English Bossuetism which he needed to meet. In a letter of 6 October 1847 (OM) he asked whether Newman still held to his 'development', and then pleaded that it was Catholic to suppose a development of institutes and of conquest, but not of faith. To the latter belong 'accession of new truths, the faith or Christian religion as a seed developing in its very substance, definitions of successive Councils so many points of new faith introduced not confirmed, *constituere dogmata* meaning imposing new doctrines on the faithful not confirming and guarding the old, truths unknown to the Apostolic Fathers discovered in process of time by the subsequent Church, or as I have heard it expressed by an advocate, like the law of the motion of the earth round the sun, unknown to antiquity, discovered by modern experience and science, nay even contradicted in antiquity by the maintenance of the opposite theory (!)'.

For the reputation of the Oratory, cf. Newman's letter to Formby, 19 October 1848 (*LD*, vol. XII, p. 302)—'If there is any province which does not directly belong to the Oratory it is that of dogmatics—and if there is anything which we must avoid, and which some people, recollecting the history of the French Oratory, are apprehensive of in us, it is new views in Theology. This consideration has so weighed with myself that, many as were the misrepresentations that have been published of my Essay on Development, I have written nothing on the subject since I was a Catholic, and shall not without the greatest deliberation and caution.'

Letter in the *Tablet* of 14 September 1852, conveying also a very strong formula of submission to ecclesiastical authority on the matter. The cause was another attack by Brownson, who replied on 5 October. Brownson claimed that Newman's silence was what was continuing American suspicions. 'Dr Newman's doctrine of development was submitted here to a close and rigid examination, not by me only but by Bishops and professional theologians. I have only censured what they bid me censure, and I am responsible only for the manner in which I have done what they have instructed me to do.... The only thing that operates here to Dr Newman's disadvantage is his refusal to explain himself publicly with regard to his doctrine, which has been publicly controverted, and his apparent disposition to regard attacks on his doctrine as attacks on his person. His silence in this respect is not edifying...' (*LD*, vol. xv, p. 165).

The attack of 1852 was stimulated by J. B. Morris' book on the Incarnation: cf. 'Morris on the Incarnation', *Brownson's Quarterly Review* (n.s.), vol. vi.

## PAGE 186

1 *Difficulties of Anglicans*, vol. i, pp. 344–6; *Idea of a University* (1947 ed.), pp. 197–8; *Tracts Theological and Ecclesiastical* (1874 ed.), p. 287, originally published in 1858—'Every Catholic holds that the Christian dogmas were in the Church from the time of the Apostles; that they were ever in their substance what they are now; that they existed before the formulas were publicly adopted, in which, as time went on, they were defined and recorded....' Passages like these were quoted by some Catholic critics (even Marín-Sola, p. 362) to show that Newman had in effect retracted the theory as he originally expressed it.

The chief passage of the *Discourses on the Scope and Nature of University Education*, as it was called when he first published it in 1852, ran thus:

'The notion of doctrinal knowledge absolutely novel, and of simple addition from without, is intolerable to Catholic ears, and never was entertained by anyone who was even approaching to an understanding of our creed.... Christian truth is purely of revelation, that revelation we can but explain, we cannot increase, except relatively to our own apprehension' (original ed. p. 348: slightly revised in the later versions, 1947 ed. pp. 197–8). Newman's friend Richard Simpson did not fail to draw Brownson's attention to the importance of this paragraph, Simpson to Father Hecker, 4 April 1853; Hecker passed the letter to Brownson and it is now in BP.

Newman to Acton, 8 July 1862, CUL Add. MSS. 5463, *LD*, vol. xx, p. 223:

'What is *meant* by development?...

'Is it a more intimate apprehension, and a more lucid enunciation of the original dogma? For myself, I think it is, and nothing more. If I have said more than this, I think I had not worked out my meaning, and was confused. I think it is what an Apostle *would* have said, when on earth, what any of his disciples would have said, according as the occasion called for it. If St Clement, or St Polycarp, had been asked whether our Lady was immaculately conceived, I think he might have taken some time to understand the meaning of the question, and perhaps (as St Bernard) he might have to the end misunderstood the question; but if he did ever understand it, I think he would have said "Of course she was". Whether the minute facts of history will bear me out in this view I leave to others to determine. Accordingly, to me the words "development in dogma" are substantially nothing but the process by which, under the magisterium of the church, implicit faith becomes explicit.

'I should hold that the *substance* of the *res credenda* or dogma of Christianity was just what it was in the Apostles' day, and that the difference between the creed then and the creed now was only *quoad nos*—one of *apprehension*. I should like to say that *the Church* apprehends it more clearly; and I almost think that Bossuet countenances such a notion. When I suggested it to Father Perrone, he disliked the idea. But what is the Church as separate from pope, councils, bishops and faithful?'

Yet even here it will be seen that Newman cannot help allowing as a theory, in the moment when he is asserting his improbabilities about St Clement or St Polycarp, the primacy of historical inquiry. 'Whether the minute facts of history will bear me out in this...'—was the sort of sentence most calculated to irritate Acton.

Gondon's translation of the *Essay* appeared at last in 1848. The preface enjoined the reader not to forget that the author was an Anglican, and 'indépendamment de cette position de l'auteur, n'oublions pas qu'en Angleterre le langage philosophique et théologique ne brille, pas plus qu'en Allemagne, par sa clarté'.

Deferrière's translation of the selected *University Sermons* appeared in 1850.

2 Cuttings from the pastoral charges of Archbishop Sibour of Paris and Dr Brown the vicar-apostolic of Wales in OM, B.8. iii. Cf. Stanton to Newman, 7 August 1855.

The *Apologia* (Everyman, p. 227) contains the strangest passage upon the subject which Newman ever wrote: after asserting that infallibility does *not* extend to 'mere logical conclusions' from the articles of the deposit, he went on: 'Nothing, then, can be presented to me, in time to come, as part of the faith, but what I ought already to have received, and have not actually received (if not) merely because it has not been told me. Nothing can be imposed upon me different in kind from what I hold already—much less contrary to it. The new truth which is promulgated, if it is to be called new, must be at least homogeneous, cognate, implicit, viewed relatively to the old truth. It must be what I may even have guessed, or wished, to be included in the apostolic revelation; and at least it will be of such a character, that my thoughts readily concur in it or coalesce with it, as soon as I hear it. Perhaps I and others actually have always believed it, and the only question which is now decided in my behalf, is that I am henceforth to believe that I have only been holding what the apostles held before me.'

### PAGE 187

1 CUL Add. MSS. 4990, 176.

2 The note continues: 'The argument seems to be this. Christianity is an objective fact or supposed fact and a very manysided multiform fertile productive fact. Such extraordinary facts make a deep impression on the minds of those who come across them, which impression may be called the subjective idea of them. But from the vastness, richness etc. no individual mind more than partially embraces it, thus it makes a different impression or idea on different minds—the same indeed but incomplete and therein different—also arranging differently and making different points the most important.' This summary is in part based on 1845, pp. 94–5: compare the corresponding passage of 1878, pp. 55–6.

### PAGE 188

1 Cf. Newman to Plummer, 11 October 1877, 'I am half re-writing, or rather whole-re-arranging, my Essay...'; Newman to Coleridge, 5 November 1877 and 13 November 1877; Newman to Aubrey de Vere, 20 January 1878; LD, vol. XXVIII, 247, 264, 268, 304.

2 'In the new edition of the Essay various important alterations have been made in the arrangement of its separate parts, and some, not indeed in its matter, but in its text.'

A manuscript note, evidently part of a hypothetical draft for the preface, expressed it a little differently. 'I have tried to simplify the arrangement which was very unsatisfactory, but it still has great defects.

As there was no object here, as in other books before I was a Catholic, to preserve the original, I have not scrupled to allow or insert, as well as to transpose passages, as I thought best.'

Notice how the alignment of this new edition with the other publications of *non-Catholic* works, projected here, was removed in the published preface.

PAGE 189

1 In the front cover of the copy which he used for revision in 1877, he wrote a curious note headed *Development equals translation into new language*. It runs:
'Revelation is not of *words*—from the derivation of the term it is addressed to the *sight*.

E.g. I may have a new truth, e.g. the doctrine of induction, or the wealth of nations etc. conveyed to my intelligence by one set of words, then by another, then by a third—I may get the idea simply into my mind, independent of any one sentence of all that has been said to me. And then, when called upon, I may enunciate the doctrine, the very same doctrine, but again and afresh in my own words, and not in those which were used to teach it to me, and again on another occasion a second set of words, or a third in another. Here there is an idea communicated, not indeed except thro' words, but not in dependence of any formula. Such is the nature of that communication to us afresh of the truth of what we call revelation. It *may* be given also in formulas, as "The Father is God, the Son is God, the Holy Ghost is God: yet these three are one God", but this is not necessary for the revelation. Or knowledge is Power (?) which is an after reflection.'

The note shows how far he was from the traditional idea of translation into clearer language even when he was casting about for possibilities along this line.

PAGE 190

1 The chief rearrangement is simply to remove the 'tests' for distinguishing between development and corruption, which in 1845 had appeared as general tests for such distinguishing without any particular relation to Christianity, into the part at the end where they are applied to Christianity. This is a considerable improvement in coherence. But with individual paragraphs Newman was much more drastic in his rearrangements than he was with the general scheme.

2 Examples: faulty phraseology, 1845, p. 138 and *passim*. Historical concessions of something now known to be *de fide*: western consecration prayer versus eastern epiclesis, 1845, p. 365 (1878, p. 379); origins of bishops and popes, 1845, pp. 165–7, 'First local disturbances gave rise to bishops, and next ecumenical disturbances gave rise to popes'; 1878, p. 151, 'First local disturbances gave exercise to bishops, and next ecumenical disturbances gave exercise to popes...'. Cf. Purgatory (1845, p. 51; 1878, p. 48): baptism (1845, p. 412; 1878, pp. 129 and 384): consecration at eucharist (1845, p. 365; 1878, p. 379).

Alterations perhaps due to recent ecclesiastical history, cf. 1845, pp. 367–8, horror of heresy, etc. are principles which 'have entirely succeeded in preventing innovation upon the doctrine of Trent for 300 years': but 1878 'succeeded in preventing departure from the doctrine of Trent'. But other phrases which the course of history had affected he did not trouble to alter: cf. the passage about infallibility in 1845, p. 368 which he transferred bodily, though in a different context, to 1878, pp. 179–80.

It may be said that he had a compulsive reason for maintaining *some* of the historical objections which to Roman Catholic theologians appeared to be so liberal. Part of the *Essay* was a polemic against traditional Anglican ecclesiology. He must destroy the credit of the Vincentian Canon and of George Bull—because in order to justify the Council of Trent he had to prove that there was no continuous tradition of Trinitarian theology leading to the Council of Nicaea. It may therefore be alleged that the polemic conditioned the historical objections, the historical objections did not condition the polemic: on the ground that Newman had not changed from Bull to Petau by further historical research but by the 'antecedent probability' established by his loss of faith in the Church of England. This view, though doubtless containing truth, does insufficient justice to the truly historical sense in Newman's mind. This historical element had been kept in control by his faith in Bull and the Vincentian Canon as supports of the *Via Media*. Once the faith which controlled the historical sense was subverted or transformed, a genuinely historical recognition entered in—perhaps sharpened, exaggerated, and overstated, by the polemical needs. And although it is true that the *Apologia* gives the impression that historical investigation had little enough to do with his swing of opinion, and although many other considerations unquestionably entered in (*inter alia* the power of scepticism, the resistance to him by Oxford and the bishops, the divisions among the Tractarians themselves) his correspondence shows that out of the study of the Fathers came more than the flimsy parallels between ancient and modern, between Anglican and Donatist, which the *Apologia* suggests. See for example *Letters and Correspondence of J. H. Newman*, vol. II (1891), p. 292 (Newman to Mrs J. Mozley, 17 November 1839, some two months after the 'stomach-ache' which he received from Wiseman's celebrated article in the *Dublin Review*). 'The question of the Fathers is getting more and more anxious. For certain persons will not find in them just what they expected. People seem to have thought they contained nothing but the doctrines of Baptismal Regeneration, Apostolical Succession, Canonicity of Scripture, and the like. Hence many have embraced the principle of appeal to them with this view. Now they are beginning to be undeceived....'

It cannot therefore be said *simpliciter* that the historical investigations were controlled by antecedent and dogmatic probability. But if this is true of the

1845 *Essay*, it is less obviously true of the 1878 edition, which so weakened the 'freedom' of the appeal to history.

1 *Diary* for 5 August 1847, compared with note of this date in Newman's rough note-book on development, OM.

2 Changes allowing a clearer place for theological reasoning: cf. 1845, p. 4 with 1878, p. 6 (weakness of historical evidence): 1845, pp. 56–7 with 1878, p. 53 (omitting the strong passage from the *University Sermons* about the propositions being inadequate to the idea). 1878, p. 327, removed a negative sentence against reason, cf. 1845, p. 328, and in the same direction cf. 1878, p. 330 with 1845, p. 331. 1878 omitted altogether a passage from the *University Sermons* about faith as presumption, cf. 1845, pp. 131–5. For new paragraphs on theology, see 1878, pp. 336–8. The old paragraphs of 1845, pp. 388–96 were omitted or rewritten. But he kept quotations from Butler and Huet on probabilities, he kept a phrase of 1845 that we are only 'morally certain' that the apostles are infallible, he kept his verdict that the evidence was partial rather than demonstrative.

He removed negative passages which denied that logic could 'discover' as opposed to 'propagate' truth. He introduced positive assertions about logic as the organization of thought, and the security for faithful development when the development is intellectual, and the same in all ages. But logic is still a subsequent test of consistency and congruity; cf. 1878, pp. 189 ff. (1845, pp. 80 ff.): 1878, p. 195 (1845, p. 77): 1878, p. 190 (1845, p. 81). In 1878, p. 191 he omitted a passage of 1845 quoting Tract 73 to the effect that to rationalize is to receive nothing but revealed truth. But he kept the next paragraph which granted that 'the spontaneous process which goes on within the mind itself is higher and choicer than that which is logical'. Newman's historical instance of logical development is still the whimsical theory, so warmly espoused by Hurrell Froude, that Strauss and Kant are the 'logical' development of Luther's thought.

Changes away from the 'idea' and towards revelation in propositions: he removed the phrase 'an instance of the mind of the Church working out dogmatic truths from implicit feelings'; he occasionally removed the word *idea* and substituted *type* or 'statements of the doctrine'. But much more commonly he retained the original language, cf. 1845, p. 417 with 1878, p. 390; 1878, pp. 33–4, 37, 42, 207; 92–3; 53, 55, 77, 89, 195. He usually, though not quite always, kept the language about 'growth' and 'unconsciousness', and he added one passage in which the 'unconsciousness' was asserted. Partial removals of the suggestion, cf. 1878, p. 390 with 1845, p. 417

(where the unconsciousness is removed from the Church and attributed to 'the faithful', as in the *Difficulties of Anglicans*), 1878, p. 444; the final paragraph of the *Essay* removed one sentence which might have suggested 'dormancy' too strongly. But the paragraph as it survived kept the general idea. Cf. 'reason ever awake', 1878, p. 338 (added), cf. p. 383.

New assertions of identity through change—1878, pp. 99, 106, 127, 206, 324. At the last minute of correcting the proofs in 1878 he thought of substituting the word 'enlargements' for the word 'accretions' but refrained. The pencil marks on his revising copy also show that he contemplated removing an 'assimilating' passage of 1845, pp. 337-9 but in fact kept nearly all of it except the 'external' doctrine.

PAGE 194

1 CUL Add. MS. 4987, 7.

# INDEX

# INDEX